THE QUESTION OF THE ANIMAL AND RELIGION

The Question of the Animal *and* Religion

THEORETICAL STAKES, PRACTICAL IMPLICATIONS

Aaron S. Gross

COLUMBIA UNIVERSITY PRESS   NEW YORK

COLUMBIA UNIVERSITY PRESS
Publishers Since 1893
New York   Chichester, West Sussex

cup.columbia.edu
Copyright © 2015 Columbia University Press
All rights reserved

Library of Congress Cataloging-in-Publication Data

Gross, Aaron.
   The question of the animal and religion : theoretical stakes, practical implications /
Aaron Gross.
      pages cm
   Includes bibliographical references and index.
   ISBN 978-0-231-16750-5 (cloth : alk. paper) — ISBN 978-0-231-16751-2 (pbk. : alk. paper) —
ISBN 978-0-231-53837-4 (e-book)
   1. Animals—Religious aspects.   2. Meat animals—Religious aspects.   I. Title.
   BL439.G76 2014
   205'.693—dc23

2014014716

Columbia University Press books are printed on permanent and durable acid-free paper.
This book is printed on paper with recycled content.
Printed in the United States of America

C 10 9 8 7 6 5 4 3 2 1
P 10 9 8 7 6 5 4 3 2 1

JACKET AND BOOK DESIGN BY VIN DANG

FOR MY PARENTS,
who taught me that *rachamim* is more than human.

Contents

Acknowledgments

This book is the product of a long intellectual journey, with core ideas that started marinating more than twenty years ago, and so I begin by thanking my earliest academic mentor, Harold Kasimow at Grinnell College, and my mentor during my masters work at Harvard Divinity School, Jon Levenson, for helping me fall in love with the study of Jewish traditions and leaving me space to find my own path. The individuals who have contributed more directly to this book along the way are too numerous to list in any comprehensive manner. Nonetheless, some individuals and institutions were especially noteworthy. The incredible support and encouragement I received from the Department of Religious Studies at the University of California Santa Barbara, especially my Ph.D. committee—Barbara Holdrege, Richard Hecht, and Elizabeth Weber—cannot be overstated; conversations about the question of the animal with Tom Carlson, Nathaniel Rich, Anne Taves, and Colleen Windham-Hughes at UCSB also shaped parts of the book. I was similarly fortunate that a Leverhulme fellowship allowed me to spend nine months at the Theology and Religious Studies department at the University of Chester in the UK, and the colleagues I met there, especially David Clough and Celia Deane-Drummond, provided tremendous insight and good coffee that were crucial to the completion of this book. Other important conversation partners while in the UK were David Grummet, Rachel Muers, Krithika Srinavasan, and Daniel Weiss. I am similarly grateful for the numerous opportunities to present early versions of chapters of this book through the auspices of the Animals and Religion Group of the American Academy of Religion, and the incredible group of scholars I've had the privilege of working with through this program unit, especially David Aftandilian, Barbara Ambrose, Heather Eaton, Laura Hobgood-Oster, Kimberley Patton, and Paul Waldau. I similarly wish to thank the Society for Jewish Ethics, especially for affording opportunities for rigorous conversations about AgriProcessors with Geoffrey Claussen, Jonathan Crane, Elliot Dorff, Moses Pava, Julia Watts-Belser, and Jonathan Schofer among others. A special thanks to Tim Ingold for being willing to read and offer feedback on the chapter dedicated to his work, and to Devora Kimelman-Block, Joe Regenstein, and Philip Schein for reviewing particular sections. Finally, I am grateful to my home department of Theology and Religious Studies at the University of San Diego for their steadfast support for my study of animals and religion and this book project. And though he won't be able to appreciate it, Fletcher, my canine companion, and all the dogs and cats that have linked me intimately to the more than human world, *thank you.*

THE QUESTION OF THE ANIMAL AND RELIGION

Introduction

THE EVENT IN POSTVILLE

Although I did not know it at the time, this book began in 2004 when a bland manila envelope arrived at my home by overnight post, a rectangular bulge revealing its content as a VHS tape.[1] The tape contained footage of cattle slaughter at one of the world's largest religiously identified slaughterhouses, a kosher abattoir oddly located in a historically Lutheran town in rural Iowa. The community of previously urban Hasidic Jews who moved to the town to run the slaughterhouse stood out against the backdrop of an economically struggling farm town like a proud anachronism. Black hats and gabardines amid swaying corn and heartland churches also proved journalistically and cinematographically irresistible, an easy symbol of America's pluralistic promise. Well before the footage I was about to view was taken, Postville had inspired a thoughtful book by Stephen Bloom and an educational Iowa state government film on diversity that portrayed the town as a multicultural success story in progress.[2] Despite some critical comments in Bloom's book, the town's reputation remained pristine enough that it had even become the subject of a Hallmark channel special, *The Way Home*.[3] By the time the slaughter footage arrived, I was anticipating something ugly, but, even as someone who had seen a great deal of undercover footage taken by animal advocates, I found the video unusually disturbing.

Today, extensive reporting in national and international media (the *Forward*, the *Jerusalem Post*, the *Los Angeles Times*, the *New York Times*, *NPR*, the *Washington Post*, and others) has meant that hundreds of thousands, more probably millions, of people have seen a clip or at least read a description of the routine violence revealed by the tiny hidden camera on the investigator planted by People for the Ethical Treatment of Animals (PETA). The Internet-driven proliferation of the slaughter images has become an important part of what happened "in Postville." In addition to still images depicted in major print and Internet media sources, parts of the video I was about to watch were rapidly made available on PETA's Web sites and on YouTube. Five years later the clips had been accessed roughly seven hundred thousand times.[4] When I first saw the footage, however, aside from a few insiders (people employed by AgriProcessors, the USDA inspectors, and the half-dozen Orthodox Jewish kosher oversight agencies), no more than half a dozen eyes had witnessed the practices shown on the tape. The "interior chambers" of American slaughterhouses of all kinds,[5] and the "kill floor" most of all, are strictly guarded from view and virtually invisible to the general public.

The violence documented on the video included workers systematically cutting and partially removing the esophagi and tracheas of cattle after *shechitah*—the biblical word for slaughter used today to designate the cutting of the animal's neck required by kosher law—but, in more than one out every five slaughters, before the animals lost consciousness. This is simply the most disturbing of a handful of procedures that were later deemed to be illegal under the one U.S. law that provides some modest legal protection for cows and pigs at the time of slaughter.[6] Dr. Temple Grandin, the nation's most influential humane slaughter expert and a meat industry insider who has designed more than half of all cattle slaughter facilities in America, explained, "Removal of the trachea and other internal parts before the animal has become insensible would cause great suffering and pain. Many of the cattle on this tape had this dressing procedure performed when they were still fully sensible. Several cattle were walking around with the trachea and other parts hanging out of them."[7]

As a Jew myself, I felt shame well up inside me in an irrational surge that, as the scandal unfolded, was surely repeated inside tens of thousands of Jews—an unwelcome lightning flash of Jewish identity.[8] I did not feel ashamed only as a Jew, however, but also simply as a person. "How embarrassing to be human" as Kurt Vonnegut has it.[9] Competing with the critical voices in my mind that wielded academically honed attentiveness to particularity and context, another part of my imagination melted away such analysis. The specificity of my religious location as a Reform Jew—an identity rather distant from that of Postville's Hasidic Jews—was forgotten. I was no longer American, or Jewish, or, in a certain way, human. I was a mammal, a body, a creature of evolution whose mind, programmed for empathy as much as the potential for indifference, could not help but wince at the pained animal faces. Something unfathomably old inside me responded. What neurologists call von Economo neurons and mirror neurons fired and danced.[10] As much because of my biology as because of my culture, I could not help but empathize and sympathize with those suffering others.[11] I was held hostage to whatever "it" is one wants to name that philosopher Jacques Derrida invokes as the "possibility of sharing the possibility of this nonpower . . . the anguish of this vulnerability" of being flesh.[12]

The practices depicted on the tape drew swift, strong, and diverse reactions from American Jewish and animal welfare communities, especially where these two communities overlapped in persons like myself. Much of what follows in this study is an attempt to interpret the intensity and meaning of the Jewish responses to the suffering depicted on the video, responses to animals.

These responses are significant not only because of what they reveal about Jewish self-understanding and ethics but because of what they reveal about us Americans and, in the end, all of us who call ourselves human, *humano* (Spanish), *humain* (French), *Mensch* (German), and so on. The events at Postville have a traceable pragmatic influence that lives on in USDA memos, a changed U.S. kosher cattle slaughter industry, and an energized Jewish food movement. But the deeper charge these events carried and that brought them into discussion far beyond the Jewish fold is not about kosher slaughter in particular but about religious slaughter in an age when farms and slaughterhouses have come to be managed like factories. In the end this "religious slaughter" of which I speak is not limited to, as usually thought, what kosher or halal slaughterhouses do, but arguably what happens in American slaughterhouses of all kinds as they help bring billions of animal bodies into three hundred million American bodies as food every year with hardly anyone seeing a single farmed animal die. While I will be primarily concerned with the specificity of the Jewish response to these events, the final implications of this discussion is about all of us who live in industrial and postindustrial societies where eating animals is commonplace.

The practices that the undercover video depicted were regarded by a small minority of Orthodox Jews as high piety—the "highest standard" and "glory" of kosher slaughter, as AgriProcessors manager Sholom Rubashkin put it.[13] "This is the way we did it in the Holy Temple all those years. This is basically the exact way that God asked us to do it," explained the rabbinic supervisor for kosher slaughterhouses for the Chicago Rabbinical Council.[14] To others, like Grandin, a longtime gentile advocate of the potential humaneness of kosher slaughter,[15] they were "an atrocious abomination"[16]—a profanation of sorts.[17] For most American Jews, the animal suffering captured on the video was at least worrisome and almost always condemned. More significantly, the video ignited broader conversations about the contemporary meat industry as well as ethics more broadly. *Who are we when we do this to them?*

The video was both exposé and window into a normally hidden "holy of holies" in which animals were supposed by most American Jews to be receiving a "good death"—a contemporary echo of the sacrifices that the ancient Israelites offered in the Temple in Jerusalem. Kosher practice, which includes detailed rules for slaughter but little in the way of explicit rationale, was generally supposed to embody a benign human dominion over a good creation. But the video, which implicated not only this individual slaughterhouse but the entire infrastructure of kosher certification and secular humane slaughter laws, revealed what appeared to most as "grisly" (the *Washington Post*) and "egregious" (USDA) animal abuse.[18] The events that followed in the years after the video's release tended to confirm suspicions that the plant, kosher supervision, and U.S. government regulators more generally are no longer able to uphold (or never sufficiently upheld) ethical standards widely agreed upon by most Americans. Two subsequent undercover investigations documented mistreatment of animals by AgriProcessors, and a series of additional investigations also revealed worker abuse steeped in racism toward undocumented (and non-Jewish) immigrant workers. In 2008 a fuller picture of the scope of these human rights abuses came to light when the federal government conducted the largest single-site immigration raid in U.S. history at the plant, arresting 389 people, including 285 Guatemalans. After arrest, workers were held in fairgrounds normally used for cattle until they were processed by immigration. The corruption and violence at AgriProcessors became an even bigger national news story, later inspiring both a play,

La Historia de Nuestras Vidas, and a documentary, *AbUSed: The Postville Raid.*[19] Even then Senator Barack Obama commented on the event: "When you read about a meatpacking plant hiring 13-year-olds, 14-year-olds—that is some of the most dangerous, difficult work there is. . . . They have kids in there wielding buzz saws and cleavers? It's ridiculous."[20] The plant went bankrupt in the face of this scandal and is now under new ownership and called, curiously, Agri Star.[21] Apparently the plant no longer works in processing but dwells in the majesty of the night sky; its work is not about bloody earth but the light of heaven.

SOMETHING EXTRAORDINARY

[handwritten: What does it to be mean "human"]

Even before it became well known that the plant was not only mistreating animals but also its own workforce, the American Jewish community responded to the 2004 video by debating the meaning of humane slaughter and, ultimately, the meaning of humanity. The release of this video was surely not the first time the pleading faces of animals—and tales about them—had gripped people and become an entry point for wider discussions. The Talmud relates that no less a giant of the rabbinic world than Judah ha-Nasi, the editor and redactor of the Mishnah, Judaism's most sacred text after the Bible, was once confronted by a calf being led to slaughter.[22] The calf broke away from the person leading him, buried his head in the folds of the Rabbi's garments, and wept. Judah ha-Nasi's response to this unusual plea from a bovine, which I will return to in the final chapter of this study, shaped his life for thirteen years, the Talmud reports. Of the many things this Talmudic story might mean, the most basic is this: an animal resisting slaughter is both a powerful sight and a site of meaning. Our responses to such an animal matter.

As Jewish responses to AgriProcessors accumulated, an extraordinary charge became evident in them that connected these events with older streams of thought and practice. As this charge grew I put down my petitions, put on my scholar's cap, and realized that I had found an event that not only called forth energetic responses but also called for scholarly analysis. The events at AgriProcessors originally demanded my attention as a Jew and as an animal protection advocate, as they still do, but soon my response to the event demanded less engagement and more *epoché*—the suspension of judgment in order to understand—the labor, in short, of a historian of religions.

As a historian of religions I had already been working on the question of the animal and religion and I saw that the theoretical work I was doing could help interpret the AgriProcessors "events," by which I mean both the abuses that took place there and the responses to them.[23] At the same time, the event offered a powerful opportunity to clarify the significance of animals and the category "animal" for our understanding of religion. This is so not only because of the unique drama of the AgriProcessors events but because food animals constitute 98 percent of the animals contemporary Western people interact with over the course of their lives (mostly by eating them).[24] Any theorization of animals and religion that wants to have a meaningful relation to the particular historical moment in which we find ourselves must give considerable attention to the question of the *food* animal.

Theorizing animals and religion, on the one hand, and understanding the animal abuse scandal at AgriProcessors, on the other, are the two tasks of this book. To engage them will require that we carefully consider the broader meaning of animals and the category animal. It will necessitate probing not only the meaning of animals in Jewish traditions but also in the study of religion. In the end, interpreting the events at AgriProcessors in this broader context will mean exploring something fundamental about how modernity has altered our relationship with animals in that "dimension of depth" we name religion.[25]

RELIGION, THE STUDY OF RELIGION, AND ANIMALS

Many religious traditions, as well as the study of religion itself, share a presupposition so basic that it often goes unnoticed: the existence of essential distinctions between humans and all other animals. Although the imagination of animals and the human/animal border are fundamental to a surprising number of religious traditions and to the academic study of religion generally, this significance has been largely ignored.[26] Only in recent years, following increased political consideration of animals' welfare, has the discourse coming to be known as "animal studies" (a category that some will further divide into "human-animal studies" and "critical animal studies," the latter being more explicitly political) begun to expose the importance of animals.[27] This critical turn toward animals is now evident in numerous scholarly disciplines within the social sciences and human sciences, including anthropology, classics, comparative literature, critical theory, gender studies, geography, history, media studies, philosophy, psychology, sociology, religious studies, and women's studies. Still, at the time of writing, no monograph has taken up the task of theorizing the study of animals and religion as such. While this book begins with and analyzes a particular incident, its larger task is to both expose the absent presence of animals in the history of the study of religion and clear a space for their future—inside and outside the academy.

How does the scholarly, cultural reconsideration of animals—this critical turn toward animals—bear upon the study of religion? How does it impact the study of different traditions differently? How can critical attention to animals help us better understand religion as a scholarly category and advance theory and method in its study? How can the lens of religious studies help us better understand cultural events that involve animals—the animals we eat, the ones we keep as pets, and the animals we conjure to tell ourselves who we are? How can religious studies play a role in clarifying the nature and significance of animals by analyzing their religious "charge"—their sacrality and their intimate interwovenness with religious practice? These questions, unintelligible not long ago, now command considerable attention.

What is needed, and what chapters 3 through 5 of this study seek to provide, is a theorization of "the animal" as an abstract category in the study of religion that *at the same time* attends to the animal individuals in its view—a conceptual engagement with animals that avoids, in Levinasian terms, becoming a totality: a calculated dogma rather than an always incomplete movement.[28] We require a way of speaking about the depth dimension we share with animate life that does not overconfidently think we can simply make animals fully present by coming into physical proximity with them. Ethology, the study of animal behavior, can help us in this confrontation with animals, but is inadequate to the questions of meaning that face us. Our failure to think animals and religion is a failure of imagination, not a lack of information. Looking the horse in the mouth will not be enough. Yet, *at the same time*, we need a way of speaking that remains responsive to the immediacy of the animal lives bound to us, for example, the fact that I must now pause in my writing to take my dog, a named and beloved companion, out for a walk.

We would do well to bring together, on the one hand, a theorization of religion that does not homogenize the diversity of, for example, the religions of the contemporary Cree of Northern Canada and fourth-century Christians in Rome, and, on the other hand, a theorization of the animal that no longer levels the profligate heterogeneity of nonhuman beings as diverse as the gorilla and the snake. We need a discourse that is grounded in awareness of its own historical unfolding in human minds and, at the same time, is grounded in the present ecological-political moment. We need to move within the tension and curiosity of this at-the-same-time, on-the-one-hand-and-on-the-other-hand movement of thought and let it clear "space for the event of what we call animals."[29] We need to allow animals to be seen, to see them, and, as Jacques Derrida puts it, allow ourselves to "be seen seen" by them.[30]

   If this feels a bit dizzying, there is good reason. The question of the animal and religion is a question not only about the foundation of the study of religion but the foundation of the human sciences, even the foundation of thought itself. There are many ways one might conceptualize the line between the human sciences and the life sciences, but, however one imagines it, the distinction of the human sciences is its employment of methods that apply to—and only to—the human. Ecosystems, "brute" physical phenomena, the human (animal) body, and animals themselves (which are viewed as all body) are left, at least to a large extent, to the life sciences. At a structural level, the binary human sciences/life sciences *is* the human/animal binary. The isolation of the human in the human sciences is predicated upon various arguments for human uniqueness that are not intelligible without animal others. Frits Staal provides a helpful summary of this dominant view, which he here attributes to Wilhelm Dilthey: "In some of Dilthey's work . . . the uniqueness of the humanities is related to the unicity of man, which is, in turn, related to a tradition of discussions on 'subjectivity' in modern philosophy. The argument runs, briefly, as follows. 'Man' is so different from stars, rocks, molecules and even other animals that he cannot be studied by the same methods by which these other things are studied. He is, after all, not a thing: he is the unique studying subject himself."[31]

   It requires some imagination to remember that there is nothing inevitable about the creation of special disciplines that deal exclusively with the human. In an alternate history, we might have had an academy that was structured around a "primate sciences"/life sciences or "mammal sciences"/ life sciences binary, viewing all primates or all mammals as requiring unique methods of study and the isolation of the human as unjustified. The question of the animal is so fundamental in Western thought (though not only Western thought) that it functions as a question about what it means to ask a question, draw lines, and create categories—a question about what thinking itself means. Thinking itself, or so the dominant Western logic has gone, begins with humanity breaking from animality. Could we, instead, "think thinking" as beginning in the liminal space that connects and at the same time separates sentient life? Are, for example, the Paleolithic cave paintings that are, nearly without exception, dominated by animals and hybrid creatures—the most ancient surviving human artistic expression—evidence of the *uniquely human* mind or *merely humans* joining the conversation of the sentient in a new way? Is the world a "collection of objects" thought only and exclusively by the human subject or what Thomas Berry, speaking as much as a historian of religions as a Catholic priest, calls a "communion of subjects"?[32]

Rigorous attention to animals disrupts, without displacing, the very categories and terms that religious practitioners and scholars of religion have developed over generations. At the same time, as has long been noted in scholarship on this topic, the question of the animal evokes strong emotional currents and is tied to ethical questions that face virtually everyone everyday.[33] To raise the question of the animal is often to enter the vertigo-inducing realm of what Sigmund Freud theorized as *Das Unheimliche*, the uncanny. As we will see, the shadowy, forgotten animal haunts the very categories that are used to organize the study of religion, including this study.[34]

The categories we use to study religion, starting with "religion" itself, are made intelligible against the background of (and on the backs of) animals. The primary burden of chapter 3 is to illustrate this insinuation of animals in the nontheological study of religion. This will be accomplished by considering how animals figure in the theorization of religion by a handful of foundational theorists—Ernst Cassirer, Émile Durkheim, and Mircea Eliade—and a contemporary historian of religions, Jonathan Z. Smith, and also by considering how the category "myth" is bound to animals.

Attending to this insinuation has an inherent value in illuminating a usually unnoticed feature of religion scholarship. In the case of the present study, it also has a propaedeutic function: understanding how animals have constituted the study of religion is a basic precondition for the project of theorizing animals in the study of religion, a task to which the present study aims to contribute. Finally, it is also a precondition for the analysis of the 2004 AgriProcessors scandal that grounds and stands watch over this theorizing.

To interpret the significance of the events at the AgriProcessors abattoir and their ongoing aftermath, I will first explain the details of the event in the context of the American kosher industry (chapters 1 and 2), review the "absent presence" of animals in the history of the study of religion (chapter 3), and provide critical, theoretical purchase on the category "animal" through an engagement with the insights of contemporary anthropology as discussed by Tim Ingold (chapter 4) and the insights into Western thought brought to us by Derrida (chapter 5). We will then be in a position to proceed to a deeper consideration of the AgriProcessors event (chapter 6) and, in the epilogue, the broader implications of this entire study.

Christian theology has approached religion by privileging questions about the divine. The nontheological study of religion, religious studies, approaches religion by privileging questions about the human. The present work proposes a study of religion that, by becoming critically aware of the excluded, forgotten, or disavowed "animal," simultaneously gains a critical vantage on previous approaches to religion and offers a third way: approaching religion by way of the animal, the creature, the sentient—by way of our forgotten ancestors.

FORGOTTEN ANCESTORS

It will be helpful to ask precisely what or who are these animals that I propose to attend to in this study. We will consider three "species" of animals: "actual" animals, the category of the animal as a root other or antitype of the human, and symbolic animals. First, my study is concerned with "actual" biological animals, including not only animals literally running about in the world but "actual" animals that are represented in texts and oral traditions (as opposed to imaginary animals such as frogs as large as cities). As my use of quotations suggests, there are times when the meaning of this apparently common sense term breaks down. As our understanding of the category animal shifts, so does our understanding of what we mean to do when we insist on talking about actual animals. In any case, these actual animals stand in contrast to the second species of animals that I consider: the category of "the animal," which configures animals as the root other of the human. For example, it is more the animal than actual animals that Saint Augustine speaks about when he says that in the afterlife "there will be no animal body to 'weigh down the soul' in its process of corruption; there will be a spiritual body with no cravings, a body subdued in every part to the will."[35] What will not be of concern to us, is what I would call "symbolic" animals, animals who are invoked—whether in the world or in texts—overwhelmingly or at least primarily because of some other specific meaning that they designate for humans.

This threefold preliminary schema helps us see the complexity of these three types of interrelated animals, but the beings that populate the landscapes of disciplined reflection on the phenomena of religion are not so easily domesticated. Who, for example, has the authority to speak about, in the phrase of novelist and Nobel laureate J. M. Coetzee, the "lives of animals"?[36] Is it ethologists or philosophers or advocates of an interdisciplinary approach? And where, for example, would one place in this threefold schema the animals and human-animal hybrids of Franz Kafka's tales? Or what of Walter Benjamin's articulation of animals as burdened sites of forgetting?[37] Consider the difficulties in trying even to juxtapose Benjamin's animals with Claude Lévi-Strauss's animals, who are, as he famously quips in *Totemism*, "good to think,"[38] indeed foundational for thinking. Perhaps even more disruptive is our knowledge of the Cree and other northern hunters who, Ingold explains in his classic essay "Hunting and Gathering as Ways of Perceiving the Environment," reject "an absolute division between the contrary conditions of humanity and animality. . . . Personhood for them is open equally to humans and nonhuman animals (and even nonanimal) kinds."[39] What of Donna Haraway's "companion species" who invite us "to enter the world of becoming with, where *who* and *what are* is precisely what is at stake"?[40] "I am who I become with companion species," Haraway explains, "who and which make a mess out of categories in the making of kin and kind."[41] Should we count as actual or symbolic the animals Wendy Doniger invokes when she reminds us that we humans engage not only in anthropomorphism but the more complex process of "zoomorphism" in which "although this time a human being is the explicit object, the bestial qualities imputed to the human usually reveal an observation of animals more detailed (if no more accurate) than that of anthropomorphism, and the text teaches us simultaneously what sort of person it thinks that animal is like and what sort of animal it thinks that sort of person is like"?[42]

And where would one locate Martin Heidegger's animal, who, dwelling in the liminal space between the worldless stone and world-building human, is "poor in world [*weltarm*]," indeed both "*has and does not have world*

[Somit seigt sic him Tier ein *Haben von Welt und zugleich ein Nichthaben von Welt*]."[43] Where would one locate Emmanuel Levinas's faceless animals that are nonetheless able to recognize the human face at times more faithfully than other human beings?[44] Where within this schema would we place an exchange of glances between Martin Buber and a cat, which leads him to declare: "No other event [!] has made me so deeply aware of the evanescent actuality in all relationships to other beings, the sublime melancholy of our lot, the fated lapse into it of every single You"?[45]

Can this threefold framework contain Giorgio Agamben's animals who are products of the machinelike process of "anthropogenesis" whereby the division within man between man and animal produces "the human" in a mysterious operation of separation?[46] And where might we set the cat whose glance catches Derrida "naked" and embarrassed in his seminal text *The Animal That Therefore I Am*? As Derrida notes, this cat that confronts him is a singular animal. She "does not belong to Kafka's vast zoopoetics. . . . Nor is the cat that looks at me . . . Hoffmann's or Kofman's cat Murr. . . . This cat I am talking about, which is also a female, isn't Montaigne's cat either . . . [or] Baudelaire's family of cats, or Rilke's, or Buber's."[47]

The thought of trying to herd together the cats Derrida alone invokes is daunting, but nevertheless a central aim of this study is simply to *attend*—a verb I wish to gloss in a moment—to animals. Beyond the discrete interpretation of the religious dimensions of the AgriProcessors events and the animals that feature within them is a more basic call for scholarly attending to animals.

THE ANIMAL AND ANIMALS

While I will often distinguish between the animal (as concept, category, word) and animals (as biological individuals, creatures, flesh), the invisible threads that bind the category animal to animals are never wholly cut, no matter how thin they may be worn. Derrida is so concerned to emphasize the endless interrelations that proliferate between animals as flesh and as word that he playfully (in a *certain* sense midrashically—that is, in the spirit of canonical rabbinic scriptural interpretation) combines the French words *animaux* (animals) and *mot* (word) into *animot*.[48] In French *animaux* and *animot* would be indistinguishable when pronounced, which is exactly Derrida's point: just as the difference between *animaux* and *animot* is inaudible in speech, so the line between *words about* and *the presence of* animals is ultimately unstable. To avoid the cumbersome phrase *the animal and animals* throughout the present work, I will sometimes use (and already have used) the word *animals* to refer to the entire complex of *the animal, animals,* and their symbolic charges. This is in fact what happens all the time in ordinary speech, where, as in Derrida's pun, *animaux* and *animot* are indistinguishable.

ATTENDING

As a strategic countermove to the myriad of tendencies to render absent, forget, or disavow animals, I propose *attending* to them. By this verb I mean simply attention to animals in roughly the same manner scholars train themselves to be attentive to gender, sex, race, or theological nuances. I specifically choose the term *attending* because it contains within it the word *tending,* which can mean both tending flocks and a kind of mental attention. This is a useful image of the sort of attention to animals that is required— an attention attentive to both the proliferation of meanings that surround animals and the fleshy, practical, economic relationships with which these meanings are always intertwined.

Attending to these multiple levels allows us to see that when scholars deploy the human/animal boundary to theorize religion we do not select a neutral binary. The human/animal binary has been inflected by a dominant discourse that is particularly influenced by certain streams of Protestant Christianity (as is the case with so many categories). Imagining religion as a strictly human phenomenon—which, I will argue, is to imagine religion as the *nonanimal* part of the human—may have been useful, but it is also correlated in Western Christian cultures with a series of hierarchical dichotomies that not only privilege the human over the animal but also mind over body, transcendence over immanence, spirituality over materiality, spirit over letter, faith over law, modern over primitive, West over East, Christian over Jew, and so on.[49]

When I share with colleagues who have not reflected much on animals that I work on "religion and animals," whether they find the topic intriguing or banal, they tend to view the intersection of religions and animals (at least at first) as an obscure area of study—a narrow margin on the outskirts of the most important concerns of both religious traditions and the field. I do not wish simply to refute this view but to suggest that the strong impulse many of us have to dispute and downgrade the significance of animals, especially in relation to religion, is precisely because of the impulse to disavow the in fact significant charge of animals. A complex intellectual-cultural apparatus constantly hides the importance of the animal, thus making the category human, which is so decisive to the study of religions, appear natural and relatively unproblematic (despite all our postmodern gesturing).

The category animal, connected by a thousand "adjustable threads" to the category human,[50] has exerted a discernible if not always decisive influence on virtually every major theorist of religion—and not only on theorists of religion, as the human/animal binary is fundamental to Western discourse in multiple ways. The animal and animals have always been present *invisibly* in our studies and in our prayers, chameleoning themselves into our thinking of religion.

As long as animals are approached uncritically, the historically entrenched hierarchical dualisms that privilege particular kinds of Christian orientations—historically more modern than ancient, more Protestant than Catholic, more Western than Eastern—will continually reassert their pull. Animals are, to borrow a phrase from Benjamin's readings of Kafka, the forgotten ancestors of our field. To take up the question of the animal, then, is not so much to pick a theme—although it is also that—but to select a location of resistance to a "schema of the dominant" and, perhaps more profoundly, a location of resistance to the "dominant schema of subjectivity itself."[51]

Significantly, we cannot say that all peoples even draw the human/animal binary as we know it. The human/animal binary does appear in a striking array of cultural contexts—which is intriguing—but it is not invariably present.[52] There are human communities, most notably those named hunter-gatherers,[53] for whom the human/animal binary is absent or, if known, understood as an error. This ethnographic fact has immense and underappreciated significance. It is not a coincidence that scholars from and of Native American traditions have been among the most active in advancing the discussion of animals and religion at American Academy of Religions annual meetings.

To move forward in considering the positive utility of critical attention to the category animal and the significance of actual animals for the study of religion in the remainder of this study, we need to get a little bit dizzy. For a robust consideration of religions and animals to grow, in or outside the academy, we must return to our roots and wrap our minds around the manner in which the very discourses we use to understand religion and animals have already been shaped by animals.

To think seriously about animals and religion requires an indirect approach, one that involves always keeping part of our attention on ourselves rather than on the animals we are inquiring after. Unexpectedly, this sharpens our attention to actual animals as it also reveals features of our self-imagination. Borrowing an image that Holocaust historian Omer Bartov employs in a different context, to address the question of the animal is to attempt to slay a gorgon. The gorgon—a creature of the ancient Greek imaginaire that is ambiguously suspended between human and animal—cannot be fought by any frontal attack. Any glance at the monstrosity of the gorgon will turn one to stone.[54] To face a gorgon, the myth proceeds, one must look at the creature indirectly. Thus Perseus looked at the gorgon only in the reflective inside surface of his shield as he fought the creature and, in doing so, could not help but see his own reflection at the same time. The only way to look at the gorgon requires one to simultaneously look at oneself.

We are caught in a hermeneutical circle: inquiry into animals is also inquiry into thought itself. I want to follow this circular movement as it produces a knot in which the human sciences, the study of religion, the human, and, of course, the animal are tied together. I want to follow the contours of this knot at its "most economical torsion"—and at the beginning of its unraveling.[55]

also w/ others
"absent"
from
dominant
schema of
binary systems

Ethical Tropes in American Kosher Certification

Tellingly, if one looks up *kosher* in an English dictionary, there are typically two meanings listed: first, *kosher* describes food that meets traditional Jewish legal requirements. Second, *kosher* means that which is "proper," "genuine," "legitimate," "permissible," or "authentic." In this way the production of kosher food is inevitably related to the production of Jewish ethics. Thus, even though important ethical values are often understood tacitly, it will be helpful to ask: *What were the ethical themes expressed by the kosher certification agencies charged with ensuring that AgriProcessors' meats were properly and legitimately produced?*

To begin we should recognize that "ethics" is a notoriously difficult-to-define concept. Indeed, both the question of what should count as Jewish ethics and the larger question of the role of normative values in the academic study of religion are at stake in this volume. For these reasons, we must defer an attempt at a comprehensive definition of ethics here. Nonetheless, we can say that ethics deals with the domain of values rather than descriptions, the "ought" rather than the "is." By "ethical themes," then, I mean to indicate primarily discourses that provide second-order grounding and justifications that supplement first-order moral standards or rules of conduct—discourses that, necessarily, imply anthropologies and function to shape characters.

This understanding of ethics blurs, without erasing, a line often drawn by professional ethicists between procedural-based ethics and character-based ethics. Procedural-based ethics, in this understanding, responds to the question "How should I act?" and considers the procedures of analysis and thinking that lead to particular actions. This category would include ethics based on rules (deontological ethics) and ethics based on an estimation of the effects an action will have (consequentialist ethics such as utilitarianism). Character-based ethics, on the other hand, responds to the question "What kind of person do I want to be?" and reflects on the rightness or wrongness of particular actions in the context of forming qualities of character such as patience or compassion.[1]

In the case we will be considering, these two forms of ethics are best thought of as interlocking gears in a single machine. Particular procedures and rules—for example, a requirement to slaughter an animal by the throat rather than the nape of the neck[2]—can be compared to the tip of an iceberg. The rest of the iceberg, the part usually unstated and only implied, is analogous to the aspect of ethics that works from particular anthropologies to shape certain kinds of character—for example, from the understanding that human compassion is a limited resource that can easily be used up to the conclusion that we therefore must discourage robust compassion for animals lest there be insufficient compassion for other humans (a common critique against animal activism). This chapter along with chapter 6 are an attempt to describe the entire iceberg—not only the rules, but the implied anthropology and strategy for shaping human character that are enmeshed with the rules.

KASHRUT AND ETHICS

The modern American kosher industry represents one of the most visible traditional religious systems of dietary practice in the West. Of the approximately 500 billion dollars in goods on supermarket shelves in America in 2010, more than 200 billion were certified kosher. While kosher practice is widespread and thus easily observed, the values underlying kosher food, like food in general, usually go unstated.

Crises like the AgriProcessors scandals, however, tend to force the articulation of ethical ideas that might otherwise remain implicit, radiating their influence unconsciously. If what we mostly see is the tip of the ethical "iceberg," crises can expose the submerged mass. This ability to make implicit values explicit is part of the unique significance of the response to AgriProcessors' misdeeds.

Readers less familiar with Jewish studies may be surprised to learn that there has been a long-standing question within the academic study of Jewish traditions about the extent to which applying the category of ethics to classical Jewish texts is helpful. Some would question whether ethics is an appropriate category to apply to *kashrut* at all, and an examination of this objection will help clarify the understanding of ethics I employ. Concern over whether there is Jewish ethics typically stems from difficulties in trying to satisfactorily distinguish between Jewish law (understood as what a Jew is commanded to do because God commanded it) and Jewish ethics (understood as what a Jew ought to do even if it is not explicitly commanded).[3] If there is no clear distinction, some scholars challenge, in what sense can we speak of a separate domain appropriately called Jewish ethics? A small minority of Jewish studies scholars ultimately do not accept that there is a domain independent of Jewish law that could be called ethics—at least, they argue, not in the most authoritative texts of Jewish traditions, particularly the Talmud. Thus David Weiss Halivni argues that the "notion that the Rabbis of the Talmud were aware of a possible conflict between morality and religious law, and consciously resolved in favor of morality [that is, ethics] cannot be defended historically. Historically, they gave other [nonethical] reasons for their interpretation."[4] For a scholar like Halivni, the logic of modern ethical discourse, particularly the typical way law and ethics are imagined in opposition, is simply too much in tension with the logic of rabbinic texts to justify speaking of a distinct domain of rabbinic ethics.

The vast majority of Jewish studies scholarship has, unlike Halivni, recognized a domain of rabbinic thought and practice independent of Jewish law and, further, have been comfortable associating this domain, to varying degrees, with "ethics."[5] These scholars, and I include myself in their number, follow a long-standing trajectory in Jewish thought that has sought to go "beyond the letter of law"—*lifnim meshurat hadin*—while retaining the law itself. In a famous Talmudic passage, Rabbi Yochanan declares that Jerusalem was destroyed (the archetypal catastrophe of Jewish thought) precisely because the population made decisions only on the basis of the letter of the law and did not perform actions that would have gone beyond it.[6] Contemporary Jewish ethicists follow the lead of Rabbi Yochanan in concluding that acts not obligated by law may nonetheless be essential for the world to continue to function—an essential part of the divine plan. In sum, ethics (beyond the law) matters—and matters in distinctively Jewish ways.

The charged disagreement (what the rabbis of the Talmud would call a *machloket*) in Jewish studies around whether ethics is an appropriate category for *describing* Jewish traditions is a distinctive way of raising a basic human question about the ground of "ethical truths." Are ethical truths fully accessible to human faculties like reason? Or, alternatively, is some kind of revelation—or even religion—required to reach this ground? Moreover, even if fundamental ethical truths may in principle be discerned with human faculties, is the character of the human such that she will, in the imperfect world in which we live, find sufficient confidence in these "merely human" ethical conclusions to be motivated to live an ethical life?

These more general questions about the nature of ethics and ethical motivation mirror a pervasive tension throughout rabbinic texts about the value of seeking *normative* explanations for *mitzvot* (the divine commandments around which Judaism has organized itself). Since it is precisely such explanations (for example, "we slaughter the animal this way so as not to cause it pain" rather than "we slaughter the animal this way because it is commanded") that scholars like myself prefer to call ethics, this traditional ambivalence about explanations of mitzvot can translate into an ambivalence about ethical discourse. The resistance to explaining the commandments is most acute in relation to the category of Jewish laws known as *chukkim*—"statutes" that are regarded as having no rational explanation. *Chukkim* are understood in contrast to *mishpatim*, "judgments" that are understood to be self-evident even if there had been no revelation, such as prohibitions on murder and theft.

Of great significance for our inquiry is the fact that traditional Jewish texts regard the laws of kashrut as *chukkim*, and so resistance to ethical discourse about kosher practice can be (but is by no means always) robust. American Orthodox Jews—today constituting a little more than 20 percent of affiliated American Jewry but who control virtually the whole of the kosher industry—generally resist the notion that kashrut should be discussed in ethical terms. There is an Orthodox consensus that the "underlying divine reason" (this is the phrase many Orthodox employ) for kashrut is inaccessible and therefore, at the most fundamental level, one cannot claim that the dietary laws are rooted in ethics. That said, Orthodox Jews, at different

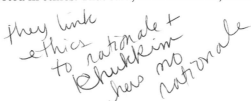

levels in different communities, also accept that while the "underlying divine reason" is unknown, there are beneficial outcomes to *chukkim* that can be discerned by humans and explained. This more modest exercise of explanation and inducement (rather than providing underlying reasons)—which can look a lot like what most of us would call ethics—is often viewed as useful by Orthodox communities, for example when communicating to children or as a strategy of outreach to Jews who are considering returning to traditional observance. In some cases, though, even this humbler exercise of explanation may be viewed with suspicion; today this is especially true in the case of the kosher laws that deal with animal slaughter.[7]

Thus, as I map the ethical landscape of kashrut articulated by Orthodox pundits, the first feature that must be noted is how small a place ethics—or rational explanation generally—plays in contemporary public declarations by kosher certification agencies. The overwhelming emphasis is on the ritual nature of kashrut and on adherence to rules that no one attempts to defend other than on the basis of their being commanded. A statement by Rabbi Yacov Lipshutz, a Talmud scholar who has worked in the kosher industry for twenty-five years, captures this sentiment: "many have attributed *kashrut* to either hygienic or social separation purposes. However, these extraneous motivations fail to stand up before the onslaught of human temptations. . . . Only when the Jew observes *kashrut* as a matter of faith does his commitment permeate his entire life."[8] The same emphasis on commandment is seen in this more bland statement in "The Kosher Primer" found on the Web site of the nation's largest kosher certification agency, the Orthodox Union's Kashrut Division (OU Kosher): "Though an ancillary hygienic benefit has been attributed to the observance of kashrus, the ultimate purpose and rationale is to conform to the Divine Will."[9] Even in articles and statements that are focused on providing a more rational understanding of kashrut and inspiring practice on the basis of some spiritual, ethical, or health benefit that may be obtained, disclaimers are frequent, such as this one from the Web site of another one of the nation's four largest kosher certification agencies—the so-called Big Four[10]—OK Kosher Certification:

> We therefore [to stave off nonobservance] offer some of the insights into the mitzvah of kosher provided by Jewish tradition. These insights satisfy our need for understanding and motivate us to keep the mitzvoth of the Torah in the face of opposing values from contemporary culture. Nevertheless, it should

be understood that the commandments are Divine in origin and can never be fully comprehended by human intellect. We keep the mitzvoth because they are G-d's gift to the Jewish people.[11]

[handwritten margin note: "divine can be used as excuse"]

ETHICS UNDER ANOTHER NAME

In practice today, this emphasis on *mitzvah* amounts to a rhetorical emphasis on the ritual aspects of kashrut at the expense of long-standing rabbinic traditions that did indeed emphasize ethics in connection with kosher practice (despite the tendency among some contemporary Orthodox leaders to deny this). From the dominant Orthodox perspective, only someone who believes that an all-seeing God commanded the laws of kashrut would be a reliable guardian of them; a concern for ethics *as discerned only by human actors*, many Orthodox will argue, simply will not have the same motivational power.

[handwritten margin note: "Orthodox = divine"]

We also see in this Orthodox Jewish emphasis a reaction against liberal Judaism, particularly Reform Judaism, which highlights the centrality of ethics to Judaism. Reform Judaism—now the largest denomination in America, constituting nearly 40 percent of affiliated American Jewry[12]— went so far as to champion ethics as the very essence of Judaism[13] and argued that kashrut is, to use the famous words of early Reform Judaism in the movement's 1885 Pittsburgh Platform, "foreign to our present mental and spiritual state."[14] The Orthodox emphasis on commandment and ritual precision over ethics and rationality is, in fact, the mirror image of the strong rhetorical emphasis on ethics found in the Reform movement—both historically and as Reform leaders have, to a limited extent, encouraged a return to kashrut (although not quite a traditional kashrut).[15] As is the case with many issues of Jewish observance, the Conservative movement—the second largest movement, constituting one third of affiliated American Jewry—finds itself located between these two poles.

[handwritten margin note: "Reform = ethics"]

This Orthodox ambivalence about ethics notwithstanding, there is ample discussion of the "spiritual," social, and, indeed, ethical potential of kashrut in these same Orthodox sources. References to the idea that kashrut is beneficial to the Jewish soul and, conversely, that *treyf* (nonkosher) food may damage the soul at a subtle level are found sporadically.[16] Often mentioned in this connection is the fact that kosher law forbids the consumption of carnivorous animals, as this would subtly transmit their aggressive, immoral nature to humans.[17] Socially, it is frequently noted that kashrut observance makes assimilation less likely. The idea that kosher food is more healthful than nonkosher food is generally absent today, and indeed much energy is spent to counteract the idea (kashrut is still occasionally associated with healthful food but not as explicitly).[18]

ELEVATION ABOVE AND KINDNESS TO ANIMALS

In my study of the ethical tropes found throughout the copious texts produced by the big four kosher certification agencies shortly before the AgriProcessors scandals, two emerge as dominant: discipline and kindness. While this chapter exclusively cites statements made before the 2004 exposé, the pattern has not meaningfully changed nearly a decade later. On the one hand, kashrut is rationalized as an ethical discipline that elevates humans above the animal by transforming the animalistic act of eating into a response to divine commands. On the other hand, kashrut is rationalized as embodying a certain kindness to animals. It is not always easy to differentiate these two sentiments, as the concern for animals itself can be understood as a moral discipline that elevates the human, but they nonetheless are typically presented as independent (or even competing) concerns.

The theme of kindness to animals has generally pointed to the humane intention perceived to be behind the laws of *shechitah*—the traditional Jewish method of slaughter. In the literature of the big four, the claim that shechitah is humane is common, although not ubiquitous.[19] More generic assertions that kashrut promotes kindness to animals are slightly more common. For example, an article on the Web site of another of the big four kosher certification agencies, Kof-K Kosher Supervision, asserts that "keeping kosher is supposed to produce a heightened sensitivity to *Hashem*'s [God's] creations. . . . The dietary laws remind the Jew of some of the ideals of *'kedusha'* [holiness], which are discipline, restraint, the avoidance of inflicting pain—even on animals—minimizing the pain of any living thing."[20] Another article on the OU Kosher Web site is more direct: "*Kashrut* undoubtedly projects sensitivity towards animals and plants."[21]

The second main ethical trope speaks of the power of kashrut as a moral discipline that suppresses and transforms something "animal" in human beings and moves humans toward the divine. A set of value-laden binary oppositions is established: animal/human, physical/spiritual, and human/divine. The discipline of kashrut does not simply deliver the ethical benefit one might see as inherent in all discipline, but rather it is a very particular discipline that moves the practitioner from the left side of the binaries (animal, physical, human) toward the right (human, spiritual, divine). Consider this rabbinic statement published by yet another of the big four, Star-K Kosher Certification: "We serve our Creator meaningfully by sublimating our appetites, disciplining our instincts, channeling our hungers, harnessing our animal drives according to the dictates of the Jewish law. . . . How we deal with all of our *animal instincts* is an important litmus test of our *humanity*."[22] The statement calls our attention to the classic Jewish imagining of the human as suspended between the animal and the divine. Approximately the same idea is articulated in an article found on the Kof-K Web site:

> In order to acknowledge G-d and follow His laws, one must first recognize that there is a higher authority than that of our own judgment. Once we do that, the potential to elevate ourselves from the performance of mere physical acts to acts that make a spiritually significant impact on our lives becomes real. . . . It is interesting to note that most of the animals and birds that Jews are not permitted to eat are aggressors. Permitted foods are more spiritual in nature, and thus more alike in essence to the soul of man. Unclean foods are those whose nature contains less of the Divine. The dietary laws, therefore, are supremely important in raising man to G-d, and in achieving the ultimate goal of the world—its return to its Divine source. . . . Eating can be a battle. We must uplift our animalistic urges to eat and drink and transform our meals into a refined and exalted endeavor—characterized by mastery and discipline over our passions. We must subject our instincts to a higher force and elevate ourselves.[23]

Note the centrality in both these statements of chain-of-being imagery, which urges us to become fully human by suppressing and transforming those aspects of our nature that are associated with animals.

Previously we saw how the animal is often understood as an object of divine concern in relation to the dietary laws. Now the animal reappears as an image of the darker side of the human—an aspect in need of elevation. The OK Kosher Certification Web site is not as explicit in its use of chain-of-being imagery, but offers basically the same vision:

> Forbidden foods are referred to in the Torah as abominations to the G-dly soul [the special soul believed to be found in Jews], elements that detract from our

spiritual sensitivity. Birds of prey and carnivorous animals, having the power to influence the eater with aggressive attributes, are among the foods that are forbidden. . . . To explain the power of kosher food, we must turn to Chassidic teachings based upon the mysticism of the Ari-Zal (Rabbi Yitzchak Luria). The Ari-Zal gave a literal interpretation of the verse, "Man does not live by bread alone, but by the word of G-d" (Deuteronomy 8:3). He explained that it is not the food itself that gives life but rather the spark of G-dliness—the "word of G-d"—that is in the food. All matter has within it some aspect of the "G-dly sparks" that give life and existence to the world. When we eat, the digestive system extracts the nutrients while the *neshamah* [soul or spirit] extracts the G-dly spark found in nature.[24]

This chain-of-being imagery, while common, is not found in all cases. For example, this imagery was not to be found anywhere on OU Kosher's Web site.

A quite similar idea, however, is expressed on the OU Kosher Web site in an article entitled "Thinking Kosher." While the article agrees that the idea that kashrut enhances discipline is important—"much of Torah is disciplinary in nature and self-discipline is vital in one's religious life"[25]—the author wishes to emphasize instead "the idea that what we eat . . . affects what we are. . . . Samson Raphael Hirsch, the great modern interpreter of Torah Judaism, explains that the massive complex of *mitzvos* is designed to make the Jew capable of, and sensitive to, his spiritual task. Indeed, the Jewish record for endurance, spiritual creativity, and God-centeredness is unparalleled."[26] The idea expressed here is softer than the idea expressed on the Star-K Kosher Certification and Kof-K Kosher Supervision Web sites sites. Kashrut is understood as preparatory—as providing an opening and sensitivity to the greater task of "endurance, spiritual creativity, and God-centeredness"—rather than, as the Star-K and Kof-K texts imply, as actually constitutive of a spiritual elevation. In all cases we have the common idea that kashrut allows the activity of eating—normally a base "animal" activity—to advance a larger spiritual task.

In these highly pubic discourses about humane treatment of animals and moral elevation of human animals, a vision of what it means to be both human and ethical is articulated. Humans are obligated both to be kind to animals and, partly by means of this very kindness, to surpass them, thereby achieving the distinctive dominion over external animals and internal animality that is the human's privilege. Although, as we have seen, concern for animals is a common trope in explanations of kashrut, it is constrained and informed by the fact that kashrut is simultaneously understood as a suppression and transformation of all that is "animal." The texts oscillate between viewing animals as fellow creatures that must not be indiscriminately harmed and the animal as an ideal type, representing the unethical nature into which the human is born and above which God commands him to rise.

Ultimately, the practice of eating animals according to the laws of kashrut symbolically orders the cosmos—particularly the human being's place in it in relation to human and nonhuman animals. It avoids not only "matter out of place"—to invoke the apt phrase of Mary Douglas[27]—but helps ensure that the human and the animal are "in place."

This analysis of the ethics of kashrut provides a framework within which to understand the AgriProcessors event—an event that broke into contemporary Jewish discourses when some animals that were supposed to sit still as steaks on our plates, representing a benevolent dominion, stood up and, with the help of an undercover video, issued a protest. Leaving their hidden place on distant ranches and slaughterhouses, these creatures began, so to speak, walking through homes and synagogues. The eyes and bellows of cattle being slaughtered confronted the Jewish public. If a functioning kosher infrastructure helps keep the human and animal in place, then the events at AgriProcessors can be understood as a disruption of the proper order of things. The force that accomplished this disruption was not simply the fact that American Jews unused to seeing slaughter were presented with a video of it or even that the video depicted acts that were especially abusive. The video accomplished more: it made the animals present for a public that had forgotten them. It brought the reality of the kill floor into the comfort of living rooms. The eyes of the cattle in the undercover video rolled in pain and blinked when the animals should have been insensible and, in the minutiae of these movements, released a charge that cannot be denied—"yes, they suffer, like us."[28]

2

The Event and Response

The public scandals associated with AgriProcessor's Postville plant have become iconic in many quarters of American Jewry. They have become "extraordinary magnets of meaning with a religious cast."[1] The scandals have not only received abundant attention in the popular press but generated substantial discussion in rabbinic circles, become a point of reference for Jewish food, environmental, and animal activists, and, as we will see, helped to generate infrastructural change. *AgriProcessors* and *Postville,* while hardly meaning any one thing, have come to stand for what is wrong or, at least, what can go wrong in American kosher practice. Despite this prominence, a full narrative of the inaugurating events and their subsequent unfolding has never been printed.[2] This chapter provides exactly that, answering the question "what happened" in an essentially commonsense manner—what traditional Jewish exegetes would call a *pshat* reading.

Our story begins November 30, 2004, when an article appeared in the *New York Times* online: "Videotapes Show Grisly Scenes at Kosher Slaughterhouse," followed by a less provocatively titled print version on December 1 entitled "Video Cited in Calling Kosher Slaughter Inhumane." The article launched the systematic animal abuse at AgriProcessors into public consciousness. Hundreds of news stories followed in the coming months, and discussions of AgriProcessors have continued to appear even as this book went to press almost a decade later.

THE EVENT

AGRIPROCESSORS BEFORE THE EVENT

AgriProcessors was not simply a business venture; the company was also conceived as a service to the Lubavitch community: both by providing kosher meat and by bringing money into the community. The Rubashkin family who owned and managed the plant was known in the Chabad community for its intracommunity charitable work and for the political influence it exerted through large contributions, mostly to Republican political candidates and campaigns.[3] A story is told that "the Rebbe"—the seventh and late leader of the Chabad-Lubavitch community, Rabbi Menachem Mendel Schneerson— asked Sholom Rubashkin to provide kosher meat to Jews in smaller towns where it had been difficult or expensive to obtain. The Rubashkins' labor in creating AgriProcessors was understood by them and much of the Orthodox community as godly work. Godly or not, the venture was a financial success and, for a time, a public relations triumph as well. Some estimate that at its peak AgriProcessors provided 60 percent of kosher beef and 40 percent of kosher poultry in the United States.[4]

Before going further, it is important for me to be clear that the fact that my original involvement in AgriProcessors was primarily as a Jew concerned with animal abuse has provided me a *particular* angle of vision on the events that preceded the *New York Times* article and requires that I write myself into the first part of this narrative. Some months before PETA conducted the undercover investigation, I was invited to participate in an internal discussion the organization was having about whether it should devote investigatory resources to animal abuse in kosher slaughterhouses. Undercover investigations have been a central part of PETA's work since its founding by Ingrid Newkirk, who continues to lead the organization, and Alex Pacheco in 1980, but the organization had, as a kind of unofficial policy, never campaigned on the ethics of kosher slaughter or abuses in kosher slaughterhouses. This is noteworthy, as an earlier incarnation of animal protection movements in the European context historically targeted "ritual"—that is, Jewish and Muslim—slaughter, which remains controversial in the European Union today. Newkirk had a keen awareness of the history in which anti-Semitic attacks on shechitah masqueraded as concern for animal welfare and consciously wanted to avoid any association with this form of anti-Semitism.

PETA has never argued that shechitah is inherently more problematic than any other method of slaughter, and Newkirk appears, prior to AgriProcessors, to have chosen to steer her organization away from exposés on aberrant animal abuse that just happened to be at kosher facilities. It was a reconsideration of this latter policy while retaining the former that led PETA to contact me in 2004.

This reconsideration had been prompted primarily by an observant Jewish assistant of Newkirk's, Philip Schein, who was eager to be able to address concerns pertaining to animal abuse in his own community. When I was invited into the discussion, two questions were posed to me. First, did I, as a person active on farmed animal protection issues and a young scholar of religion who presumably had some familiarity with broader Jewish attitudes toward the ethics of eating animals, think that it made sense to do such an investigation?[5] Second, assuming it was the right thing to do, was it possible to do so without appearing anti-Semitic?

As it was evident that PETA leadership had no interest in attending to (let alone critiquing) shechitah as such, I could not see how such an investigation could be construed as anti-shechitah, which has always been the focus of anti-Semitic attacks. Furthermore, it became clear that beyond reaching the Jewish community with their message (which was the motivation for the campaign that was especially important to Schein), part of the reason the idea of investigating a kosher plant made sense to PETA from the point of view of resource allocation was because of the public impression that kosher slaughter was particularly humane—something PETA (and myself) doubted would hold up under scrutiny. Some PETA staffers felt that the aura of decency around kosher meat gave meat eaters a way out of acknowledging the "real" conditions of modern slaughter. Someone could eat kosher meat and say that all the documentation PETA had amassed of problems at nonkosher slaughterhouses simply did not apply to the meat they ate. PETA, which takes an abolitionist stance that raising animals for slaughter is inherently inhumane, thus had a certain inclination to address problems of animal abuse in kosher slaughter for the same reason they wanted to address problems of animal abuse on allegedly humane "free-range," "organic," or other kinds of specialty farms: to argue that modern meat production—even at its best—remains cruel. Thus ceasing to avoid kosher slaughter plants was broached not out of a sense that they were particularly bad, but rather a sense that even though these companies might be slightly better than average (that was the guess before the AgriProcessors investigation began) they were still unacceptable. PETA staffers I spoke with, such as then PETA director Bruce Friedrich, saw truth in the idea that kosher was "less cruel" because, they reasoned, any additional level of certification and supervision, such as that required by kosher law, could work to reduce animal abuse. Precisely the fact that it was reasonable to assume kosher slaughter might be, from PETA's organizational perspective, slightly "less cruel" helped legitimate the idea of an investigation of a kosher slaughterhouse. Some of PETA's leadership was attracted to the possibility of being able to advance their vision of animal ethics in the Jewish community while also being able to say to Americans at large, "if this happens in a kosher slaughterhouse, imagine what happens elsewhere."[6] Taking all these factors into consideration, I did not see any credible way PETA could be accused of anti-Semitism and I told the PETA leadership so.

Did I also think it was a good idea for them to do an investigation into "a kosher slaughterhouse" (all discussions were abstract at this point, as no particular plants had been mentioned)? Ultimately I said yes. In the discussions in which I participated, with the exception of Friedrich,[7] PETA's top leadership initially expressed reservations rather than enthusiasm about engaging kosher slaughter practices, and it appeared to me that without Schein's pressure PETA would have dropped the idea. The person then in charge of investigations and whose support was crucial, Mary Beth Sweetland, PETA's then director of research, investigations, and rescue, was especially skeptical. Kosher was, in her perspective, a tiny market and, given the immense resources that must go into any investigation with no guarantee it will be successful she was unsure an investigation made sense. Schein and myself, however, were asked to put our heads together and report back to Friedrich, Newkirk, and Sweetland our best analysis of what such a campaign might accomplish. We argued—and we were really guessing—that if a PETA investigation obtained video footage of what modern industrial kosher slaughter looks like, even barring any exceptional abuses, it would upset the Jewish community's image of animals being humanely slaughtered and start a public discussion that concerned Jews already active on animal issues could advance totally independently of PETA.

Beyond our primary observation that such an investigation would advance PETA's concern with animal protection in the Jewish community, Schein and I further noted that the market for kosher food was growing and that such an investigation would make less plausible the idea that kosher slaughter avoided the problems of modern industrial slaughterhouses. This abstract conversation about the feasibility and appropriateness of an investigation at kosher plants came to a close in July 2004. Not long after I was told that Newkirk and Sweetland, the ultimate decision makers, thought an investigation made sense if there was an appropriate facility to investigate. I (surely among others) was then asked if I had suggestions for possible sites. Originally I had none and told them so. Another thread of events becomes important to relate at this point.

In June of 2003 PETA had received a whistleblower complaint about AgriProcessors from a prominent animal welfare expert whose name was shared with me confidentially. PETA, as it often does, sent the company a letter, now publicly available, asking that the issues be addressed—in this case by hiring the nation's most well-known expert in the humane slaughter of cattle, Dr. Temple Grandin. The PETA letter further offered to keep the exchange confidential if AgriProcessors moved to address the concerns.[8] PETA's request was modest, given standards in the industry, and ultimately AgriProcessors, under pressure from the OU, did allow Grandin into the facility after the investigation had gone public. Nonetheless, at the time of sending (well before the investigation), PETA's letter was summarily dismissed. AgriProcessors' attorney, Nathan Lewin, one of the most prominent Orthodox attorneys in the nation, with special ties to the Haredi community,[9] wrote a letter back to PETA in August, which was interpreted by PETA, in retrospect it appears correctly, as indicating that AgriProcessors had no intention of addressing the concerns PETA raised. PETA nonetheless continued to make several efforts to enter into negotiation with the Rubashkins in writing and over the phone, all of which produced no results.

The difference in tone between PETA's letters and Lewin's is striking. PETA's letter opens: "On behalf of People for the Ethical Treatment of Animals . . . I am writing about a matter of mutual concern—the humane treatment of animals. I'm sure you'll agree with PETA that, in addition to meeting the most minimal requirements of *kashrut*, those who raise animals for food must not allow them to suffer any more than is absolutely necessary, in accordance with the admirable principle of *tza'ar ba'ale chayyim* [צער בעלי חיים: the traditional Jewish principle to avoid animal suffering]."[10] By contrast, Lewin responded: "You may rest assured that, contrary to the assertion in your letter, neither Jewish law nor 'common decency' is being violated in the

AgriProcessors plant. . . . Long before the rest of the world showed any 'common decency' to animals or had the slightest concern for the treatment of animals, the laws of the Torah and rabbinic teachings commanded the Jewish people to treat all living creatures humanely. Secular society—including your organization—has still not caught up with the precepts of Jewish law in this regard."[11]

I recalled this exchange with AgriProcessors at the time that PETA asked me about possible places to investigate and, looking into the company, discovered that this was not only one kosher slaughterhouse among others but the largest *glatt* slaughterhouse in the nation. At that point I suggested to PETA, through Friedrich, that since this plant was refusing to engage in dialogue when concerns were raised, and because it was one of the largest in the nation, it seemed a natural choice for investigation. Judging by the speed of Friedrich's reply that AgriProcessors was to be investigated, it appeared that PETA had come to the same conclusion internally. At this point, as far as I was concerned, PETA's investigative work was a black box, until a few weeks before the *New York Times* story was aired when PETA contacted me again. From this point forward most of the narrative I will now review is a matter of public record.

PROCEDURE

The unnecessary suffering of animals captured on video at AgriProcessors does not appear to be the result of sadism,[12] but rather standard operating procedures.[13] The procedure at AgriProcessors that attracted the most extreme negative attention was the further cutting and partial removal of the tracheas and esophagi of cattle immediately after shechitah and, in at least 20 percent of the cases, while the animals were still sensible and often in visible agony.[14] This potentially dangerous task was performed by the *shochtim's* gentile assistants by simply pulling the organs out by hand, cutting them out, or pulling on them with a hook. The procedure is not typically performed in other kosher slaughterhouses, and, according to Grandin, the real purpose behind the procedure at AgriProcessors remains unclear.[15]

There are halakhic (Jewish legal) precedents for allowing a "second cut" to facilitate bleeding,[16] but the practice is not seen as mandatory and ultimately was prohibited at the insistence of the OU. Nonetheless, this procedure was performed on virtually all the cattle that appear on the undercover video. The only exceptions were a handful of cases where the procedure appears to have been skipped because the speed of the line simply did not leave time to do it. PETA showed me all the footage obtained during the investigation—a total of five hours of footage of cattle slaughter videotaped in six sessions over the course of roughly seven weeks in August and September of 2004. All this footage has not been publicly released. In it 278 animals were slaughtered, 230 of them were clearly visible, and at least 20 percent of these animals showed behavioral signs of consciousness (for example, eye movement but not leg twitches, which can be involuntary) after having their tracheas and esophagi removed and then being released from the rotating pen in which they were held during slaughter.

The policy of systematically removing the trachea and esophagus from each animal was probably the most painful of the procedures performed at AgriProcessors, but the use of a "rotating pen" to invert and hold the animals while shechitah was performed appears to have been another serious welfare problem. In this procedure the animal enters a machine that clamps onto it from both sides and rotates the animal to expose the animal's neck so that a cut to the neck will be me made with the knife's blade facing toward the floor rather than toward the ceiling. Grandin argues that the act of being inverted is generally distressing and frightening to cattle,[17] which can have the secondary effect of prolonging consciousness after shechitah. For this reason in a 2002 *teshuvah* (legal ruling) the Conservative movement's Rabbinical Assembly formally declared the practice of inversion a violation of *tza'ar ba'ale chayyim* and the standards for kosher slaughter outlined in the welfare guidelines endorsed by the American Meat Institute and Food Marketing Institute/National Coalition of Chain Restaurants originally prohibited the procedure.[18] Certain Haredi Orthodox communities, however, require inversion before shechitah and argue that inversion is a halakhic requirement. Though the head of OU Kosher, Rabbi Menachem Genack, is an advocate of upright (nonrecumbent) slaughter, the OU defended AgriProcessors use of inversion prior to slaughter, arguing that "recumbent slaughter is considered humane and is widely practiced in the European Union."[19]

Whether or not there is some theoretical way to perform inverted slaughter that could reduce animal suffering to the levels that upright slaughter produces, the handling and slaughter methods used at AgriProcessors consistently left animals conscious for more than a minute and, in one videotaped incident, three minutes. Peer-review studies and rabbinic statements suggest sensibility should typically be lost within twenty seconds. Stephen Bloom has confirmed that problems with prolonged consciousness after slaughter existed as far back as 1996 when he was given a tour of the slaughter facility. Bloom witnessed multiple animals struggling to stand minutes after shechitah. Bloom did not actually see animals' throats slit and so cannot verify whether or not the animals' tracheas and esophagi were removed at that time.[20] However, another anonymous source who contacted PETA, and whose statement I independently confirmed, stated that she saw the trachea and esophagus procedure when she visited the slaughter line in 1998. While inconclusive, this suggests that for at least six years AgriProcessors cut the tracheas and esophagi out of animals that were frequently conscious.

While these summaries of the incidents of greatest concern can give one a general idea of the issues at hand, the very nature of a generic discussion of the events—speaking of "cattle," as if there were such an animal, instead of individual, sexed animals—can make it more difficult to understand the intense reaction to the video footage. Videos are always images of particular times and places and individuals. One will never see "the animal" on film, only this or that animal of a specific species, sex, age, state of health, and so on. For this reason a discussion of some of the specific incidents recorded on the undercover videos is helpful. Precisely such a summary was prepared by PETA's legal team as they pressed the USDA to prosecute the plant. While the USDA never chose to prosecute, they did conclude that the Humane Methods of Slaughter Act, a federal law that applies to the slaughter of cattle and pigs, was violated and further that the USDA's own employees often slept or played video games while the "abuses" occurred and even accepted "inappropriate gifts" from the Rubashkins. Significantly, this conclusion was not released to the public until a year after it was reached and then only because PETA aggressively pursued its release through the federal Freedom of Information Act.

PETA's descriptions in this legal brief are careful and consistent with the video footage, but also calculated to achieve a certain effect. Here are select descriptions:

> In scene #21 (August 27, 2004) the shochet slits the throat of a steer who is still conscious when his trachea and esophagus are ripped from his throat. When the animal is rotated out of the Facomia pen, he falls to the floor[,] then

stands and slips and slides in the blood as he maneuvers into a corner of the room; his trachea can be seen swinging from side to side as he struggles. . . . This steer languished for approximately 3 minutes in the kill room . . . yet no attempt was made by the shochet or any other employee to end the unnecessary suffering of this animal. . . . As depicted in the same scene, a second steer is slaughtered while the first animal huddles, still conscious, in the corner of the room. This animal also appears to be fully conscious when he is hoisted, as evidenced by the movement in his tongue and his tail . . .

In scene #26 (September 6, 2004) yet another steer struggles to stand after he is released from the Facomia pen. More than one minute after the initial cut, he remains conscious on the floor. The employee is unable to shackle the animal and so a second steer is dumped to the floor and bellows as he is shackled and swung to the bleed rail. . . .

In scene #43 (September 12, 2004) a steer is dumped from the Facomia pen. The animal slips in the blood on the cement floor as he attempts to right himself. An employee repeatedly kicks the animal in an apparent effort to gauge the safety of approaching the animal to attach the shackle.[21]

WAS IT KOSHER?

Did the kinds of actions described above render the meat produced by AgriProcessors *treyf*? A relative but incomplete consensus has been reached in both the Orthodox and Conservative Jewish communities that incidents like those caught on PETA's video have in no way jeopardized the kosher status of the meat from AgriProcessors. Anecdotally, I have found this comes as a surprise to most American Jews unversed in the details of Orthodox practice. Despite the fact that a—almost certainly *the*—dominant folk Jewish explanation for the laws of kosher slaughter is that they are humane, and despite the consistent trope regarding the humaneness of kosher slaughter invoked by kosher certification agencies themselves, the leadership of all of America's halakhic forms of Judaism—Modern Orthodoxy, Haredi Orthodoxy, and the Conservative movement—have, since the AgriProcessors event, emphasized publicly that any degree of cruelty, no matter how egregious, has no impact on the kosher status of the meat. For example, Rabbi Avi Shafran, representing the Haredi organization Agudath Israel of America, likened the relationship between kashrut and ethics to the relationship between poetry and hygiene. "A great poet might opt to not shower, but that bad habit does not necessarily affect the quality of his writing."[22]

This consensus was by no means assured, and the circumstances preceding its emergence suggests socially coercive measures were necessary to manufacture it. Significantly, the existence of such coercion would have no impact on the question of the meat's kosher status. What qualifies meat as kosher in traditionally observant Jewish communities is not ultimately the fact of any particular set of procedures having occurred (although this is of course not irrelevant), but rather a judgment by the relevant rabbinic authorities that the meat is kosher. No amount of documentation that a stated rule of kosher slaughter was violated has any bearing on the kosher status of meat any more than documentation that a convicted person is innocent has any bearing on the legal status of that person if that documentation is not ultimately ruled upon in a court of law.

What is more significant, given the internal standards of Jewish law, is that in the weeks following the scandal several *poskim* (Jewish legal authorities) with unquestioned credentials in the Orthodox world issued statements that the meat produced through the procedures seen on the video could not possibly be kosher. The first of these was Shear Yashuv Cohen, who has been the chief rabbi of Haifa for more than thirty years and, at the time, was serving on the Kashrut Committee of the Israeli chief rabbinate. PETA, working through a then employee with family in Israel who knew Rabbi Cohen, Tal Ronnen, arranged to have Cohen review the video before it was released to the press. Rabbi Cohen disputed that meat from the animals slaughtered on the video could be kosher, explaining that "the procedure of this shehita is definitely unacceptable by halakhic standards. . . . This procedure is not only cruel and therefore unacceptable by Jewish religious law. It also cannot be certified as kosher, as the animal must die as the direct result of the ritual cut." Note that Rabbi S. Y. Cohen makes two distinct legal observations: first that there has been a violation of anticruelty law and, second, that there has been a kashrut violation. Cohen had not been told what plant the tapes were from or that the plant in the video was certified as kosher by multiple agencies, including the flagship American Orthodox certification agency, the OU. Before his remarks made it to the press, Rabbi Cohen received a series of calls from U.S. rabbis, including Menachem Genack at the OU and Chaim Kohn from KAJ,[23] another agency certifying AgriProcessors, and backed away from his remarks without ever retracting them (despite some suggestions to the contrary).[24] Rather, Rabbi Cohen simply explained that it was not his place to issue an authoritative ruling and that he deferred to other authorities like Genack and Kohn, and he requested that his letter no longer be cited. For example, in a December 2, 2004 article in the *Jerusalem Post* he is quoted as qualifying his remarks by saying, "I'm not an expert on the laws of cruelty to animals in Halacha. . . . AgriProcessors' kosher supervisor, Rabbi Haim Cohen [Chaim Kohn], claims that tearing out the windpipe reduces the suffering of the animal. . . . If that is true, the shehita is kosher." Of course, "tearing out the windpipe" does not reduce animal suffering and Rabbi S. Y. Cohen surely knew as much.[25]

A similar incident subsequently occurred with Israel's chief rabbinate itself. On December 2, 2004, the *Jerusalem Post* reported that the rabbinate told them "it would not consider as kosher cows that appear in an undercover video of ritual slaughtering at the AgriProcessors Inc. plant. . . . The rabbinate's opinion contradicts a halachic ruling by the Orthodox Union in the US."[26] Unexpectedly, ten days after this article the *Jerusalem Post* reported that "Israeli rabbis are staging an about face. On Friday [Rabbi Ezra] Raful [head of the rabbinate's international shehitah supervision department] was quoted by a Public Relations firm contracted by US rabbis as saying that AgriProcessors' meat is kosher. As if he were refuting an inaccurate news report, Raful said that 'I never said that the shehita seen in the [PETA] video is not kosher.'"[27] It is true that Raful never said that shechitah per se was a problem according to halakhic standards, but the rabbinate did indicate that the meat was not kosher—a position they reversed for reasons that remain obscure.

BEHIND THE SCENES

It was not only rabbinic authorities who may have been pressured into backing down, if not retracting, their statements. The Iowa secretary of agriculture, Patty Judge, originally condemned the cruelty at AgriProcessors and asserted she would shut AgriProcessors down if she had the jurisdiction.[28] Then, two weeks later, after an announced tour of the plant in which three to four animals were slaughtered especially for Judge, she declared the plant humane.[29] Not long after this, Judge received a $10,000 campaign donation from AgriProcessors—fully 10 percent of the money she raised in her run for the Democratic nomination for Iowa's governor.[30]

The enormous influence that AgriProcessors and its allies seemed to wield behind the scenes may also explain some unusual circumstances surrounding the breaking of the story by the *New York Times*. The editors at the *New York Times* surely understood that reporting on PETA's 2004 video, as with so much of their reporting, would propel the scandal into national attention, and the reticence with which the *New York Times* published the article is a story worth reflecting on all in itself and one that has, as far as I know, never entered the public record. The print article had been scheduled to appear on the *front page* on Monday, November 29, 2004; this was told to the journalist, Donald McNeil, who reported it to Bruce Friedrich at PETA, who reported it to me. Late Sunday evening the article was withheld. When Monday came and went with no word from the editors, McNeil contacted Friedrich and explained his puzzlement, noting that he had never experienced anything like this with any previous story and that top editors were discussing the piece. The cause of the delay and displacement of the article from page one appears to have been the result of strong-arm tactics by AgriProcessors' lawyer, Nathan Lewin, to whom I will return shortly.

THE RESPONSE

Once the video of animal abuse at AgriProcessors was public, hundreds of news stories quickly followed, including articles in the *Los Angeles Times*, the *Washington Post*, multiple articles in the *Jerusalem Post*, and an NPR story.[31] The range of initial responses included denial by Haredi Orthodox authorities, partial denial and a limited response by Modern Orthodox authorities, and a general acknowledgment of the problems by Conservative and other liberal Jewish leadership.

DISAVOWAL

Denial of wrongdoing was most aggressive in the Haredi Orthodox community. Consider the response of AgriProcessors' top administrator, Sholom Rubashkin, who gave an impassioned speech on his company's practices shortly after the story broke. In the speech, which was subsequently distributed on the Internet, Rubashkin expounds:

> Although the media likes to present the Shechita story as an "undercover" story to gain some appeal, there is no undercover story. What hit the satellite waves

was a documentation of the Shechita process in its full glory (assuming the video is not altered, and we are in the process of trying to ascertain if it was altered.). . . . The point of this whole drasha [talk; literally "interpretation"] is this: What Agriprocessors is seen doing, is done with the supervision of the USDA and Rabbinical supervision. Every Beis Hashchita [kosher slaughter-house] should be that way. Nothing wrong was, or is being done. There is nothing to admit.[32]

Lewin was similarly strident, arguing in multiple articles that absolutely nothing inappropriate happened at AgriProcessors, that the company was a victim of anti-Semitism, and that PETA actually was aiming to end shechitah in particular. The last accusation was particularly questionable, as at the time a number of media sources, including the *Jerusalem Post* and even the Orthodox Union, had quoted PETA's explicit position that kosher slaughter was likely less problematic than nonkosher slaughter. Lewin's own narrative of events in his revealing diatribe "The Assault on Shehita," published on December 15, 2004, reflects his peculiar standards of evidence. In this article Lewin revealingly describes his interactions with *New York Times* reporter Donald McNeil just prior to the newspaper's breaking article on the incidents: "McNeil invited us into a small office where we watched the video together. The film began with a title that read 'Kosher Slaughterhouse, Summer 2004.' Then came snippets, each headed 'Incident # ___' with a specific date." These scenes correspond to the ones described in the first section of this chapter. Lewin then describes the second cut and removal of tracheas and esophagi before asserting that "there was no reason to think that the animal felt any more pain from this removal than an appendicitis victim under anesthesia feels when his appendix is removed." This remark is hard to square with the scenes, and Lewin helps us understand why he makes this claim by further explaining that he "knew that animals whose throats are cut by a shohet totally lose consciousness and any sense of pain between two and six seconds after the cut is made." This claim is not only unsubstantiated by any study, but it contradicts figures that are normally given by Haredi experts themselves whenever a precise number of seconds is mentioned (typically at least twenty seconds), a time range that is consistent with some scientific studies. It did not matter to Lewin if the animals appeared to be in pain; he "knew" without observation—without seeing the animals—that they must be unconscious whatever they appeared to be doing. Lewin goes on to express his frustration with McNeil, "Both Rabbi Kohn [of KAJ] and I noted that scientific fact [that animals lose consciousness in two to six seconds] in conversations with McNeil while the film was running. He seemed unpersuaded. 'Look at that animal thrashing around and bellowing,' he said. 'How can you say it is not feeling pain?' The first animal on the video even got to its feet and walked off into a corner before it fell over." No matter, Lewin says, nothing inhumane occurred.[33]

In this same article, Lewin also appears to reveal himself as the source of the unusual delay in the *New York Times* article. He writes:

> Very early Sunday morning I also called Reb Chaim Dovid Zwiebel, executive vice-president of Agudath Israel of America, at the Agudath Israel convention in Connecticut. . . . There was still one session left in the Agudath Israel convention, and Reb Zwiebel presented to it a strongly worded condemnation of PETA and support for AgriProcessors. The resolution passed unanimously. I e-mailed the Agudath Israel resolution and the facts regarding Rabbi Shear Yashuv Cohen's statement to McNeil at The New York Times. I received no acknowledgment.
>
> But no story appeared in Monday's New York Times. And no story appeared in Tuesday's New York Times.[34]

We have already dealt with the issue of S. Y. Cohen's statement in the first section of this chapter and will turn to the Agudath Israel resolution in a moment, but I think the congruence of Lewin's and Friedrich's recollections of the events makes it clear that Lewin had indeed been successful in delaying the story and perhaps also convinced the editors to move the story from the front page and leave out mention of Cohen's statement, which is noticeably absent from McNeil's breaking piece.

As a significant side observation, it is worth noting that Lewin issued the same kind of implausible response regarding the voluminous evidence of abuse of human (non-Jewish) workers at AgriProcessors amassed by the federal government after its May 8, 2008 immigration raid several years later. Given the arrest of hundreds of undocumented workers, Lewin conceded that AgriProcessors had employed them: "Regarding Agriprocessors having employed illegal aliens, it was a well-known fact that Agriprocessors employed illegal aliens—as does every other meat packing plant in the United States."[35] This observation is mostly fair; the employment of undocumented workers in meat processing is a public secret. However, Lewin goes on to argue that "Rubashkin treated his employees better than the employees are treated at all the major slaughterhouses in the United States. They were paid better and treated more humanely"[36]—leading Orthodox blogger Shmarya Rosenberg to speculate about the "alternative universe of AgriProcessors former counsel, Nathan Lewin."[37]

This aggressive denial is perhaps best shown in how Agudath Israel of America, a rabbinic organization representing Haredi Orthodoxy, responded to the initial publicity. As Lewin explained, the organization passed a resolution in the closing session of their annual convention condemning PETA and the video shortly after its release. As reported by *Yated Ne'eman*, a weekly Haredi news magazine: "By unanimous vote, Agudath Israel condemned what it termed a 'vicious and unethical attack on Jewish religious practice.' The resolution also noted that among the first Nazi attacks against Jews was 'peddling photographs of allegedly "cruel" kosher slaughter,' and that PETA 'now follows in that vile course.'"[38] What Lewin does not mention in his account of the Agudath Israel convention is that at least the majority and possibly no one who voted for the resolution had *seen* the video. They acted, it appears, on the basis of the phone call from Lewin himself.[39] Given Lewin's own narrative quoted earlier, it seems likely that he orchestrated the resolution with such haste precisely to use it to delay the *New York Times* story.

In contrast to these Haredi voices, the Modern Orthodox OU responded to the events in a measured way and, while certainly saying critical things about PETA, issued no condemnation of the organization and implied no anti-Semitism. However, the OU leaders also went out of their way to shield AgriProcessors from criticism, downplayed the seriousness of the problems, and for several days tried to deny that there were any problems at all. For example, in the original *New York Times* article we read: "Rabbis Menachem Genack and Yisroel Belsky, the chief experts for the Orthodox Union . . . said the killings on the tape, while 'gruesome,' appeared kosher. . . . Scientific studies, Rabbi Belsky said, found that an animal whose brain had lost blood pressure when its throat was slit felt nothing and that any motions it made were involuntary. 'The perfect model is the headless chicken running around,' Rabbi Genack said."[40] To compare the scenes on the AgriProcessors tapes to the involuntary movements of a headless chicken is one of those rare statements that is obviously absurd. To give some context, Grandin, who Genack himself now recognizes as a national expert, was quoted in the same article describing the same scenes on the tape as "an atrocious abomination, nothing like I've seen in 30 kosher plants I've visited here and in England, France, Ireland and Canada. . . . Nothing in the Humane Slaughter Act says you can start dismembering an animal while it's still conscious."[41]

Days after these denials, as coverage of the story rapidly expanded, the OU did in fact successfully pressure a recalcitrant AgriProcessors to end the "second cut" and to consider addressing the broader problems in the plant's management. It appears that, despite his public remarks, Genack, who was uniformly described to me as an honorable and ethical person,[42] was the central figure who accomplished these changes.[43] And Rabbi Tzvi Hersh Weinreb, OU's executive vice president, did acknowledge the problems with cruelty in a limited way when he was quoted by the *New York Times* on December 3, 2004, describing the removal of the tracheas and esophagi as "especially inhumane."[44] At one level it is a strong condemnation of AgriProcessors, in that the use of the adjective *especially* implies that there were other cruel practices at the plant. Still, Weinreb is later quoted in the same article saying he needs to "investigate how regularly it [the removal of tracheas and esophagi] happened."[45] Such investigation is completely appropriate, but in this context Weinreb's remarks give the incorrect impression that the removal of the tracheas and esophagi was not a standard procedure.

Official statements by the OU about the AgriProcessors events functioned to diminish or eliminate any sense that the problems at AgriProcessors were systematic or serious. In the opening sentence of the first such official statement (December 9, 2004), the word *apparent* plays a decisive role, introducing uncertainty where there really was none. The statement describes the PETA video as depicting "scenes of cows staggering in apparent agony for several minutes after their throats were cut by the shochet."[46]

The statement continues by explaining that "during the six or seven weeks during which the video was taken, approximately 18,000 animals were slaughtered by the plant in question. With such numbers, it is inevitable that aberrations do sometimes occur, and those shown in the video represent only a tiny percentage of the total number processed in that time span."[47] This statement appears calculated to mislead. At the time it was issued, the Rubashkins' own remarks (cited earlier) made it clear that the procedures on the tapes were standard.[48]

Even a month after the initial release of the tapes, representatives of AgriProcessors, the OU, and other kosher authorities repeatedly claimed or implied that the animals in PETA's video footage were not conscious. This was often accomplished simply by laying emphasis on the generic fact that animals *can* make involuntary movements, even when totally insensible. Other strategies were also used to obfuscate the situation. An OU statement issued on December 29, 2004, repeats the language of the December 9 statement: the agony of the animals is described as "apparent," the ugliness rather than cruelty of the procedures is emphasized; it is implied that the procedures PETA documented might have only occurred to a small fraction of animals and it is suggested that all slaughterhouses have similar kinds of problems. Although the December 29 statement does indicate that the OU wanted to see changes in the plant, it appears—from the statement, at least—that there was no real reason for this: "After carefully studying the video . . . [OU experts concluded] that these procedures meet all OU standards to the highest degree, and that the shochtim (rabbinic slaughterers) are all highly proficient, skilled and knowledgeable. Nevertheless . . . the trachea will no longer be removed following shechita, and . . . any animals that appear to have survived the procedure will be promptly stunned or shot."[49] This obfuscation of the cruelty of the procedures that the OU actually took steps to correct speaks to a broader sentiment that dominated the Orthodox response to the publicity around AgriProcessors: problems were not being acknowledged "to the goyim"—that is, the gentile public—but it was more acceptable to quietly address them through intracommunity means. That sentiment was most extreme among the Haredi leadership, but characterizes the Orthodox response as a whole and distinguishes it from much of liberal Judaism's response. This was true even among some of the leaders most desirous of change.[50]

The sense that non-Orthodox authorities had no place in dictating the details of how kosher slaughter should be done was perhaps the most profound barrier to addressing the problems at AgriProcessors. Haredi rabbis and community leaders like Lewin denied anything needed to be corrected in part because only intrahalakhic processes could, in their eyes, lead to any legitimate concern about the slaughter procedures. Modern Orthodox rabbis, as one would anticipate, given that movement's greater acceptance of the value of secular learning as compared with Haredim, were eventually amenable to consultation with animal welfare experts, but they did not want to publicly be seen as reprimanding their Haredi colleagues. This helps explain Genack's public defense of AgriProcessors even while privately pressuring them to change.

AGRIPROCESSORS AFTER THE EVENT

Going beyond the 2004 release of PETA's footage, a clearer picture of AgriProcessors'. management emerged in May of 2006 when the *Forward* reporter who had covered the PETA investigation, Nathaniel Popper (now at the *New York Times*), released the results of his own undercover investigation at AgriProcessors, this time focusing on worker abuse.[51] The article, "In Iowa Meat Plant, Kosher 'Jungle' Breeds Fear, Injury, Short Pay," proved a turning point in AgriProcessors' history. The extent to which the PETA investigation helped prompt the *Forward* and later the federal government's investigations into the mistreatment of humans is a question that merits further analysis. I observe here only that the relationship seems significant in that Popper's May 2006 article prominently features an interview with the PETA undercover investigator:

> He [the investigator] said that the cafeteria at AgriProcessors was in a lower class than the carpeted, climate-controlled cafeterias at the nonkosher slaughterhouses where he has worked. . . . At those nonkosher slaughterhouses, the PETA investigator said, he received significantly more safety training: a minimum of two days, while AgriProcessors only gave him one hour—with a supervisor who did not speak Spanish. The investigator said he ended up translating for the other trainees, all of whom were Hispanic. In addition, the PETA investigator—who agreed to speak with *The Forward* only if he could do so anonymously—said that when workers were injured or sick, supervisors at AgriProcessors showed little concern and were reluctant to provide access to the company's doctor.[52]

PETA had previously made public video footage showing that the investigator was denied health insurance by AgriProcessors for an obviously work-related illness, the contraction of Campylobacter, a bacteria which is abundantly present in chickens such as those he had handled immediately before his illness.[53] PETA's decision to make this information about worker abuse public happened at the insistence of Schein; PETA's slaughterhouse investigations regularly reveal violations of workers rights that PETA, as an organization dedicated to animal protection, does not publicize. After the human rights abuses were exposed by Popper and, to a lesser extent, PETA, the Conservative movement set up a task force in June of 2006, spearheaded by Rabbi Morris Allen, that earnestly followed up the accusations of abuse and ultimately led to the creation of an ethical food certification by the Conservative movement known as Magen Tzedek.

HUMAN / ANIMAL

AgriProcessors again garnered negative national attention in May 2008 when the federal government conducted what was at that time the largest single-site immigration raid in U.S. history at the plant, arresting more than 380 individuals. While the immigration raid was a moral tragedy for the undocumented workers arrested, it brought into full light the scope of the systematic human rights abuses at AgriProcessors, which, if worker reports are trusted, included unsafe working conditions, child labor, sexual harassment, sexual assault, forced labor (under threat of deportation), and cheating workers out of compensation for injuries. In September 2008 the Iowa attorney general filed more than 9,000 counts of child labor violations and by the end of October had compiled 10 million dollars in fines for tax and wage violation.[54]

Following the raid, the Conservative movement's Rabbinical Assembly and the United Synagogue of Conservative Judaism issued a joint statement condemning the abuses at AgriProcessors, but not advocating a national boycott. The question of a boycott or other actions to affect change at AgriProcessors became moot shortly thereafter in November 2008 when AgriProcessors filed for bankruptcy (the plant itself latter reopened and continues to operate as a new company, AgriStar).[55] Orthodox leaders—for example, at a panel on what it means to be kosher held at Yeshiva University on December 9, 2008—have responded to both the raid and its aftermath with cautious expressions of concern, discussion, and consistent arguments that, in their view, the kosher status of meat is not affected by unethical labor practices.

The press coverage of the immigration raid was on a much larger scale than the previous two scandals, and voices from every quarter of the Jewish world responded. Expressing a protest that, as we will shortly see, dates back to the original 2004 AgriProcessors scandal, Rabbi Morris Allen argued that the plant was neglecting Jewish ethical traditions and attending only to more technical, "ritual" aspects of Jewish law. "People want kosher food that is produced in an appropriate manner according to both ritual law and ethical law," Allen explained, expressing the view of many Conservative leaders.[56] In varying degrees, Orthodox leaders tended to defend Rubashkin or at least argue that accusations against him were overblown. For example, Rabbi Pesach Lerner, the vice president of the National Council of Young Israel, an Orthodox synagogue movement that claims twenty-five thousand member households, toured AgriProcessors' plant shortly after the raid and then described the site as "a Cadillac with top-of-the-line machinery and an emphasis on safety, security and health."[57] Many in the Orthodox community, largely Haredim, wrote letters and sent monetary donations to support Rubashkin as he faced a potential life sentence.[58] Secular leaders also weighed in. Then senator Barack Obama indirectly commented on the event in response to an inquiry about the situation in Postville: "We've got to crack down on employers who are taking advantage of undocumented workers. . . . The only reason they're hiring these folks is because they want to avoid paying people decent wages and providing them decent benefits."[59] The condemnation of AgriProcessors' management—which, even when focusing on human abuse, often gave a few words to the abuse of animals—had reached a new level.

Media coverage of the prosecution of AgriProcessors' leadership centered on the trials of Sholom Rubashkin. In late October 2008 Rubashkin was arrested on federal charges of harboring illegal immigrants and aiding and abetting aggravated identity theft; charges of bank fraud were later added. In November 2009 Rubashkin was convicted on eighty-six counts of financial fraud, and the following June he was sentenced to twenty-seven years in prison for these crimes.[60] Rubashkin was the sixth high-level manager at AgriProcessors to be convicted on federal charges; the other five individuals, who included two line managers, two financial officers, and the director of human resources, struck plea deals in exchange for testimony against him.[61] Following this conviction, prosecutors dismissed the immigration charges they had brought against Rubashkin; in a separate state trial in Iowa he was also acquitted on sixty-seven charges of child labor violations.[62] The company itself pled guilty to multiple charges of abusing underage workers; however, AgriProcessors' bankruptcy prevented prosecutors from collecting any fines for these crimes.

Ultimately some leaders at AgriProcessors were called to account for their financial crimes, but not their abuses of immigrants, minors, women, and animals. Meanwhile, the nearly four hundred immigrants who had worked at the plant endured expedited trials and subsequently served federal prison sentences of up to five months for identity theft before being deported; only a fraction of them were granted visas to remain in the United States.[63]

Tentatively, and in contrast to the dominant logic of the popular press, let us think about the various abuses at AgriProcessors—socially unacceptable treatment of animals, children, women, and undocumented workers—not as a series of separate occurrences, but as a unified pattern of abuse of vulnerable populations.[64] The thesis that these abuses are part of a unified worldview and pattern of behavior is something that cannot be adequately demonstrated until chapter 6, though we can already note that all these abuses appear to have been happening in the same time period and at the same places and were perpetrated by the same management structure. If this thesis is correct, it is worth highlighting the fact that only when the magnifying glass of media attention moved from the animal individuals wounded in this pattern of domination to the human victims did the problem come most fully into public view. Only then, for example, did figures like Obama begin to openly condemn AgriProcessors.

In the relative force of the condemnations of AgriProcessors that appeared in the news media a hierarchy was visible; speaking quite crudely, "children" are the object of the highest rhetorical concern, then women and undocumented workers, and then animals. While presenting itself as a necessary prioritization, we might ask if, in this entire process of separating out the victims as these constituencies and then allotting them each some "appropriate," relative amount of public attention and concern, the entire nature of what happened was not hidden from view, denied, disavowed.

PROTEST AND CHANGE

These larger questions aside for the moment, did AgriProcessors change its procedures? Most concerns about animal treatment raised in response to PETA's video by independent animal welfare experts were never publicly addressed by AgriProcessors or the OU. As described in the earlier quotation, AgriProcessors, under pressure from the OU, did report that they stopped the second cut in which the esophagi and trachea were removed and that they made a captive bolt gun available to (at least theoretically) quickly render unconscious animals improperly slaughtered. However, the extent to which these changes were implemented is unknown. AgriProcessors' Postville facility steadfastly refused unannounced audits (a standard if not widespread industry practice) that might have provided such evidence. Moreover, although it received surprisingly little public attention, in July 2007, and then again in May 2008, less egregious, though similar, slaughter problems were videotaped at another AgriProcessors plant in Nebraska (2007) and again in Postville (2008). In response to the 2008 footage from Postville, Grandin argued that "the undercover video clearly showed that when they think nobody is looking, they do bad things in this plant."[65] Just two months before its closing, and nearly four years after the release of PETA's undercover footage, Grandin considered AgriProcessors among the worst 2 percent of American slaughterhouses in its treatment of animals.[66]

During those four years, no major national Jewish organization called for a boycott of AgriProcessors. In May 2008, a pioneering and newly created Orthodox social justice organization, Uri L'Tzedek, announced what was to become a six-week boycott of AgriProcessors, which the group reported achieved certain improvements for workers before AgriProcessors declared bankruptcy. Unfortunately, I am aware of no evidence that this boycott achieved its aims.

Numerous individual rabbis, overwhelmingly in the Conservative movement, did declare AgriProcessors' products *treyf* following the 2004 events, but at no point did any well-established Jewish organization attempt to reduce financial support for AgriProcessors' products. (I cannot but feel a reflex of shame in this fact as I consider myself a part of the larger American Jewish community.) Given this support, it seems predictable that the basic problems with animal cruelty—and the whole package of mistreatment of workers with which I argue these abuses are linked—was never resolved.

ORTHODOX VOICES OF PROTEST

If only modest and unverified changes occurred at the AgriProcessors plant as a result of communal protest, there were nonetheless articulate condemnations of it by individual rabbinic authorities. Beyond the Haredi authorities discussed in the "Was It Kosher?" section of this chapter, at least three noted Orthodox leaders publicly condemned AgriProcessors, making statements repeatedly printed in the news media: Rabbi David Rosen, former chief rabbi of Ireland and then director of both the American Jewish Committee's Department for Interreligious Affairs and the Heilbrunn Institute for International Interreligious Understanding; Dr. Chaim Milikowsky, then chair of the Talmud Department of Bar Ilan University; and Rabbi Dr. Irving "Yitz" Greenberg, then president of the Jewish Life Network/Steinhardt Foundation.[67] Unlike Shear Yashuv Cohen and Israel's chief rabbinate, the social authority of these figures was not such that it had halakhic ramifications for Orthodoxy more generally and therefore did not provoke the same kind of concern from Orthodox leadership. Rosen's remarks attempt to build on the halakhic authority of Cohen's comments. Rosen wrote, "The manner of the slaughtering of animals as well of animal treatment generally as shown in the undercover footage taken at AgriProcessors, involves flagrant violation of Jewish halachic (religious legal) requirements. I join my greatly respected colleague Chief Rabbi Shear Yashuv Cohen in declaring that such behaviour desecrates Jewish teaching and values and the meat of the animals abused in this way is rendered totally nonkosher as a result."[68]

RHETORICAL ELEVATION OF COMPASSION FOR ANIMALS

Dr. Milikowsky's remarks accuse AgriProcessors of ignoring the ethical aspects of Jewish law in favor of exclusive attention to the ritual aspects and are still available in their entirety on PETA's Web site.[69] Milikowsky's critique of AgriProcessors received what was perhaps its largest hearing in a *Jerusalem Post* editorial by the *Post*'s then editorial page editor, Saul Singer:

> It makes little sense, as Chaim Milikowsky of Bar-Ilan University's Talmud department has pointed out, "to insist upon the most stringent requirements with regard to the ritual portion of the slaughtering process and yet, at the same time, flagrantly not insist upon stringent requirements with regard to the crucial moral aspect." To do so makes "the entire *kashrut* endeavor of that person both suspect and absurd."
>
> Further, the clear implication that "God cares only about his ritual law and not about his moral law," Milikowsky argues "is to desecrate His Name. . . . "
>
> To me, if *kashrut* is not on the cutting edge of humanity toward animals, it's not *kashrut*.

A noteworthy feature of Singer's and Milikowsky's remarks is that they not only draw attention to a violation of tza'ar ba'ale chayyim but also work rhetorically to elevate the status of tza'ar ba'ale chayyim. This is in sharp contrast to the way in which this Jewish legal mandate, acknowledged by all Orthodox Jews, was mentioned by OU leaders, who tended to *deflate* its importance.

This rhetorical elevation of the status of tza'ar ba'ale chayyim is also evident in remarks made by Greenberg. Greenberg weighed into the debate relatively late, nearly a year after the story originally broke, by appearing in a short video critiquing AgriProcessors that was released by novelist and National Jewish Book Award winner Jonathan Safran Foer. On the video Greenberg speaks of his own vegetarian practice and goes to great lengths to add prestige to concern for animal life: "The central verse [of] perhaps one of the central prayers of Jewish tradition, the Ashrei prayer . . . says 'God is good to everything because God's compassion—really God's mother love—is over all God's creatures.' [Not only] our attitude towards fellow human beings but also towards all animals, towards all God's creatures, is supposed to be mother love, a sense of compassion. Feel their pain. Feel their needs. Respect their lives."[70]

AN ORTHODOX MUCKRAKER

Shmarya Rosenberg's blog FailedMessiah.com, which I have cited several times already, also deserves mention alongside these voices. On the one hand, FailedMessiah.com is of interest to the present study as the most rigorous and thorough media source documenting the ongoing story and as perhaps AgriProcessors' most effective Orthodox critic. On the other hand, it is of interest because FailedMessiah.com has become an influential and well-known blog—what historian Jonathan Sarna described in the *New York Times* as "THE destination for those who want dirt about Orthodoxy exposed to the world"[71]—and it is by reporting on the AgriProcessors' story that the blog first became famous. The establishment of this important Jewish blog is one of the more enduring legacies of the AgriProcessors scandal.

It is telling that Rosenberg, formerly a Lubavitcher, began his controversial career as an Orthodox critic of Orthodoxy first out of concern with what he perceived as indifference to the plight of Ethiopian Jews.[72] Whereas Sholom Rubashkin combined unethical treatment of animals and communities perceived as racially other, Rosenberg's blog has combined special concern for both these vulnerable groups. Rosenberg had created his blog in 2004 only months before PETA's video footage was released, and at the time the blog had little traffic.[73] From the days after the initial undercover video was released until today, however, Rosenberg has attracted a significant following in part by collecting and commenting on virtually every event related to AgriProcessors (and now AgriStar), clarifying important omissions in the mainstream media and adding his own commentary. The overall force of

Rosenberg's journalism, like Milikowsky's and Greenberg's far more limited comments, is to elevate Jewish ethics generally and compassion for both animals and workers. This combination of heightened sensitivity to arguably the primary racial other of the American imagination—black Africans—and the primary other of the humanist imagination—animals—is, for reasons that will become clear as this book unfolds, unlikely to be accidental.

LIBERAL VOICES OF PROTEST

Several years before the incidents at AgriProcessors, the Conservative movement's Committee on Law and Standards issued a unanimously approved teshuvah that can be considered a "preemptive response" to the kinds of abuses later exposed at AgriProcessors because of the specificity with which it condemns practices that were, in the United States, unique to the AgriProcessors abattoir.[74] Although I have no reason to think the committee was specifically aware of what was happening at AgriProcessors, they were somehow guided to develop policy that responded to the kinds of methods employed at the plant. The teshuvah primarily articulates opposition to the shackling and hoisting of animals before shechitah, but it also specifically bans as cruel the practice of inverting animals before slaughter, which, to this day, is not known to have been practiced in any other U.S. kosher abattoir besides AgriProcessors and now AgriStar. "To be clear," the teshuvah reads, "in this ruling we intend . . . to ban . . . those pens that turn the animals upside down before slaughtering them. Only moving and killing the animals in an upright pen satisfies the requirements of Jewish law forbidding cruel treatment of animals."[75] I would not say that this teshuvah functions to rhetorically elevate the status of tza'ar ba'ale chayyim in the way some of the other texts we have encountered do, but it does insist that tza'ar ba'ale chayyim matters and has implications for kosher meat today.

RHETORICAL ELEVATION OF COMPASSION FOR ANIMALS

Other voices among the Conservative leadership were more emphatic and did rhetorically elevate the value of tza'ar ba'ale chayyim as they responded to AgriProcessors. For example, roughly a week after the first *New York Times* story, Rabbi Perry Raphael Rank, then president of the Conservative movement's Rabbinical Assembly, wrote: "The disturbing video that People for the Ethical Treatment of Animals (PETA) produced of incidents during *shechitah* . . . should be regarded as a welcome, though unfortunate service to the Jewish community. . . . When a company purporting to be kosher violates the prohibition against *tza'ar ba'ale chayyim,* causing pain to one of God's living creatures, that company must answer to the Jewish community, and ultimately, to God."[76] Rank's description of PETA providing a "welcome . . . service," like his emphasis that these are wrongs for which one is answerable before God, functions to heighten concern.[77]

Another example in the Conservative movement is that of Rabbi David Wolpe, widely regarded as among the most influential American rabbis.[78] Wolpe appeared alongside Greenberg in Foer's video, and, like those of Greenberg, Wolpe's comments went beyond simply asserting that a violation of tza'ar ba'ale chayyim had occurred. Wolpe spoke of a Jewish law that requires a person to send away a mother bird before taking her eggs and two divergent interpretations of it. The first interpretation he traces to Maimonides (Moses ben Maimon, or Rambam, 1135–1204), possibly the most influential of the *rishonim* (Jewish legal authorities that lived between the eleventh and mid-sixteenth century), who argues that the law is meant to relieve the suffering of the mother bird and thus teach us compassion. The second interpretation he traces to Nachmanides (Moses ben Nahman, 1194–1270), another giant of the period, who argues that the law's real purpose is not to prevent animal suffering, but to prohibit the disposition of cruelty that would be strengthened by taking the eggs amidst the mother bird's protests.[79] We again see the twofold ethical explanation for the practice of kashrut that we found in the literature of the big four kosher organizations: kindness, on the one hand, and ethical discipline, on the other. Whereas the dominant response we have traced in the Orthodox world seems to champion the tradition of Nachmanides over that of Maimonides, without any explicit denial of the Maimonidean position, Wolpe, in the video, stresses that *both* are reasons to be extremely concerned about the events at AgriProcessors. Even more, he appears to suggest, both are reasons to take this Jewish concern for animal life seriously enough to embody it in a daily commitment to vegetarianism.

The leadership of the nation's largest Jewish denomination, the Reform movement, joined Conservative leadership in immediately expressing their concern over the incidents at AgriProcessors, but the extremely low rate of kosher observance in the community and ongoing rejection of the practice, at least as traditionally conceived, gives the remarks from this quarter of Jewry a different significance. The Reform community is simply less identified with kosher practice than any other Jewish denomination. Rabbi Barry Schwartz, a rabbi who at the time sat on the task force on kashrut for the Reform movement's Central Conference of American Rabbis (CCAR), was widely quoted in the media for responding to PETA's video with the quip "If this is kosher, then we have a big problem."[80] The president and executive director of the CCAR, Janet Marder and Paul Menitoff, were among signatories to a joint statement by Jewish leaders asserting that "Judaism's powerful tradition of teaching compassion for animals has been violated by these systematic abuses and needs to be reasserted. We urge AgriProcessors to desist from these abuses."[81] The statement, which goes on to call for specific changes at AgriProcessors and for basic humane standards to be established for all kosher certification agencies, was also signed by Arthur Green, then dean of the Rabbinical School of Hebrew College; Arthur Waskow, then director of the Shalom Center; Elliot Dorff, then rector at the University of Judaism and vice chair of the Conservative movement's Committee on Jewish Law and Standards; and other leaders in all major Jewish denominations.

INFRASTRUCTURAL IMPACTS IN THE JEWISH CONTEXT

I have already noted one important addition to American Jewish communal life that was advanced by the energies released in response to the AgriProcessors incidents: the establishment of FailedMessiah.com as an important node in the online world of Jewish media. There are other more dramatic examples of infrastructural developments, including an alternative kosher meat industry, activist networks, and initiatives at the level of national movements.

THE RETURN OF ETHICS TO KOSHER MEAT   Consider the growth of purveyors of kosher meat outside the extant supermarket and butcher shop infrastructure, meat obtained from animals who are (in some but by no means all cases) raised and killed according to ethical standards—both for the animals and the workers—virtually impossible to find in the mainstream industry. The most developed and long-standing of such efforts is led by Washington, DC–based KOL Foods, which was followed into the market by a second company with considerably different ethical standards, Grow and

Behold. KOL Foods, which originally stood for "kosher, organic, and local" was founded and is run by Devora Kimelman-Block. In Kimelman-Block's self-understanding, she is not in a good position to judge how the 2004 and 2006 AgriProcessors scandals helped create demand for her product, but when the final and most high-publicity wave of the AgriProcessors scandal hit in 2008 the effect on demand was noticeable. By late 2008 she was selling as much as $20,000 in lamb and beef every month as a newly formed LLC.[82] Naftali Hanau, the owner of Grow and Behold, has been quoted explaining that the collapse of AgriProcessors created the opportunity for his own business.[83] Exactly how much the scandals at AgriProcessors drove the change is hard to say, but there is no doubt that in the aftermath of the 2004 investigation an alternative kosher industry has begun.

THE INVENTION OF THE JEWISH FOOD MOVEMENT Another important infrastructural impact is found in the Jewish environmental organization Hazon, which has since 2006 held national and regional conferences for what it calls the "Jewish Food Movement"—a phrase that appears to have been coined by Nigel Savage, the group's founder and executive director. These conferences have become major hubs for food activism in the Jewish community and, along with a range of other food-related projects, have made Hazon the most visible organization dealing with Jewish food ethics. The first conference was held in December 2006, a few months after the *Forward* released its exposé on worker abuse at AgriProcessors. The beginning and expansion of Hazon's work on food issues seems to have ridden and capitalized on the wave of concern catalyzed by AgriProcessors. According to Judith Belasco, current director of programs, Hazon was founded in 2000 to promote more sustainable communities in the Jewish world and beyond.[84] Hazon's first specific project was a cross-USA "Jewish Environmental Bike Ride." In 2004 Hazon launched a CSA in the Upper West Side of Manhattan, marking the beginning of their work to promote sustainable food systems. Significantly, this means that Hazon strengthened, and aside from the CSA began, its promotion of food ethics—one of the main issues with which it remains associated—at about the time of the first AgriProcessors scandal. The growth of its food conferences also follow the growth of the AgriProcessors scandals, rising from 158 attendees in 2006 to 560 at their December 2008 conference, held a few months after the immigration raid at the peak of the AgriProcessors scandals. When the annual conference reached near capacity with 640 participants in 2009, the organization decided to split into two conferences—one on the east coast and one on the west—in subsequent years.

Savage regularly references AgriProcessors in his construction of Hazon's identity, showcasing the group's long-standing connection with Postville. Hazon's first bike ride fundraiser in 2000 included a tour of AgriProcessors that involved seeing animals slaughtered. In a promotional article for the organization, Savage writes, "8 years before federal authorities raided the Agriprocessors' plant in Postville, Iowa, 7 years before we schechted [slaughtered] three goats at our food conference, 6 years before Michael Pollan's *Omnivore's Dilemma* was published, and 4 years before we launched the first Jewish CSA, we went to visit the Agriprocessors' plant. For me, I think that the visit crystallized and focused some of what has led to the flourishing of the Jewish Food Movement."[85] Savage, who went on this first bike ride, does not clarify what crystallized in 2000. Curiously, after extensive searching, I have found no evidence that Savage publicly criticized AgriProcessors in any manner after the ride or at any time prior to the 2004 PETA investigation. An even more explicit mythologizing of Postville as a landmark event is found in Savage's preface to an edited volume of essays on food and Judaism published by the CCAR, *A Sacred Table* (itself evidence of the surge of interest in food and ethics in Jewish circles). Savage associates AgriProcessors with one of the iconic events of American Reform Judaism, the "*t'reifah* banquet," the name given to the banquet held in honor of the first graduating class of American Reform rabbis in which all the main laws of kashrut, except the prohibition on pork, were violated. "One hundred and twenty-five years later," argues Savage, "the topic of American Jews and food was back on the nation's front pages. On May 12, 2008, federal authorities raided the Agriprocessors kosher meat plant in Postville, Iowa. If the *t'reifah* banquet heralded a century of we-don't-believe-in-keeping-kosher, what does the raid on Agriprocessors symbolize?" Again, Savage does not suggest what AgriProcessors might symbolize. I am unaware of any public writing in which he offers any kind of analysis of AgriProcessors or its implications, but this highly charismatic leader—not unlike a historian of religion—seems to grasp—and, going beyond this, deftly utilize—the charge that AgriProcessors acquired to inspire further ethical reflection on food in the American Jewish context. The important work Hazon has done and supported deserves further description, but my point here is simply to note that the organization's foray into food justice was in part fueled by the extraordinary energies unleashed by the AgriProcessors events.

RELIGIOUS ETHICAL CERTIFICATION   We could also consider movement undertakings like the Reform movements "Green Table, Just Table" initiative and the Conservative movement's Magen Tzedek program.[86] I have found the former's connection to the AgriProcessors events—while no doubt present—difficult to trace, but Magen Tzedek is a direct efflux of the AgriProcessors scandals, growing in particular out of a visit to the plant by Conservative leaders that was prompted by the *Forward*'s 2006 expose on worker abuse. Magen Tzedek offers producers of kosher food products for the retail market a certification that ensures *minimal* ethical standards are met in a wide range of areas,[87] including both worker protection and animal welfare. Magen Tzedek released its initial guidelines just before the High Holy Days in 2009 and finalized its nonprofit incorporation in January of 2011, but, as of the publication of this book, no products have been certified. The survival of the program remains unclear, but, whatever the fate of this particular initiative, I would argue that vision of a religious, ethical food certification represents the crossing of an important threshold.

Magen Tzedk was the first time and remains the only time one of the major liberal movements of American Judaism has ventured into the certification of food in the name of the Jewish religion (approximately 75 percent of American Jews who affiliate with a synagogue choose a liberal—and thus non-Orthodox—form of Judaism).[88] This has been territory ceded wholly to Orthodox Judaism (which constitutes approximately 20 percent of affiliated American Jewry).[89] Even more, this concession has been understood by many non-Orthodox Jews as the proper order of things. The general attitude among both laypeople and rabbis has been that Orthodox Jews know what they are doing when it comes to kosher law and, by extension, the rabbinic regulation of food as such. The logic has been that if a given food item is acceptable to an Orthodox certification body, with their "rigorous" standards, then surely it is acceptable for all other Jews. However, that sentiment has been weakened, and a number of liberal Jews have come to believe that often their own sensibilities require more, not less, rigor than those of Orthodoxy. This is, perhaps, one source of much of the hostility of the Orthodox establishment to Magen Tzedek: the idea of liberal Judaism claiming its own practices as more exacting, more rigorous, more stringent, more in accord with divine will than Orthodoxy strikes at the core of Orthodox identity.

This admitted speculation would explain, at least, why the Conservative movement's conceding traditional kashrut to Orthodoxy did not appease its Orthodox critics. Any kind of ethical certification offered *in addition* to a kosher certification is perhaps inherently an indictment of the present Orthodox establishment. Even if not intended, the existence of any such program exposes the extreme marginalization of Jewish ethical concerns that has come to characterize how Orthodox Judaism runs its kosher certification infrastructure. At stake is not only Jewish dietary practice but the role of ethics in Jewish life more broadly. This fundamental set of issues about ethics and identity was first lit up, we should remember, not by the 2008 AgriProcessors raid but by the suffering of animals on an undercover video. The suffering of those animals and the PETA investigator's willingness to suffer the investigation contributed to and perhaps even made possible Popper's 2006 exposé, and both the 2004 and 2006 exposés seem to have set the stage for the government's 2008 raid.

The animal abuse scandal that the undercover video of AgriProcessors first exposed by no means created *ex nihilo* the general surge of concern about the ethics of food that I have partially documented in this chapter, but, I venture, it does seem to have sparked something new. At some level there is always one domino before the next, an infinite chain of causes (in which case AgriProcessors is "no big deal," just another domino in the line). However, being the sorts of creatures humans are, certain causes stand out to us and demand our attention. Certain causes take on the aura of, and thus become, a beginning—an event.

The AgriProcessors scandals constitute just such an event. Consider a 2008 *New York Times* article entitled "Kosher Wars"—the military analogy is noteworthy and appropriate—that reports: "The PETA video was only the beginning of a long run of bad press for Agriprocessors."[90] And ultimately, according to the article, "The allegations against Agriprocessors galvanized a small but thriving Jewish environmental movement and took its concerns to a much wider audience."[91] Undercover video → run of bad press → galvanized movement → wider audience.

In highlighting the significance of AgriProcessors, I do not mean to suggest that it—or any single "event"—itself creates historical change. It is impossible to imagine that AgriProcessors could have become an event without decades of grassroots activism, the patient transmission of values by parents, and the building of an American Jewish social infrastructure. Interest in adapting kosher laws and practices in response to the new ethical problems created by modern industrial agriculture has been evident in both Orthodox and liberal Judaism for decades. We could look to the Haredi rabbi Moshe Feinstein's influential rulings about veal in the 1970s in the Orthodox world or the liberal rabbi Arthur Waskow's championing of the idea of "eco-*kashrut*" beginning in the 1980s as early examples.[92] The AgriProcessors scandals simply played a role in transforming these concerns into energetic discussions and institutionally supported work to change the ethical landscape. Whatever actual influence the *events* had—for this is simply impossible to decide with certainty—it is clear that they have, at least for the moment, become part of the story Jews are telling themselves. And though public references to AgriProcessors sometimes speak as if everything began in 2008, it remains the case that AgriProcessors first became an event in 2004 with an exposé on animal abuse. Part of the labor of this description is a hope that this beginning will not be forgotten, that animals will not be forgotten.

To begin with the undercover video in 2004 is, of course, not the only way to tell the story, but in a very real way it was an encounter with animals—suffering animals totally within human control and slaughtered in the name of religion—that began this entire chain of events. Can animals have such power? Here is a test you can try yourself: of all the facts you have read in the fifty-seven pages of this book, what is the one most seared into your memory? If there is an image that haunts you from these pages, what is it? I have asked many readers of drafts of this book this question, and the answer is always the same: the cattle with their tracheas and esophagi pulled from their bodies while they are conscious. It is not sentimental to be moved by this. It is, "statistically" speaking, normal. It is one of the most established facts of my research that, for most people, the knowledge of this datum—let alone that these procedures took place for at least six years and were, and are, defended as the will of God—has power. Something—*someone*—in that image demands response. Maybe the "real" beginning of the AgriProcessors event is one step prior to the video. Perhaps it resides in the empathy and sympathy that first motivated the investigation. This then would be what drove the "Postville event" from its beginning as a censored front page *New York Times* article to Barak Obama's denunciation of worker exploitation: animals, our compassion for them, and the violation of both.

UNRESOLVED QUESTIONS

To better explain these events, we need, I suggest, to consider the events at AgriProcessors and the response to them as religious phenomena rather than merely happening to a religious community. That means attending to the broader mythology and worldview that is embedded in the practices at stake at AgriProcessors and at stake in our retelling of them. It also means attending to the fact that the Jewish community did not simply respond to a "problem" or set of "abuses" or a halakhic challenge; they responded to a religious event: the unveiling of the hidden and holy sanctum of the slaughterhouse and the presence there of something unexpected. They responded to the surprising reality of what the human relationship with animals has all too often become since the advent of the factory farm.[93] They responded to the religious event of animals who, in their undeniable suffering, were not simply seen, but who, in the wordless communication that mammals share, cried out for help.[94] The response to AgriProcessors was a response to animals, to particular animals whose faces (with the technological aid of video, activist infrastructures, and modern media) not only confronted the Jewish public, but called—and have always been among those who have called—that community forth. As we will see, Jewish traditions have long imagined the human, particularly in the ethical dimension of humanity, in relation to animals—not simply "the animal," which Jewish traditions have also done, but actual animals.

Both for Jews who defended and for those who decried AgriProcessors, to be a Jew—even to be a human—is bound up in a certain kind of relationship with animals, with creatures, at least as much as it is bound up in a relationship with the Creator. Judaism and the Jew are imagined not only through a covenant between Jews and God but also one between God, Jews, and animate creation.

As in the Talmudic story in which Judah ha-Nasi was forced to respond— and suffer the consequences of his response—to the calf that broke away from its walk to slaughter and wept in his garment, so too was the Jewish community forced to respond to animals virtually breaking out of their slaughter lines. As in the Talmudic story, the element of *seeing* an animal resist its death seems important. It is noteworthy that the problems at AgriProcessors attracted public concern only after they were captured on video. This is not because video footage was required to know that animal abuse was occurring. After all, the abuse of workers received an immense response without any such video documentation. It does, I submit, have to do with what the video made possible: a kind of virtual interaction with the animals being slaughtered. How would the events appear if we not only paid more attention to the dense locus of meanings articulated around animals but in particular to the fact that the animals are, in a certain way, actors in these events? And, as actors, they constitute an ultimately uncontrollable (that is, not fully controllable) element in a complex ritual.

Animals too responded, as they always have responded. The response of animals at AgriProcessors—their bellows, their open eyes—helped shape a contemporary incarnation of a long-standing and fundamental Jewish myth, the myth of what I will theorize in chapter 6 as the "humane subject." By theorizing this myth the events at AgriProcessors can be more fully understood. However, to accomplish this interpretation will require a modification in how dominant streams in the study of religion have conceived of animals and how the study of religion has conceived itself.

3

The Absent Presence

ANIMALS IN THE HISTORY OF THE STUDY OF RELIGION

ZOOM OUT: THE BIG PICTURE

In perhaps most places in the world where the word *religion* or some variant of this Latin term is in use today, religion is popularly imagined as something that has little to do with animals. Common sense whispers that to think about ultimate concerns is to tear one's mind as far away from animality as possible. When I suggested in the last chapter that what was religious about the AgriProcessors scandals was not simply that they happened in plants under rabbinic supervision or that many of the principle actors were Jews, but rather what happened between cattle and humans, I violated an often unstated understanding. I brought an unwelcome guest to the table of religious inquiry, a guest usually welcome on the table but not at it. It is worth inquiring how this exclusion of animals from the sphere of the religious came to appear as common sense, but our aim here is more particular. This chapter asks why those of us entrusted to be professional thinkers of religion have—why the study of religion has—largely followed this "common sense" divorce of religiosity and animality? To look at AgriProcessors anew requires we confront this conspiring of both common sense and elite discourses to exclude animals from religion. We must ask how the phenomenon of religion was reduced to the drama of humanity rather than, to gesture at just one alternative, the drama of the living.

Exploring this question and overcoming this interpretive myopia points the way toward a more intelligible, complete, and productive understanding of religion in general and the AgriProcessors scandals in particular. If we can see how, despite expectations, animals and human-animal relations often dwell in a "dimension of depth,"[1] a dimension of the "hidden in the apparent,"[2] it will become clear that the 2004 scandals at AgriProcessors are underexplained by the dominant narrative of cruelty and protest against cruelty. The first step in this task, which will occupy the rest of this chapter, is to show that while this book argues for a "new" place for animals in the study of religion, this move is not as radical as it might at first appear. Animals, it turns out, have always been at the center of the modern and contemporary study of religion, albeit in a camouflaged and forgotten manner. I do not wish to make animals more central, but rather to make their centrality more conscious, more just, and more interpretively productive. After gaining purchase on this "absent presence"[3]—this disavowed centrality—of animals in the study of religion, chapters 4 and 5 will proceed to theorize a new place for animals in our thinking about religion.

FOUR THEORISTS

My analysis of the role of animals in the history of the study of religion will focus on four important theorists that can, for our purposes, serve to represent the study of religion more generally—or at least a substantial part of it: Émile Durkheim, Ernst Cassirer, Mircea Eliade, and Jonathan Z. Smith. My choice of these four theorists to trace the insinuation of the animal in the study of religion is highly underdetermined by the primary point I wish to make here: the ongoing theoretical importance of animals and the animal to the study of religion. That said, this list is not arbitrary, and certain features demand attention before we proceed.

These four thinkers are men and from the Western intellectual tradition—native speakers, respectively, of German, French, Romanian, and English. This national diversity, albeit within the Western fold, is significant, as is the lack of gender diversity. The latter is, of course, an efflux of the sexist bias that has marred the academy and indeed almost the whole of Western intellectual history. But this bias is appropriate here, for I am, precisely, trying to trace the dominant tradition—what remains, by most reckonings, a (if no longer *the*) dominant tradition. The task of this chapter is not to affirm this tradition—though there is much worth affirming in it—but to deconstruct it and, in the chapters that follow, point the way toward its ongoing reconstruction.[4]

It is also worth pausing over the fact that three of these four thinkers are of Jewish background and, while not necessarily Jewish in a traditional religious sense, perhaps could be fairly described as secular Jews: Cassirer, Durkheim, and Smith.[5] There are at least two reasons for this: first, there is indeed a disproportionate contribution of Jewish thinkers, especially "secular" Jewish thinkers, to the task of developing a study of religion no longer dominated by the categories of Christian thought (Sigmund Freud and Karl Marx are the most prominent examples)—and it is, again, precisely this lineage of nontheological modes of studying religion that we are presently critically considering. Second, this favoring of "secular Jewish thinkers" reflects my own intellectual location as a Jewish historian of religions who, if not quite secular, nonetheless finds that his intellectual heroes are disproportionately secular or, at least, "problematically Jewish" Jews.[6] That is, the Jewishness of these thinkers represents both a certain Jewish influence on the nontheological study of religion, on the one hand, and my own socioreligious location, on the other.

Of the four thinkers, I choose to begin with Durkheim and Cassirer, not only because of their stature and influence in the academy beyond the study of religion but also because they each represent what I will characterize as a different "ethical" orientation to the human/animal divide. Moreover, they provide excellent illustrations of ideas about this divide that remain contemporary—for example, the idea of the uniquely "neotenic," plastic human. *Neotenic* is not a term Durkheim or Cassirer use themselves, but it captures an aspect of their thinking on the human/animal divide that I wish to highlight. Neoteny refers to the biological phenomenon of the retention of juvenile characteristics in adults of a given species. An evolutionary advantage of neoteny can be a lack of fixity. A mature brain, for example, cannot learn certain new modes of comprehension as nimbly as an immature brain (consider language acquisition).

Some have argued that the human may be understood as a neotenic ape. That is, the uniqueness of humanity in relation to other apes is a lack of fixity—the fact that many years after we exit the womb our minds are still maturing and, in significant ways, never mature into a fixed state. The implication of this proposal is that because the human is born into the world immature and remains so for a long time, if not indefinitely, culture must fill in the gaps left by this immaturity. Instead of a "fixed" mind formed by "natural" forces, we have a highly malleable one that is "fixed"—if at all—by cultures that are themselves products of human minds. "The human" is thus not defined by a property bequeathed to it but is rather an open structure that blurs the very line between nature and culture. The human in this way of thinking, to cite one compelling recent articulation of it by philosopher of religion Tom Carlson, is never "at home," but instead "courses in resistance to the secure placement of 'life,' as 'human' or as 'traditional,' in any pre-given niche whose boundaries would define the human by locating it."[7]

THE UNIQUELY NEOTENIC HUMAN: ÉMILE DURKHEIM

Perhaps Durkheim's most enduring and foundational contribution to the study of religion in his 1912 classic, *The Elementary Forms of Religious Life*, was to imagine the study of religion as a study of the sacred/profane binary as it arises in all aspects of social life: in economy, in governance, in family structure, in ritual, and so on. As I read him, Durkheim's achievement is not a sociology of religion that would bring the tools of sociology to bear upon religion but a religious sociology that refuses reductionist approaches (despite common readings to the contrary).[8] Durkheim's inquiry into religion is simultaneously an inquiry into the origins of conceptual thought (particularly the classificatory function), the emergence of the human out of animality, and the foundations of society. He binds each of these four inquiries intimately to the others.

For Durkheim, the human being is distinct from all other animals because the human form is uniquely formless. In particular, Durkheim argues that in the process of the animal *homo sapiens* learning to become human—for we are not, in this view, simply born human—we come to dwell in a world where everything appears to us in relation to a sacred/profane binary. For example, we think of thinking as belonging to the mind and as proximate to the divine and we think of defecating as belonging to the body and as bestial. The human form is divine or in the image of the divine; animal forms are not. This book is sacred; that one is a good read, and so on. Everything we touch must go in one basket or the other: sacred or profane.

In his earlier work with Marcel Mauss, *Primitive Classification*, Durkheim explains that "humanity in the beginning lacks the most indispensable conditions for the classificatory function."[9] "It would be impossible to exaggerate, in fact, the state of indistinction from which the human mind developed" (5). Significantly, Durkheim argues for this original state of "indistinction" primarily by showing that certain non-Western communities "confuse" the line the separates human and animal. Durkheim appears to take for granted the naturalness of the human/animal binary. A culture without this binary, he concludes, rather than illustrating the limits of our own worldview, is just in an early, "primitive" state of "general mental confusion" (6). For example, the Brazilian Bororo "sincerely imagines himself to be a parrot. . . . The [Brazilian] Trumaí are genuinely thought to be aquatic animals. . . . Animals, people, and inanimate objects were originally almost always conceived as standing in relations of the most perfect identity to each other. . . . It is obvious what a great difference there is between these rudimentary distinctions and groupings and what truly constitutes a classification" (6–7).

Without the human/animal binary, Durkheim and Mauss argue, no more advanced and properly human classificatory function will develop. The lack of this one classificatory move, the deployment of the human/animal binary, destroys, for Durkheim and Mauss, the possibility of wielding the classificatory function that allows the animal *homo sapiens* to achieve the full measure of its (potential) humanity. We see here a troubling linkage that will recur again and again when animals are used to understand humanity: strings of oppositions that, whatever their authors may wish to say, have the effect of linking the status of "primitive" humans and animals in ways that are salutary for neither.

Durkheim maintains and refines this case for the human as a uniquely neotenic animal in *The Elementary Forms of Religious Life*: "the categories of human thought are never fixed in a definite form; they are ceaselessly made, unmade, and remade; they vary according to time and place."[10] This biological indeterminacy, he goes on to theorize, demands a completion by human society. Only when the categories of thought—including the decisive categories of the sacred and profane—are socially completed does thought become "truly and peculiarly human."[11] "Conceptual thought is contemporaneous with humanity. . . . I refuse to see [it] as the product of more or less modern culture. A man who did not think with concepts would not be a man, for he would not be a social being."[12] For Durkheim, humans become human only through the socially assisted completion of our biologically indeterminate classificatory function. As we will see in a moment, this view is quite close to that of the eminent German Jewish philosopher Ernst Cassirer, who argued that the defining quality of *homo sapiens* is our uniquely flexible symbolic function.

Differences in perception of reality, Durkheim argues, flow in part from the fact that perception itself is not possible without the development of a socially engendered classificatory system of greater or lesser sophistication. This poses a chicken and egg problem. How does Durkheim imagine society arises to play this role in the first place since society is made up of the very humans Durkheim is claiming it helps create? Durkheim theorizes that society too originates in this process of completing the human; human and society are threads in the same knot.

Durkheim understands society as simultaneously constituting (society completes human biological indeterminacy) and constituted (society itself is made in the process of thus completing human indeterminacy). The sociologist Peter Berger, who is a perfect Durkheimian in this regard, explains, in his classic, *The Sacred Canopy,* "man cannot exist apart from society. The two statements, that society is the product of man and that man is the product of society, are not contradictory. They rather reflect the inherently dialectic character of the societal phenomenon."[13]

Religion, for Durkheim, is not reducible to conceptual and classificatory thought or the human or society, but is the knot itself; religion laces these three realities together. When human communities gather for ritual purposes during the obscure moment of what Durkheim calls "collective effervescence,"[14] their experience of the difference between the sacred and profane (beings, space, times, and actions) founds "the religious idea."[15] The individual, in a state of exaltation and surrounded by particular sancta in particular times and places, becomes religious by acquiring an understanding of the community's sacred/profane binary. Acquiring this binary and other categories, Durkheim theorizes, is nothing other than the formation of conceptual thought itself, and with this the human emerges from animality and society is constituted (and, dialectically, constituting). Religion—understood as the coproduction of conceptual thought, the human, and society by means of the entrance of the sacred/profane binary and thus the classificatory function into the interactions of *homo sapiens*—is therefore, in Durkheim's estimation, a universal characteristic of properly human culture. It is necessitated by our uniquely neotenic biology. Religion is not something humans produce, but the very production of the properly human from the fodder of the indeterminate animality into which we are born.

Interestingly, while Durkheim (and, as we will see, Cassirer too) ultimately is arguing for a radical break between the human and all other animals, he does not rest this difference in biology. For Durkheim, nature, as it were, provides only differences in degree between human and animal. Human biology may be unique, but it is not uniquely unique; at the level of body there is no ontological distinction between *homo sapiens* and other species. "From a physical point of view . . . and from the mental point of view . . . [man] differs from the animal only in degree."[16] "And yet," Durkheim continues, "society conceives him and requires that we conceive him as being endowed with a *sui generis* character that insulates and shields him from all reckless infringement—in other words, that imposes respect. This status, which puts him in a class by himself, seems to us to be one of his distinctive attributes, even though no basis for it can be found in the empirical nature."[17] While human uniqueness is constructed, this does not make it any less real for Durkheim. Human uniqueness—and thus a special moral and ethical status of human life *predicated on a demotion of the animal*—is simply grounded in a different kind of reality than brute biological facts.

Durkheim here offers a secular, scholarly position that parallels a wide variety of theological arguments for the human distinction from animals that suggest that human uniqueness is not found in the animal body but rather in the unique human soul, unique divine mandates, unique abilities of humans to transcend themselves, and similar conceptions—in sum, that human distinction lies in the sphere of religion. In place of these explicitly "classical" markers of the human/animal border, Durkheim provides his interwoven understanding of conceptual thought, society, and religion. What remains consistent in both cases is the articulation of "the human" through a dramatic division between animal and human, and a related deployment of this binary to gesture at the most essential meaning of "religion" (and related terms).

The degree to which Durkheimian and, for example, Abrahamic theological articulations of the human/animal binary overlap in their functions presents something of a problem for those who would wish to use Durkheimian theory to articulate a nontheological study of religion. One reason Durkheim has been so useful to scholars of religion is precisely because he is believed to provide an approach to understanding religion relatively free of theology, but attention to the role of the animal in his work puts this in question. Durkheim certainly has moved in the direction of an understanding of the human less driven by Christian theology. Still, on the question of the animal his view is strikingly close to both Jewish and Christian theology and, as his own views would suggest (this is part of their enduring utility), problematically bound to the categories imposed by a particular community. Durkheim's views on the human/animal border, despite his humanism and desire to elevate the status of non-Western cultures, nonetheless reproduces an understanding of religion that views many hunter-gatherer communities—who lack a human/animal binary—as "confused." He promotes a view that subtly privileges modern (conceptual thought) over primitive (confusion), and spirit (formless neotenicity) over flesh (fixed biology), thereby implicating himself in a series of interlaced binary oppositions.

There are knots to sort out to further explicate Durkheim's binding together of religion, conceptual thought, the properly human, and society. For our purposes, though, the crucial detail has been more than established: the observation that, for Durkheim, society and religion are inextricably bound together and imaginable only on the assumption of a radical break between the almost infinitely malleable human and "animals," who, he maintains, have a fixed nature and thus are utterly cut off from any participation in the phenomenon of religion, conceptual thought, or society. Although this is hardly the way Durkheim is remembered, the question of the animal and the difficulties associated with it turn out to be at the very heart of Durkheim's foundational contribution to the scholarly study of both religion and society. If Durkheim's views on the human/animal binary do not seem peculiar, it is because later scholars have so often shared the same culturally specific imagination of the relationship between humans and the rest of animate life.

THE UNIQUELY SYMBOLIC HUMAN: ERNST CASSIRER

HUMAN/ANIMAL/MODERN/PRIMITIVE   For Cassirer, the distinction of the human is our unique ability to create worlds through a symbolic function and, even more, move between—ideally at will—these different worlds. Unlike Durkheim, Cassirer emphasizes that this unprecedented human function is embedded in a material substrate—in our organic, biological bodies as they have evolved through natural selection. I am not suggesting that Durkheim would deny this, but it does not appear to interest him. Cassirer imagines a small alteration in the symbolic function that gives rise to a sort of cascade effect that generates the uniquely human mode of being. Cassirer writes:

> Obviously this [human] world forms no exception to those biological rules which govern the life of all the other organisms. Yet in the human world we find a new characteristic which appears to be the distinctive mark of human life. The functional circle [theorized by the biologist Johannes von Uexküll to inter-pret animal life in its relation to its environment] of man is not only quantita-tively enlarged; it has also undergone a qualitative change. Man has, as it were, discovered a new method of adapting himself to his environment. Between [Uexküll's theorized] receptor system and the effector system, which are to be found in all animal species, we find in man a third link which we may describe as the *symbolic system.* . . . As compared with the other animals man lives not merely in a broader reality; he lives, so to speak, in a new *dimension* of reality.[18]

For Cassirer, as for Durkheim, the human is not born but unfolds—is pro-duced and produced again and again. And, as in Durkheim, this production is not merely a brute evolutionary distinction—just one more example of speciation[19]—but a decisive, epochal event that has transcendent signifi-cance. For Cassirer, biology surpasses itself in the human symbolic function: reactions morph into responses; sign becomes symbol; mere being becomes being radiant with meaning;[20] we are not only thrown into the world, but construct it; fixity gives way to a versatility, which is reminiscent of infin-ity[21]—and what all these binaries amount to is that the animal *homo sapiens* becomes "man."[22]

Cassirer draws the line between human and animal by making a subtle distinction between the brute biological capacity with which any typical human would be born, on the one hand, and the actual deployment, or un-folding, of this capacity especially in relation to the structures of language, on the other. "Human culture derives its specific character and its intellec-tual and moral values, not from the material from which it consists, but from its form, its architectural structure. And this form may be expressed in any sense material."[23] In the same way that the "primitive" is not always granted a fully human status in Durkheim, so in Cassirer's perspective the human child before speech and the person who is born without the capacity for lan-guage and the person who loses the capacity for language are not properly human.[24]

Much like Durkheim, for Cassirer the "primitive," while human, is imagined as a kind of stunted version of humanity that has symbolic (or categorical) capacity, but is barely aware of it and thus closer to animal fixity: "A genuine human symbol is characterized not by its uniformity but its versatility. It is not rigid or inflexible but mobile. It is true that the full awareness of this mobility seems to be a rather late achievement in man's intellectual and cultural development. In primitive mentality this awareness is very seldom attained" (36). Thus, once again, we see the human/animal binary linked with the status of "primitive" human and all the troubling implications this carries.

In this connection we must note that, even more than in Durkheim, this denigration of the primitive is also accompanied by a robust humanistic concern that pervades Cassirer's work. While perhaps preoccupied with the modern-primitive binary, Cassirer at times seems at pains to increase the status of the primitive and in places seems to be pointing to superior features of primitive thought (80)—for example, the dignity of its embrace of life. "Primitive religion is perhaps the strongest and most energetic affirmation of life that we find in human culture" (84).

This does not undo the troubling racist implications of his discourses, but it mitigates and complicates critiques that might be justified with other thinkers. In any case, none of these problems provide cause to ignore the enormous accomplishment of Cassirer's broad ethical embrace. As I emphasized with Durkheim, my point is simply that the human/animal binary becomes an occasion that, intentionally or not, inscribes a violent disavowal of animals at the heart of humanism, and it is far from clear that this violence can really be kept from overflowing, if you will, into the human realm.

THE QUESTION OF THE ANIMAL AND RELIGION Religion then, which Cassirer associates with myth and art, becomes understood as one among a multiplicity of modes, determined by different instantiations of the symbolic function, through which reality as we experience it is constituted. There is, Cassirer argues, a certain inevitability about this unfolding of the symbolic function into myth, art, and religion. "Man cannot escape from his own achievement. He cannot but adopt the conditions of his own life. No longer in a merely physical universe, man lives in a symbolic universe. Language, myth, art, and religion are parts of this universe" (25). Here we see how Cassirer, like Durkheim, has ultimately woven the emergence of the human out of animality together with the generation of religion and—significantly—*myth*. As we will see shortly, Eliade and Smith after him will also argue that the human and myth arrive in the world together. In Cassirer's system, some of the most important categories in the study of religion—for example, "symbol," "myth," "human," and "religion" itself—all arise together and only together. As in Durkheim, we encounter a knot in which a richly imagined vision of the human as inherently religious is wound together with a particular understanding of the animal.

Cassirer lays more emphasis on evolutionary continuity with animals than Durkheim—for example, in the attention he gives to primate studies and his detailed parsing of minute differences between "anthropoid apes." This more robust consideration of human continuity with animals, especially apes, does not diminish Cassirer's concern to make an emphatic, ethically charged case for human ontological uniqueness, but it constitutes a set of countervailing gestures through which Cassirer leaves open a door for a more critical consideration of animals. Cassirer clearly deploys the animal to define the human, but he devotes more than a little attention to actual animals.

Perhaps most significantly, Cassirer constantly attempts to restrain his theorizing in light of "empirical, scientifically ascertained" information about particular animal species produced by the biological sciences. At juncture after juncture in his analysis of the human, while he always insists on a sharp animal/human divide, he gives ground to animals. Apes, for example, are granted the ability to engage in "certain symbolic processes" (31)—a strong claim given the weight Cassirer lays on the symbolic function and one that seems to suggest that apes would have a religion of sorts (although Cassirer never asserts this as far as I know). Moreover, his engagement with scientific exempla of animal behavior suggests that he would have remained open to revising his arguments as new kinds of scientific evidence about animals came to light. His negative conclusions about particular animal species would thus be falsifiable, which makes animals more interesting and their study more important to the task of interpreting religion as he defines it.

In sum, the greater emphasis Cassirer lays on biological continuity with, concern for, and scientific study of animals constitutes what I would consider a broad countergesture to his constant deployment of the difference between humans and animals in order to theorize religion. Cassirer, like Durkheim (and, as we will see in chapter 6, like much of Abrahamic thought), lays his emphasis on human ascendancy over animals (not only our difference, but our superiority). However, unlike Durkheim, he also finds ways to attend to our similarity in kind to animals and to the feelings of kindness toward or solidarity with them that have so often been expressed historically.

I emphasize this "kinder" (in the sense of both similarity in kind and concern) approach to animals I note in Cassirer, in contrast to Durkheim, to suggest that we find in him a movement toward the sort of critical attention to animals that I am ultimately concerned to advocate in this study. So far I have hastily summarized only a general difference in tone, emphasis, and style between Durkheim and Cassirer on the question of the animal. We also have more vivid evidence of Cassirer's "kinder" approach to the human/animal binary.

Both Durkheim's *The Elementary Forms of Religious Life* and Cassirer's *An Essay on Man* have abundant references to animals and provide more than enough text to get a clear picture of the general status the authors attribute to animals in relation to religion. In Karen Field's translation of *Elementary Forms* the word *animal,* let alone references to animals, appears on more than two hundred pages; in Cassirer's considerably shorter work "animal" appears on more than fifty pages. The abundant references to animals in these two works—what I theorize as animals' "absent presence"— is partly due to the unavoidable (and anything but absent) presence of animals in the "primitive" religious traditions they use as exempla. "In Australia," Durkheim observes, "animals and plants are in the highest rank of sacred things. Even among the Indians of North America, the great cosmic deities that are beginning to be the object of a cult are very often conceived of in the form of animals" (64). When considering hunter-gatherer traditions especially, a "modern" Western theorist like Durkheim or Cassirer is so constantly confronted with "animals"—for example, as "totems," which Durkheim calls "the very archetype of sacred things"[25]—that it becomes impossible not to say *something* about their abundance. Some explanation is needed, and both Durkheim and Cassirer offer such explanations. They often reveal not only what they think about religions and animals but also core features of their understanding of religion itself.

For Durkheim, the near constant engagement with animals (and plants) by the Arunta and similar communities has almost nothing to do with animals' sentience, their power, their charge, or any quality they possess; animals are so present in religions simply because their natural division into species provides an excellent *receptacle* (any one would do) for the projection of classificatory/conceptual thought as it coarises with humanity. Primordial *homo sapiens* use social relations as a model for understanding nature: social order is imaginatively imposed on animals and plants, generating conceptual thought, society, the human, and religion simultaneously. Durkheim is insistent that nothing but society could play the role of model for classificatory/conceptual thought: "In all probability . . . we would never have thought of gathering the beings of the universe into homogeneous groups, called genera, if we had not had the example of human societies before our eyes."[26] "Only in society," he asserts, "do superiors, subordinates, and equals exist," and therefore only society could have "furnished the canvas on which logical thought was worked."[27]

Significantly, the claim that hierarchical relations are unknown in the animal world rather straightforwardly contradicts common sense observations of certain animal species, but it is easy to see why Durkheim feels confident asserting the contrary with no need to attend to animals themselves. By definition, for Durkheim, animals are incapable of classificatory/conceptual thought. There is thus no need to bother oneself by looking in the horse's mouth—the gulf between human and animal has been determined in advance of any analysis. In one of the most constraining moves in his theorization of religion, this viewpoint suggests that animals—and, by extension, any member of the species *homo sapiens* that is not fully human, like children[28]—have no place in the study of religion (at least as themselves). If he appears to speak of animals a great deal, he insists that this is only because animals are so useful as receptacles of human categorization. Animals, for Durkheim, fade into hollow meaningless shells whose only participation in religion is the convenient receptacles they provide for human categorization.

If we lived in an alternative world where animals were, as in Descartes's infamous assertion, nothing but machines and their cries no different than the creak of a door, both religion and society, in Durkheim's understanding, would have unfolded in exactly the same manner. If we lived in a nearly dead universe and the only living things were human beings, once again Durkheim's theory would suggest that society and religion would be fundamentally untouched—presuming that other objects would be available for the projection of human thought. In these regards, Durkheim's basic conclusions about religion differ radically from those of Cassirer.

Cassirer arrives at his conclusions about human/animal relations in dialogue with the biological sciences, which seem to function as a check on the humanistic assumption of an ontological divide between human and animal. He concludes that a conviction of the "solidarity of life" is nearly synonymous with early religion and is never done away with (though it is radically reoriented over time). "No religion," he asserts, "could ever think of cutting or even loosening the bond between nature and man. But in the great ethical religions this bond is tied and fastened in a new sense."[29]

Both Cassirer and Durkheim find human uniqueness located in a mental-perceptual development that opens up new modes of engagement with the world, including religion. This development is conceptual thought in Durkheim (which animals possess in Cassirer's view) and a uniquely flexible symbolic function in Cassirer. Both theorists also insist on the radical, epochal nature of the human break with animality, but their views resound with strikingly different ethical tones. We could say that when considering "the animal"—the animal as a construct of humanity's root other—Durkheim and Cassirer differ only slightly, but in regard to animals—the biological beings—they represent distinct trajectories of thought. For Durkheim, animals are ultimately meaningless in themselves (despite what religionists may say). For Cassirer, in contrast, one of the keys to myth is understanding that in the mythical world—which is ultimately the religious world—there is always "the deep conviction of a fundamental and indelible *solidarity with life* that bridges over the multiplicity and variety of its single forms. . . . The consanguinity of all forms of life seems to be a general presupposition of mythical thought."[30] For Cassirer, religion is always fundamentally engaged with the drama of the living.

Cassirer seems well aware of the brute fact that human/animal relations are peculiarly charged, and we will revisit his views in this connection after considering Jonathan Z. Smith's essay "I Am a Parrot (Red)." Durkheim not only does not see this fact as important, but works actively to devalue the importance of animals themselves even as he constantly must make reference to them; he absents animals even as he brings them before us. He does this in part, understandably, to disentangle himself from earlier theories of religion, but he also simply appears to lack sufficient insight, imagination, or empathy to conceptualize animals as *significant* (and he would not be unusual in this regard). This deficiency pervades and mars the entirety of *The Elementary Forms of Religious Life,* but is expressed directly only on a few occasions. For example, when working to dispute the dubious idea that "natural things truly had become sacred beings by virtue of their imposing forms or the force they display," Durkheim maintains that if this were so then "we would observe that the sun, the moon, the sky, the mountain, the sea, the winds—in short, the great cosmic phenomena—were the first to be lifted to that status; none are better equipped to dazzle the senses and the imagination. But in fact, the great cosmic phenomena were not identified until fairly recent times. The first beings to which the cult was addressed . . . are humble plants and animals in relation to which man found himself on an equal footing at the very least: the duck, the hare, the kangaroo, the emu, the lizard, the caterpillar, the frog, and so forth. *Their objective qualities surely could not have been the origin of the religious feelings they inspired.*"[31] At this stage of our discussion, our reply to Durkheim can be pithy: Why not?

VERTICALITY, TECHNOLOGY, CARNIVORY: MIRCEA ELIADE

Both Mircea Eliade and Jonathan Z. Smith have followed Durkheim and Cassirer in intertwining the study of religion with a demarcation of the properly human from the animal. Eliade and Smith also rely in crucial ways on the Durkheimian conception of a sacred/profane binary, which, as we have seen, is intimately interwoven with the human/animal binary. Significantly, whereas in Durkheim the sacred/profane binary is "produced," in Eliade it is "discovered." Eliade's discovery takes the place of Durkheim's production of the sacred/profane distinction, but for both thinkers this awareness of distinction is what distinguishes the human from the animal and what makes humans inherently religious. For Eliade, human consciousness of the sacred/profane binary is discussed in terms of "myth," which Eliade argues always involves the narration of a breakthrough of the sacred into profane life (among other characteristics).[32] In this narration, or mythologization, the sacred is dis-covered and becomes the basis for making meaning of any kind. Both mythmaking and meaning making in Eliade's view are uniquely human activities, and the human "transcendence" of the animal becomes for Eliade the beginning of religion itself.

In both *The Quest* and the preface to the first volume of *A History of Religious Ideas,*[33] Eliade writes, "It is difficult to imagine how the human mind could function without the conviction that there is something irreducibly *real* in the world; and it is impossible to imagine how consciousness could appear without conferring a *meaning* on man's impulses and experiences. Consciousness of a real and meaningful world is intimately connected with the discovery of the sacred."[34] Appealing to our most fundamental intuitions, Eliade argues that we cannot imagine consciousness without the prior assumption of the existence of the sacred that gives it meaning. "The 'sacred,'" Eliade continues, "is an element in the structure of consciousness and not a stage in the history of consciousness" (xiii). Eliade here triangulates conceptions of "the sacred," "consciousness," and "meaning" to articulate a break between human and animal. To be human is to be an "animal plus"—plus the sacred, plus consciousness, plus meaning, and so on—and this "plus" is achieved through the act of mythmaking. In the "primates" there is no sacred/profane binary (1), no experience of the sacred, and thus no difference can be perceived between "what reveals itself as being real, powerful, rich, and meaningful and what lacks these qualities, that is, the chaotic and dangerous flux of things, their fortuitous and senseless appearances and disappearances" (xiii).

This view implies that animal life has no meaning: the animal part of the human is imagined as a blank slate of pure biology upon which the neotenic human in the throes of its emergence from animality inscribes the myths that complete *homo sapiens* as *homo religiosus* and make meaning possible. Given this, it is perhaps not surprising that in *A History of Religious Ideas* Eliade gives the distinction between humans and animals, or, more particularly, humans and "primates," the pride of the opening line. Here Eliade addresses the centrality of the demarcation between human and primate to the study of religion, while, oddly, simultaneously insisting that he will not discuss this binary. Eliade writes, "Despite its importance for an understanding of the religious phenomenon, we shall not here discuss the problem of 'hominization.' It is sufficient to recall that the vertical posture *already marks a transcending of the condition typical of the primates*" (3, emphasis added). For Eliade, the "vertical posture" is bound with *homo sapiens'* propensity to make myths: *homo religiosus* transforms a meaningless series of postures into meaningfully differentiated orientations (vertical and horizontal, for example), which are then further invested by myth. Even if an animal stood and walked upright, it would not achieve what Eliade calls a vertical posture. Eliade is here pushing roughly the same point Durkheim had in mind in his insistence that the categories of space and time are constituted not by biology but in the completion of our biology through the classificatory function. Verticality "*already* marks a transcending" because verticality itself—directionality itself, the *meaningful* organization of space itself—is already uniquely human.

Thus, from the first page of Eliade's masterwork, animals play an important theoretical role. Yet, in another sense, animals are not considered at all. As we will see, the presence of animals to theorize *homo religiosus* seems to require their absence as the complicated individuals we have come to know in, for example, our relationships with animal companions, in primatology, and in ethology more generally.

Eliade proceeds with his articulation of the human/animal binary in *A History of Religious Ideas* by enumerating three basic differences that separate primate and human: (1) verticality (which I have already introduced); (2) tools (technology); and (3), most intriguingly, the decision to kill and eat animals. Verticality, Eliade argues, is the beginning point for the human capacity to view some space as sacred space. Animals may have territory, mating grounds, and other intimate relations with land, but only the human creates sacred space—only the human, for Eliade, fuses space, memory, and meaning.

The use of tools—fire especially—Eliade continues, further distinguishes human and animal. Eliade asserts that even though other animals do make tools, only the human "use of tools is not confined to a particular situation or a specific moment, as is the case with monkeys" (4). Since Eliade mentions a specific class of animals, "monkeys," he might be alluding to some kind of scientific research on animal tool use. If so, he never tells us. As best I can tell, Eliade never takes such ethological data seriously. Here we can detect in the background, once again, the notion of animality as biologically fixed in contrast to the neotenic, inherently myth-and-meaning-making human. Contrary to Eliade's assertion, the balance of evidence available today suggests that some nonhuman animals can improvise tool use. The remarkable diversity of the use of tools by chimpanzees is well known. Significantly, since this tool use varies among communities and is transmitted generationally, primatologists such as Christophe Boesch, director of the Max Planck Institute of Evolutionary Anthropology in Leipzig, have used it as evidence for the existence of chimpanzee cultures.[35] The true scope of animal tool use is still largely unexamined; for example, the discovery of tool use by fish is comparatively recent.[36] I would argue that Eliade felt confident in denying sophisticated tool use to animals not because he had been persuaded by the scientific information to which he vaguely alludes but because such a conclusion was preordained by his very imagination of the human/animal, fixed/ open boundary.

The final demarcation Eliade presents holds special interest for the present study. "Man," Eliade argues, "is the final product of a decision to kill in order to live. In short, the hominians succeeded in outstripping their ancestors by becoming flesh-eaters."[37] This decision to kill, Eliade continues, ultimately leads to the production of gender differentiation and the structure of sacrifice. This sacrificial structure emerges, Eliade speculates, because "the ceaseless pursuit and killing of game ended by creating a unique system of relationships between the hunter and the slain animals. . . . [A] 'mystical solidarity' between the hunter and his victims is revealed by the mere act of killing: the shed blood is similar in every respect to human blood."[38] A special kind of killing is then required—what we might call following Derrida "a noncriminal putting to death"—and sacrifice emerges.[39]

How can we understand this conclusion? The notion that flesh eating is a defining characteristic of the human sounds odd in a way that arguing for uniquely human capacities to organize space or use tools and technology does not. I believe the importance that Eliade attributes to flesh eating is best understood in light of the close relationship he imagines between myth and ritual. Myth is not accomplished by the mere recording of a creation narrative, but involves the association of that narrative with special bodily actions—with rituals.

If the act of mythmaking is what lifts *homo religiosus* out of animality, that myth must be embodied in ritual action, and what better way to embody an ontological break between the human and animal that makes the human an "animal plus" than by the human ritually sacrificing and consuming animal flesh and thereby transforming it into human flesh? This is why, I believe, Eliade calls flesh eating "a decision" instead of attributing it, as he easily could have, to the spontaneous unfolding of a biological drive or the fulfillment of a basic biological need. This "decision" would of course not be the everyday, conscious kind, but rather an organic coemergence of the myth and its embodiment in ritual. I do not think Eliade means to suggest that the need to embody the myth-generated demarcation of the human from animality is the only reason human communities tend to eat flesh, but he sees this as a nontrivial factor.

Eliade further argues—and this is lucid in his prose—that anxiety pervades the act of drawing a line between human and animal, especially at the moment of killing when it is clear that their blood "is similar in every respect to human blood."[40] The human may constitute—by its neotenic, mythmaking nature—a radical break from animals, but that fact does not prevent the emergence of "a unique system of relationships between the hunter and the slain animals" that leads to a sense of "'mystical solidarity'" with them. For Eliade, this mystical solidarity itself is part of another myth and ritual complex. Myth separates the human from the animal—tying together the unique status of the human and the human's decision to eat flesh. But myth also binds humans with animals—tying together a sense of similarity in kind and obligations of kindness toward animals (for example, the hunter's mystical solidarity expressed in rituals of apology to slain animals). We saw a similar set of ideas in Cassirer, in his placement of a certain feeling of "solidarity of life that bridges over the multiplicity and variety of its single forms" at the center of myth,[41] and we will encounter them again in Smith.

I have so far tried in my discussion of Eliade, as with Durkheim and Cassirer, to present the ways in which, for him, animals are constantly implicated in the first moments of his imagination of religion and therefore by implication are insinuated throughout his works. I have further, here and there, pointed out some peculiarities and problems with Eliade's views, but I do not aim to present a full evaluation of the use Eliade makes of animals in his theorizing. Rather, I have simply attempted to show *the fact of* the radical—in the sense of root—significance of animals for Eliade's imagination of the study of religion.

Perhaps the most significant way that Durkheim, Cassirer, and Eliade are utterly dependent on animals in their theorization of religion is their shared argument that the phenomenon of religion can be found persistently through time and space because it is rooted in the uniquely religious character of the properly human. This is perhaps what brings theorists of religion together as such.[42] Religion, almost by definition, begins where the animal ends. "In other words," as Eliade frames it, "to be—or, rather, to become—*a man* signifies being 'religious.'"[43]

Despite the significant role animals play and confident assertions about their abilities—for example, on the question of tool use—as far as I know Eliade, like Durkheim but unlike Cassirer, never concerned himself with serious observations of animals or any disciplines in the sciences that consider animal life. Eliade, like so many otherwise subtle thinkers, simply drops empirical rigor in discussions of animals. Despite their centrality to his imagination of religion, he has little compunction about making sweeping assertions about animals with virtually no evidence. This lack of substantiation regarding his claims about animals is perhaps one reason why he opens *A History of Religious Ideas* by deferring the problem of how the nonhuman becomes human,[44] that is, the problem of an animal—the primate—becoming human. To have a rigorous discussion of hominization would expose the lack of evidence for the kind of break between human and animal that Eliade articulates.

Why would a thinker of Eliade's caliber expose the entirety of his corpus to critique by resting it on the shifting ground of the human/animal binary without providing evidence from actual observations of animals? We could ask the same of Durkheim. Why not look in the horse's mouth? Durkheim and Eliade seem to imagine—and this is the decisive (and surprisingly common) conceptual error—that since their real concern is human beings, they can give short shrift to the animals they invoke to clarify their theories. *It's not about animals*, I imagine the ghost of Durkheim or Eliade would insist. *If it turns out, for example, as you say, Dr. Gross, that animals do use tools spontaneously, I simply have failed to articulate the unique nature of human tool use properly. I'm not concerned with what animals do, but with what they do not do. I'm not really talking about animals, but men by way of an imagined "animal."* Fair enough, but it clearly would be a problem for Durkheim or Eliade if, even after ad hoc modifications to their work to fit better with evidence from contemporary ethology, animals could be said to possess the qualities they deny them; it undermines their entire persuasive strategy. If humans cannot be reliably distinguished from animals in the specific ways Durkheim or Eliade argue, then they have failed to identify religion as a distinct phenomenon. "Actual" animals are not irrelevant for the views they articulate, even though they are clearly more concerned with the *idea* of the animal. In any case, while relevant, the empirical study of animals is not sufficient to determine conclusively whether some animals possess the kinds of elusive capacities (meaning making, for example) that Durkheim, Cassirer, Eliade, and others want to deny them.

My complaint about the lack of engagement with animals is more fundamentally a plea that animals matter. We cannot escape their disruptive potential simply by noting that they have been invoked as foils to the human any more than we could avoid the disruptive potential of feminist thought by noting that in making various troubling comparisons between women and men we were really only talking about men. When "woman" or "the animal" is used to define man, the perceptions of actual women and actual animals are also affected. Defending Eliade's lack of consideration of animals on the grounds that he "really" is only talking about humans, in fact, points precisely to the importance of animals: we seem unable to imagine the human without them in exactly the same way that we are unable to imagine man without woman. Again, more patience would be needed to fully do justice to Eliade's views, but the important point for the present study is more basic: to show that Eliade's foundational imagination of religion and the key categories he invokes to understand it, such as myth and sacred space, are intimately bound up with his views about animals.

Such philosophical positions have immediate practical consequences for scholars of religion. For example, Eliade's perspectives on the human/animal binary, as well as those of Durkheim, would appear to suggest that ethological studies cannot teach us anything of interest about religion. (Cassirer's views are more complicated on this point.) Such an approach would most likely reject the controversial and problematic—but I think productive—proposals of scholars such as Frits Staal in *Rules Without Meaning* or Walter Burkert in *The Creation of the Sacred*,[45] who have attempted to understand ritual practices as sharing certain continuities with particular animal behaviors. Anything religious, Eliade, like Durkheim, insists, is already a product of leaving animality behind in a total fashion.

At one level we can note that Durkheim's, Cassirer's, and Eliade's choice to begin their respective theorizations of religion with the emergence of the human is an attempt to undercut—if not radically eliminate—evolutionary, Eurocentric, and often racist views. None of them, for example, deny "true" religion to any human group. In their work religion ceases to be a privilege of Europe or "civilization" and is first of all a human activity. While their deployment of the primitive/modern binary is no doubt problematic, their uses of it when compared to their contemporaries tend to highlight broad human continuity rather than to isolate Western culture more emphatically. However, as we will discuss in the next section, this humanism is purchased through an exclusion of the animal and therefore serves as a means of legitimating a series of fraught and interrelated binaries: human/animal, male/female, culture/nature, modern/primitive, insider/outsider, people-like-us/people-not-like-us, and so on. In the end this humanism—which is precisely the humanism that has defined the "human sciences" against the "life sciences"—ultimately and ironically threatens the dignity of the *homo sapiens* it sought to protect. As should become more clear with each of the remaining chapters in this study, deploying the human/animal binary, which inevitably shores up other binaries like modern/primitive, threatens the best of what the human/animal binary was (in a sympathetic reading of these thinkers, at least) in part intended to achieve: the grand idea of the inviolability of *homo sapiens*.

Part of the enduring value of the works of Durkheim, Cassirer, and Eliade—and why their works are ascribed a positive significance in this study as well as being the subject of critique—is that they invest the perception of space and time with social processes. How we understand space and time, let alone more narrow categories, they insist, is bound up with often obscure social processes: what we call myths and rituals. This insight is productively disruptive. It undermines a simplistic separation of human nature (biological endowment) and human culture, hinting that there is no secure moment of pure biological perception that is free of the taint of social-mythological influence. However, the productivity of this disruption is limited, as these thinkers end up reinscribing the nature/culture binary in their shoring-up of the human/animal binary. In important ways the human/animal binary is a stumbling block before these giants.

IMAGINE THE HUMAN: JONATHAN Z. SMITH

Smith can be viewed as advancing the humanistic legacy of Durkheim, Cassirer, and Eliade by underscoring that the study of religion is, at bottom, the study of the human. Perhaps most famous is his declaration from the introduction of *Imagining Religion*: "while there is a staggering amount of data . . . that might be characterized in one culture or another, by one criterion or another, as religious—*there is no data for religion*. Religion is solely the creation of the scholar's study."[46] So if religion itself does not present data to us, where does the scholar look for the exempla that Smith argues are central to her endeavor? Quite simply, we are to look at *human* activities—the human is the horizon of our work. There is, for Smith, no natural or necessary line to be drawn between the study of religion and the study of the human but only the lines drawn by scholars for their various intellectual purposes.

Smith's strategy in the declaration with which he begins *Imagining Religion* is one of what he calls *defamiliarization*. Smith's view, as he himself tells us later, is that scholars have forgotten that the entire idea of a study of religion located in the human sciences was once so radical as to appear a contradiction in terms.[47] Titles such as "religion and the human sciences" are so *familiar* that we no longer appreciate "their daring" and their "highly polemical" nature.[48] The study of religion became possible only when it became intelligible to pull "religion" from the divine side of the human-divine binary over to the human side (at least partially), thus making it plausible to use the tools of the human sciences where once only the methods of "divine sciences," or theology, appeared appropriate. This move's very purpose was to "domesticate" religion,[49] to transform it into a subject accessible to reason.[50] As Smith emphasizes, the inclusion of religion in the human sciences was once so disruptive because the human sciences were defined precisely in opposition to the divine sciences; the deeply rooted human/divine binary had to be reconsidered (in much the same way the present study proposes a kind of reconsideration of the human/animal binary). But what does this move really accomplish? How would our appreciation of its significance change if we were to critically attend to "the animal" that shadows it?

Smith's declaration has a radical feel to it, and no doubt Smith intended it as part provocation, but the sentiment he expresses is quite conservative—even Protestant, and certainly Enlightenment—in character insofar as it reinforces an old line of humanistic thinking, one that Smith feels we have become so familiar with as to have lost a sense of its power. Smith succeeds in challenging hastily drawn lines between religion and nonreligion, but at the expense of treating the line between human and animal, or, more broadly, human and nonhuman, as (almost) given. As expansive as this view is, in that it finds religion not only in the sphere of divinity but also humanity, Smith's view, if left unmodified, is problematically constraining. The cost of its expansiveness, as with humanism more generally, is the exclusion—or at least the marginalization—of what scholars of religions Kimberley Patton and Paul Waldau have called "the religious implications of animal subjectivities" and a tendency (though not strictly necessitated) to forget the shadow role of animality in making humanity intelligible.[51]

One could even argue that Smith and those who advanced this direction of theory before him have failed to fully shift religion from the sphere of the divine sciences. After all, it is exceedingly difficult—and I tend to think impossible—to argue for an ontological distinction between humans and all other life that would justify limiting the study of religion to the sphere of the human without an appeal that extends beyond the domain of reason. At the very least, as even Cassirer seems to acknowledge, we would have to be rather expert in our understanding of the great apes—perhaps more expert than the present state of primatology even allows—to make such a distinction with any confidence if we claim to be using arguments that are accessible to reason, as Smith does. It may well be that Smith's observation that we have forgotten the radicalism of the shift of the study of religion from the divine to human sciences can be explained precisely because it is not so radical after all. When we consider the extent to which Western thought has divinized the human (Hegel or Feuerbach are exemplary in this regard)—which is arguably already implied wherever an ontological gulf between human and animal is asserted—to shift the study of religion from divine to human may really be little more than a shift from one understanding of divinity prevalent before modernity to a more modern conception of the divine that ascribes attributes once considered exclusively divine, such as infinity, to the human—as in, for example, the idea of the infinitely open human that can never be fixed. Perhaps the only way to truly create a study of religion that would be properly distinct from the divine sciences is to open the question of animal participation in the phenomenon of religion.

Smith, to his enormous credit, seems conscious of this basic problematic and, if we take into account his larger oeuvre, we see that he brings critical metareflection to the human/animal binary that is absent in his predecessors. Whereas at one level Smith, like Durkheim, Cassirer, and Eliade before him, appears to establish the theoretical foundation of his scholarship on this obscure distinction, he at times highlights the problematic nature of the distinction. Smith incisively argues that the division of the world into human and nonhuman (which includes, but is not limited to, its division into human and animal) frequently threatens to become a distinction between people-like-us and people-not-like-us. Here he demonstrates a sensitivity to the links I have noted in Durkheim and Cassirer between the human/animal and modern/primitive binaries.

With great perceptiveness Smith argues in his 1978 collection of essays, *Map Is Not Territory*, that one of the ironies of our intellectual history is that in an attempt to understand "those activities of man which are unique" to the human we have split the world into "human beings (who are generally like-us) and nonhuman beings (who are generally not-like-us), into the 'we' and the 'them.'"[52] Despite mitigating this legacy in the contemporary era, Smith argues that the study of religion has not escaped it: "The twentieth century interpretation suggests, at best, that the primitive is another kind of human. . . . On the conceptual level it robs them of their humanity, of those perceptions of discrepancy and discord which give rise to the symbolic project that we identify as the very essence of being human" (297). Without speaking of animals directly, Smith here recognizes the violent potential of reliance on the category human, which is precisely its intimate and often hidden relation with the animal: when one splits the world into "human be-ings . . . and nonhuman beings," the threat of being placed on the wrong side of that binary always looms. In this regard Smith's thought comes closer to the critical stance I propose than Eliade's.

Smith's sensitivity to the proximity of the human/animal binary to racist articulations of the primitive/modern binary is also evident in his important essay "I Am a Parrot (Red)." In this essay Smith playfully proposes, "There are some animals which have played so decisive a role in the history of the history of religions that they may truly be seen as emblems (if not totems!) of our discipline" (265). Smith proposes that no animal could fill that role as well in "our time" as "the Brazilian parrot in the tradition of the Bororo tribe" (265). His focus is on a much-cited statement by Karl von den Steinen first published in 1894: "The Bororos boast of themselves that they are red parrots (Araras)," and, von den Steinen insists, they mean this literally. Con-sequently "we must put totally out of our minds the boundaries between man and the animal" (266). Von den Steinen's statement, especially under the in-fluence of Lucien Lévy-Bruhl, became the paradigmatic example of just how far "primitive mentality" differs from the modern—especially with respect to their inability to make proper distinctions, classifications, and taxono-mies—a view that now appears tainted by racist biases. Smith is concerned with this racist problem, but he is also concerned to ask, "How should the historian of religion interpret a religious statement which is apparently con-trary to fact?" (267).

Taking the Bororos' statement as an example, Smith shows just how thorny an issue this is: how difficult it is to honor the puzzling nature of some statements without either arrogantly assuming we know better or na-ively assuming that every apparently unintelligible statement must a priori be a result of our confusion or some bafflingly different mode of thought. In the history of its interpretation, Smith shows, "I am a parrot" was first an absurdity, than later came to be seen as a serious statement of truth, quite intelligible once properly and nonliterally understood. "The solution to the

Bororo's seeming plurality of beings, advocated since Evans-Pritchard, is the assumption of a plurality of languages and, by implication, a plurality of truths" (266). This is surely an improvement, Smith argues, but it too has limitations. Smith sets Evans-Pritchard's view against that of Ernest Geller. Geller, pointing at the hidden assumptions of even this improved view, remarks that "no sane conduct . . . can be, by definition, self-contradictory. Therefore it becomes an *a priori* assumption of functionalism that no society may hold absurd beliefs" (284). Smith goes on to cite Steven Lukes as providing a useful summary of what is at stake in the Evans-Pritchard versus Geller debate: "'The problem comes down to whether or not there are alternative standards of rationality" (285). That is, are there modes of apprehending the world that, while defying our usual understanding of rationality, are nonetheless rational in some "alternative" manner? Is there a middle ground between rational and irrational that we could call "alternatively" rational? For Smith, the problem is not settled. He ends this important essay not with a final solution to the dilemmas he finds in previous scholarship, but instead he calls historians of religion to join "both philosophical hermeneutics and anthropology" in this ongoing discussion (287). I understand the present study to be taking Smith up on this suggestion and will be engaging anthropology and philosophical hermeneutics in the next two chapters.

We are all indebted to Smith for his identification of the pervasiveness of the exemplum of the Bororos' parrots, who remain a fitting emblem for the field of religious studies because they continue to recall what remains a horizon of thought in the study of religion: the human/animal border. Smith identifies the significance of the Bororo exemplum by looking at it as a case study in "how . . . the historian of religion . . . interpret[s] a religious statement that is apparently contrary to fact" (267). While Smith does not emphasize it, I would suggest that it is not accidental that this potent example of the "apparently counterfactual" deals directly with the human/animal border. It is no accident that, for Smith, the question of "alternative standards of rationality" is arrived at through confronting a worldview that does not respect the human/animal border in the way with which we are familiar. The limits of intelligibility and rationality are tested by cultures that confront us with different taxonomic breakdowns of human and animal. Here we can begin to see, as I suggested in the introduction to this study, that the question of the animal concerns thinking itself. It is not clear to me that this was Smith's intention, but his essay in fact demonstrates enormous sensitivity and attention to the question of the animal and its implications for the very meaning of rationality, a point we shall revisit throughout this study.

Beyond Smith's sensitivity to the questions about rationality that are raised by animals, he follows Cassirer's and Eliade's thinking about human/animal relations in one of its most productive streams: the observation that human power over animals is, historically speaking, shadowed by a discomfort with the violent exercise of that power, or, alternatively framed, a sense of human distance from animals is bound with a feeling of intimacy with them. We, as readers, are asked to face this paradox.

As I noted in my discussion of Cassirer in relation to Durkheim, Cassirer places a feeling of the "solidarity of life" at the core of the history of religions, while Durkheim, in contrast, denies its significance and, as we have seen, suggests that animals have no importance as animals, let alone as fellow subjectivities. To a large extent Eliade and Smith follow Cassirer in wanting to acknowledge this same significance of animals. We have already noted that Eliade speaks of a "'mystical solidarity' between the hunter and his victim" parallel to that found in Cassirer. In different ways both Cassirer—by arguing that no religion could "ever think of cutting or even loosening the bond between nature and man" and placing a "feeling of a natural or magical solidarity of life" at the origin of religions[53]—and Eliade—by similarly placing a "mystical solidarity" with animals at the beginning of religion's unfolding—honor the religious charge of human-animal relations. Both scholars honor the fact that, as Patton argues, human-animal relations are "something charged, something holy."[54]

Cassirer is also among those who cite Karl von den Steinen's quotation of the Bororo's "I am a parrot." Cassirer's view, however, is not easily slotted into the two problematic camps Smith articulates—views that slide into either an accusation that the Bororos are absurd or an accusation that they are so distant from us in their thinking as to be untranslatable. Cassirer carefully and methodically posits a distance between the likes of the Bororo and the modern, while at the same time, with equal care, articulating a continuity. Again, we are asked to face a paradoxical tension.

While Cassirer does not entirely avoid problematic articulations of triumphalist and evolutionary ideas, he quite elegantly avoids the horns of the dilemma Smith traces by understanding human-animal relations as something fundamental that must be a starting point for scholars and, in addition, by positing a movement from "primitive" worldviews rooted in an affirmation of the "solidarity of life" to later traditions, such as the Abrahamic traditions, that develop a sense of "universal ethical sympathy."[55] There are many problems with this formulation, but some of those concerns can be rehabilitated by simply bracketing the evolutionary question and considering "solidarity of life" and "universal ethical sympathy," as Cassirer also does to some degree, as two intimately related metaorientations that ground the worldviews of particular religions by binding them to "nature" in distinct ways (solidarity or sympathy, preethical or ethical, and so on). Leaving aside the question of how or *if* these two abstracted moments of religion should be organized in a chronology or hierarchy (Cassirer himself recognizes that the allegedly later ethical view is also found in "a very primitive stage"),[56] the lens through which Cassirer approaches "I am a parrot" functions as follows: human-animal relations are understood as fundamental and often marked by extreme solidarity and thus nothing is even unusual for Cassirer about statements of identification with animals. No risk of the first horn of the dilemma Smith reports—seeing the "apparently counterfactual" as absurd—ever presents itself. Cassirer's perspective is radically different from the path Smith charts through Cassirer's contemporary Lévy-Bruhl, who sees the Bororo as exemplarily "prelogical" and therefore ultimately "incomprehensible."[57] Cassirer, in contrast, finds nothing in the "ancient" view of solidarity that renders translation impossible, although he too—and rightly—emphasizes that the view of "solidarity" is in contrast to dominant sensibilities that prevail in the modern West. Cassirer's analysis fully acknowledges the "equality" of humans and animals in the stance of "solidarity," but instead of seeing that equality as the marker of a radically foreign intelligence or even the marker of a radically different taxonomy of thought, he understands it as a variation on a theme of "the bond between nature and man" that runs right through the whole of religious life, uniting primitive and modern.[58] Thus no risk of the second horn of the dilemma Smith reports—seeing the statement as incomprehensible—presents itself either.

The accuracy or helpfulness of Cassirer's view of religion aside, it accomplishes several things of interest to the present study: it moves in the direction of acknowledging the fluidity and cultural specificity of the human/animal boundary; it acknowledges the religious charge of animals; and, not incidentally, it engages the question of the "primitive" in relation to the human/animal border in a less problematic, more sympathetic manner than Cassirer's contemporaries, who Smith reviews in his essay "I Am a Parrot

(Red)." In interpreting von den Steinen, Cassirer, in fact, does an exemplary job of "making the strange familiar," in large measure simply through careful description.

> We see from these examples how the firm belief in the unity of life eclipses all those differences that, from our own point of view, seem to be unmistakable and ineffaceable.[59] We need by no means assume that these differences are completely overlooked. They are not denied in an empirical sense but they are declared to be irrelevant in a religious sense.[60] To mythical and religious feeling nature becomes one great society, the *society of life*. Man is not endowed with outstanding rank in this society. He is a part of it but he is in no respect higher than any other member. Life possesses the same religious dignity in its humblest and in its highest forms.[61]

At no point does Cassirer malign or exoticize (though this risk always looms) this different conception of animals and religion, but he also, with a fine sense of balance, notes its distance from "our own point of view."

Interestingly, the passages that follow the mention of the Bororos are some of the moments in *An Essay on Man* when Cassirer describes the "primitive" in such strongly positive terms of life affirmation ("the strongest and most energetic affirmation of life that we find in human culture")[62] that one senses in his prose a tremendous effort to elevate the status of primitive religions—a subversive seed that challenges other moments in his prose where the modern/primitive binary is wielded in more worrisome ways. Moving on from the Bororo exemplum, Cassirer articulately defends a stance in which binary oppositions are relative and every *yin*, so to speak, contains a piece of *yang*. In his writing on the religion/myth binary, Cassirer is especially concerned to complicate a simplistic opposition:

> There is no radical difference in this respect between mythical and religious thought. Both of them originate in the same fundamental phenomenon of human life. In the development of human culture we cannot fix a point where myth ends or religion begins. In the whole course of its history religion remains indissolubly connected and penetrated with mythical elements. On the other hand myth, even in its crudest and most rudimentary forms, contains some motives that in a sense anticipate the higher and later religious ideals.[63]

Cassirer problematically maintains a certain hierarchy where religion supersedes myth, but he so relativizes, mixes, and blurs the two that he almost eliminates the hierarchy in favor of a view that sees only the play of differences. Almost. I do not wish to pretend that these views do away with the problems presented by Cassirer's deployment of primitive/modern or human/animal binaries, but I have gone into some detail here to show how Cassirer's willingness to present views that are more open to the significance of animals and more positive in their imagination of the "primitive" rise and fall together. The charge of "racial" and species difference are bound together.

While I am unaware of any move Smith makes that explicitly places human-animal relations—and a regard for and feeling of similarity to animals—at the origin of religion as Eliade and Cassirer do (whether or not they get their history right), he continues their reflections, drawing on many of the same scholars, on the widespread nature of a stance of "solidarity" with animals. He does this tellingly in an article entitled "The Bare Facts of Ritual" that, as Smith surely intends, could also be appropriately entitled "The *Bear* Facts of Ritual." As in "I Am a Parrot (Red)," I would attribute special significance to the exemplum Smith chooses to explore the category of ritual, in this case "bear-hunting rituals as reported, especially, from paleo-Siberian peoples."[64] Smith could have chosen any exemplum to reflect upon ritual; that he chooses ones intimately bound to animals already suggests Smith's greater interest in, and more critical stance toward, the role of animals in the study of religion.

Smith's essay provides a precise, critical engagement with Eliade's views about the foundational significance of the hunter's "mystical solidarity" with the animals he hunts. Smith offers a more contextualized and conservative version of Eliade's imagination of the hunter's regard for the animals he kills. Eliade, in contrast, tends toward considering all ancient hunters as a homogeneous group. Smith, like Eliade, finds a widespread anxiety regarding the killing of animals. "Among almost all of these northern hunting groups, there is a disclaimer of responsibility recited over the animal's corpse immediately after it has been killed."[65] However, Smith, unlike Eliade, is concerned first and foremost with concrete historical communities—"paleo-Siberian" hunters in particular. Beyond this critique pushing for greater contextualization, which constrains rather than contradicts Eliade's stance, Smith points toward the conflicted and idealized nature of these apparent articulations of a sentiment of "solidarity." He notes, for example: "The Nivkhi *say* that 'in order not to excite the bear's posthumous revenge, do not surprise him but rather have a fair stand-up fight,' but the same report goes on to describe how they *actually* kill bears: 'a spear, the head of which is covered with spikes, is laid on the ground, a cord is attached to it and, as the bear approaches [the ambush] the hunter [by pulling up on the cord] raises the weapon and the animal becomes impaled on it."[66]

Smith's observation that textual evidence for rituals imagining a "solidarity of life" should not be taken at face value is crucial, and his reflections in this connection represent a significant advance over those of Eliade or Cassirer. Smith's move is toward the local and the historically specific, to be sure, but it is also, more importantly, in the direction of "actual" animals. Smith's scholarly rigor insists on reflection on the interaction of the idealized representations of animals that appear in texts and the actual biological animals that are engaged in religious practices. This rigor significantly disturbs the notion of a historical evolution from a time where there was a sentiment of solidarity to a time where that solidarity has been eliminated or transformed. Given Smith's example, the actual practice of an embodied, lived "solidarity" with animals (whatever that might mean) becomes more doubtful, at least as the usual state of affairs. Smith shows us that even where we find robust articulations of solidarity with animal life we can by no means assume that those ideas are implemented, at least not in *obvious and simple ways*, in practice.

Although Smith's views could be more fully explicated, we have already learned more than enough for the purposes of the main argument I wish to make. We have yet another theorist for whom the demarcation between the human and the animal creates the horizon of what may be considered religion. The crucial difference is that in Smith's case we have frontal, critical reflection on some aspects of the violence inherent in the human/animal binary and a critical eye toward the complex gaps between what religious communities say about their interactions with animals and what they do.

THE HISTORY OF RELIGIONS AND ANTHROPOLOGICAL MACHINES

Taken together, these four thinkers—Durkheim, Cassirer, Eliade, and Smith—represent a century-long intellectual arc in the study of religion that at bottom imagines religion as that aspect of the human that is not shared with the animal. I do not mean to single these particular thinkers out as particularly wrongheaded in their theorizations of animals. My own research gives me the impression that the overwhelming majority of theorists of religion at some point in their works find themselves uncritically invoking the human/animal divide for support. Moreover, as I have noted, we find both moments of critical attention to animals and moments of forgetting them in these thinkers. The "problem of the animal" is more polyphonous and pervasive than any survey could hope to capture. As this chapter approaches its close, turning to the work of Giorgio Agamben may help us gain a better perspective on the full significance of the human/animal border that we have been tracing in religious studies scholarship and, more specifically, the incessant drawing of this border to separate the (prereligious) species *homo sapiens* from the "properly" (religious) human.

In *The Open* Agamben has called this structure that we have encountered in theorists of religion, in which the human/animal binary generates the human subject and other crucial categories of thought, an "anthropological machine" that executes the fundamental operation of "anthropogenesis." Rather than defining the human positively, the anthropological machine is "an ironic apparatus that verifies the absence of a nature proper to *Homo*, holding him suspended between a celestial and a terrestrial nature, between animal and human—and, thus, his being always less and more than himself."[67] Agamben calls it ironic because, as we have noted, the mechanism of separation is often executed in the name of preserving human dignity, of identifying, as Smith had it, "those activities of man which are unique,"[68] but ends up accomplishing something quite different. Rather, it splits the world into "human beings (who are generally like-us) and nonhuman beings (who are generally not-like-us), into the 'we' and the 'them.'"[69]

Agamben's innovation is to point out that drawing the line between animal and human, unexpectedly, creates the imagination of a *third kind of creature* that is neither animal nor human, but is what we might call the prehuman "human"—a liminal being upon which the anthropological machine can go to work to create the properly human by, for example, subtracting fixity or adding the symbolic function. From an evolutionary perspective, this third creature is the so-called missing link between human and animal—the ape that was not quite yet a human but, following some decisive leap forward, was soon to become "the first human." This overlooked third being is imagined in a wide variety of ways in Western culture. In Western intellectual lineages that laid important foundations for today's life sciences (which are

especially important to consider for those wishing to create bridges between
the life sciences and human sciences), Agamben points to, for example,
Edward Tyson's 1699 treatise "Orang-Outang, sive Homo Sylvestris: or, the
Anatomy of a Pygmie," a text he describes as "a sort of incunabulum" (that is,
a primer) of contemporary primatology.[70] Though this text is, according to
Agamben, the first to distinguish what we now know as apes and humans "on
the solid grounds of comparative anatomy," the text also nevertheless represents the pygmie as "a sort of 'intermediate animal' between ape and man,
to who it stands in a relation symmetrically opposite to that of the angel" (the
reference to angels is explicit in Tyson's text).[71] Another example is found in
Carl Linnaeus, the eighteenth-century founder of modern taxonomy, who,
Agamben points out, includes in his taxonomy "the enigmatic . . . *homo
ferus,*" which, Agamben speculates, is Linnaeus's way to address then-fre-
quent popular reports of "the *enfants sauvages,* or wolf-children."[72] In the
nineteenth century Agamben points us to Ernst Haekel's 1874 hypothesis of
"a peculiar being that he called 'ape-man' (*Affenmensch*)" or the "*sprachloser
Urmensch*" that constituted "a form of passage from the anthropoid apes (or
man-apes) to man."[73] Or, to move from the elites of European science whom
Agamben focuses on to twentieth century popular science fiction, consider
the iconic opening scene of Stanley Kubrick's *2001 A Space Odyssey,*[74] where
humanlike ape creatures (literally humans in animal costume, as if modern
day shamans) first discover something like tool use (à la Eliade),[75] and, the
implication is, the march toward humanity is begun.

The space between human and animal generated by the anthropological
machine is filled variously with Tyson's pygmie; Linnaeus's *homo ferus, enfants sauvages*; Haekel's *Affenmesch* (ape-man) or *sprachloser Urmensch*;
Durkheim's, Cassirer's, and Eliade's primitive; or Kubrick's prehominians
discovering tool use, but, Agamben shows us, is invariably a dangerous place
to find oneself. In this space dwell beings locked in a "state of exception,"
who are often reduced to a "bare life" that is "neither an animal life nor a
human life."[76] Different political regimes populate this imagined space of
indeterminacy with different persons and treat them in different ways, but
almost never benignly. In a stunning combination of intellectual history and
genealogical inquiry, Agamben traces in detail how the Nazi machine imagined "the Jew [as] the non-man produced within the man" interdependently
with their imagination of this third space of bare life.[77] Crucially, Agamben's
point is not to single out this movement in Nazi thought *as an anomaly,* but

to show us how, unexpectedly, the dangerous operation of the anthropological machine that allows the Jew to become less than human in Nazism is
at work throughout intellectual history. In fact—this is the most disturbing
and profound hypothesis Agamben puts forth—it is at work wherever we divide the world into humans and animals, that is, wherever the anthropological machine is in operation. A driving thesis throughout *The Open* is that
dividing the world, as Smith put it, into "human beings . . . and nonhuman
beings . . . into the 'we' and the 'them,'"[78] contains a seed of the most extreme
forms of violence. This thesis perhaps seems almost unbelievable, but we
should not judge its veracity too quickly. Patience is required.

In any case, it is easy to see, at least, that the division of the world into
human and animal is all around us—the pervasiveness of the anthropological machine is not in doubt. Ultimately, Agamben shows its operation
in a much broader arc of Western theological, philosophical, and literary
thought: Western understandings of life itself—and the basic divisions of
life (vegetal and relational, organic and animal, etc.)—depend on a more primary and intimate division within the human species between the animal
and the human, "a mobile border within living man" without which "the very
decision of what is human and what is not would probably not be possible."[79]
It is this fraught border that Agamben rightly asks us to attend to with new
vigor. "We must learn," Agamben insists, to read the Western tradition as
creating the human "from the incongruity of these two elements [humanity
and animality], and investigate not the metaphysical mystery of conjunc-
tion, but rather the practical political mystery of separation."[80]

What I have called the question of the animal and religion is not parallel
to other knotty points in the imagination of the human or religion. "It is as if
determining the border between human and animal were not just one question among many discussed by philosophers, theologians, scientists and pol-
iticians, but rather a fundamental metaphysico-political operation in which
alone something like 'man' can be decided upon and produced."[81] "Perhaps,"
Agamben ponders, "the aporias of the philosophy of our time coincide with
the aporias of this body [which is also "the body of the slave"] that is irreducibly drawn and divided between animality and humanity."[82]

Still, Agamben—and I would follow him here—does not suggest it is any
simple matter to avoid this fundamental distinction and division. The response cannot be to simply toss out the human/animal binary. The closing
and haunting question of *The Open* is whether there is, in fact, a way to stop

the anthropological machine. This is a pertinent question for scholars of religion, especially those working on the question of the animal and religion.

The task of a "postanimal" study of religion—which is nothing more or less than the task of finding ways to responsibly and carefully think about religion, ways to think about those things that we deem "religious"—may be more difficult than simply taking into account, as Waldau and Patton have helpfully suggested, "the religious implications of animal subjectivities."[83] Or, to put it another way, it may be more complicated than it appears to take into account "the religious implications of animal subjectivities." If we simply labor to demonstrate that *animals are religious subjects too* and proceed to win a space of discussion for the subfield of "animals and religion," we may remain fully in the grip of the anthropological machine with all its attendant potential for violence. At very least we would do well to attend to how animals and human conceptions of them found the intellectual space in which the study of religion operates. The force of feminist and womanist scholarship is not a simple plea to include women and attention to them in the same old conversation, but to change the nature of the conversation itself. Animals demand no less.

In sum, I am arguing that although the category "animal" has not generally been imagined as a "great word" in the study of religion, it should be. It always has been a great word, but we scholars have somehow forgotten or disavowed this. If we are successful in following the animal down this rabbit hole, shifts in perspective become possible that will cast the study of religion in new hues. The greatest value of our study of AgriProcessors is not to introduce new facts to the study of religion, but to apprehend religion and religions in new modalities. It is to such new angles of vision that I turn in the next two chapters, and such angles of vision will illumine the AgriProcessors event in the final chapter.

When the depth of the question of the animal is fully appreciated, it may no longer be sufficient to simply think of new and better ways to talk about "humans, animals, and religion"—ways more informed by primatology and ethology, more free from racist basis, more critical about sex and gender, less ableist, and so on. The challenge of Agamben's work—and the challenge of several other thinkers whom I am not able to adequately engage in this volume such as J. M. Coetzee, Wendy Doniger, and Donna Haraway[84]—is that we may need to cease thinking in terms of the human/animal binary altogether or, since that may be impossible, somehow learn to hold this binary in a new way.

4

After the Subject

HUNTER-GATHERERS AND
THE REIMAGINATION OF RELIGION

WHAT COUNTS AS RELIGION

As we have seen in the Durkheim to Smith lineage reviewed in the previous chapter, the nontheological study of religion has imagined itself as an inquiry into the human subject at the very moment the human is distinguished from the animal and thus becomes properly religious. Rather than an inquiry into types of phenomena that are best understood as religious, the study of religion, at least in its dominant modes of inquiry, has limited its purview to types of *human* phenomena that are best understood as religious. The aspects of the human that are perceived to be shared with animals and, of course, animals themselves are outside the circle delimiting the proper subjects of the scholarly study of religion. This limitation not only excludes animals, but obfuscates, among other things, our study of numerous indigenous traditions and our attention to the religious dimensions of childhood. That is, the religious life of human communities who have been historically seen to be close to animals, such as children (who are viewed as in a transitional state between the human animal body and the fully human adult) and indigenous peoples (who are understood to live in or close to an "animal" state), becomes distorted when animals are "absented" from the imagination of religion.

To reimagine animals from the critical vantage being proposed here is inevitably to reimagine religion (and vice versa). A critical approach to animals ultimately forces us down a path that requires us to reimagine the subjectivities and subjects that count as religious and may ultimately lead some of us to reject the entire discourse that delineates "subjects and objects," "subjectivity and objectivity" in the first place. To embark on just such a reimagination is the aim of this and the following chapter.

The present chapter pursues this reimagination by marshaling the resources of the anthropological scholarship of Tim Ingold. Ingold represents an anthropological ethos that, following Claude Lévi-Strauss, has paid careful attention to both the human/animal binary and the closely associated culture/nature binary. This anthropological ethos, also evident in Eduardo Viveiros de Castro's work on the Araweté of the Amazon and Rane Willerslev's work on the Yukaghirs of Siberia among others, is rooted in a sensitivity to the paradox inherent in the anthropological effort to interpret other "cultures" when those cultures have rejected, moved beyond, or otherwise do not deploy the nature/culture binary. The present chapter will consider this paradox and its relevance to the question of the animal shortly, but for now we can observe that whereas Lévi-Strauss's work culminates in an attempt to confront this paradox, Ingold's work begins already engaged in a hermeneutical grappling with it. Neither thinker resolves the paradox, but Ingold is valuable because of the rigor of his confrontation and the robustness of his attempts to provide a glimpse of a "culture" without reference to the idea of culture or nature, a community that has moved beyond or, in any case, operates without the human/animal binary. Following the seam of this paradox in the next chapter, I will move from Ingold's work to Jacques Derrida, who, also responding to Lévi-Strauss, can help us continue the deconstructive work essential to this reimagination.

To anticipate, motivating this reimagination is the hypothesis that the kinds of subjectivity that count as religious should not be limited, without specific qualification, to the human. That is, the religious dimension that the academic study of religion analyzes and works over is not so much a dimension of human culture as a dimension of a unified field of relations that (can be, but) need not be divided into human and animal. As Ingold has described it, "Relations that human beings have with one another form just one part of the total field of relations embracing all living things."[1] In particular, I hypothesize that religion is a dimension of reality that might be seen, for example, not only in relations among members of the species *homo sapiens*, but in relationships *homo sapiens* have with nonhuman (and nondivine) beings, and in relationships among nonhuman species themselves.[2] Religion is productively thought, I suggest, not only as something that is experienced or practiced by religious subjects but also as the matrices within which the agents of religion engage and are tangled up with a virtually infinite array of agencies (animal agencies and others) that face all of us and demand response.[3] Religion is a dimension not of culture but of who we "become with companion species, who and which make a mess out of categories in the making of kin and kind."[4] Religion not only binds human societies but also weaves and webs the living into lives shot through with concern for life.

These "agencies," "companion species," and "lives" can be a productive refinement of our understanding of the "subjects" and "subjectivities" that count as religious. Of course, what "subject" and "subjectivity" would then mean will have changed. A strategy I have hinted at throughout this book has been, precisely, to stretch our present understanding of subjectivity so as to encompass animals, most especially the animal actors in the AgriProcessors scandals. This entails, paradoxically, imagining kinds of subjectivity that do not cleave reality into "subjects and objects" (as usually implied by the idea of subjectivity) but rather view the subject as a knot, node, or nexus that allows a self to emerge as person rather than thing.

As we will see, the direction in which Ingold points is even more radical, at least rhetorically. In the end, Ingold would have us give up the language of subjects and objects, subjectivity and objectivity altogether. Rather than reimaging subjectivity, he would argue that there are no animal subjects and no human subjects—no subjects and objects at all—because dividing the world in this way just isn't useful. Ingold directs us toward a new (for Western scholarship, at least) way of moving in the world that isn't about having a particular "view," but about, to paraphrase Ingold, enskilling ourselves so as to constitute and be constituted by diverse fields of relationships, some of which would count as religious. Indeed, Ingold argues that to "re-describe the ontological commitments of non-western peoples as world-*views* is at once to accommodate them on naturalism's terms [i.e., the dominant vantage of scholarship] and to neutralize the challenge they pose to its own hegemony."[5] At times I will follow Ingold in avoiding these freighted words, but, at other times, I think we will need to transform our apprehensions of religion by reimaging religious subjectivities rather than the far more disruptive (and potentially productive) task of developing a more radically new model that does not require anything like the old idea of the subject. We will do well, I argue, to reimagine the subject after rejecting the classical idea of the subject—a process long underway in the academy in general.

It is worth noting here that despite the fundamental changes I am proposing to the theoretical foundations of the lineage in the study of religion that I have traced from Durkheim to Smith, the present study still proceeds in many important ways within this lineage. I am not arguing that this lineage be supplanted with an absolutely different kind of study. Rather, I am suggesting that the most fundamental phenomena with which the Durkheim to Smith lineage is concerned—the diverse phenomena that scholars, religious practitioners, and many reflective people have variously identified as "religious"—never were, despite recent scholarly and popular understandings, exclusively a phenomenon of the human subject. The grand idea of a scholarly study of religion, a "science" of religion that stands independently of any particular traditional religious heritage,[6] never required the exclusion of animals and, in fact, has suffered from their exile.

THE SCHOLARSHIP OF TIM INGOLD

As we will see, certain features that arise commonly among hunter-gatherers that Ingold highlights can help the Western academy more authentically reimagine a scholarly study of religion. In particular, Ingold draws upon ethnographic literature concerning (1) tropical hunter-gatherer peoples (Batek Negritos of Malaysia, Mbuti Pygmies of the Ituri Forest, and Nayaka forest-dwelling hunter-gatherers of Tamil Nadu), (2) northern hunters, especially the Cree (northeast Canada), (3) aboriginal Australian peoples (especially the Pintupi of the Gibson Desert of Western Australia), and (4) peoples of subarctic Alaska (especially the Koyukon). The most important characteristic of these hunter-gatherer communities is not something they have but something they reject, move beyond, or do without: the human/animal, culture/nature binary. Attending to this absence of the animal, like attending to animals, will make visible and help us gain purchase on our own scholarly modes of thinking and ultimately reassess the adequacy of the (human) religious subject that is the primary subject of religious studies.

This *absence* of the animal among hunter-gatherers is the polar opposite of the *absenting* of animals that I have critiqued in the Durkheim-to-Smith lineage. The absence of the animal among hunger-gathers helps allow animals to be present; it is not something missing but a positive embrace of certain commonalities among the living. The absenting of animals in the academic study of religion, on the other hand, means that even as animals are made present (for example, referred to as objects of sacrifice or as totems), they are absented as animals and transformed into mere receptacles for human projections or a convenient foil; this absenting leaves scholarship flattened and depleted. Ultimately the rejection of the human/animal, subject/object binary among hunter-gatherers gives us grounds to imagine a religious subject that is no longer a classical (human) subject, and, in a certain sense, not a subject at all.

I closed the last chapter with Agamben's articulation of an "anthropological machine." Ingold can be helpfully understood as engaging the same problematic that troubles Agamben: how can we imagine a world, like that of hunter-gatherers, without already splitting it into human and animal, nature and culture, subjects with subjectivity and objects with objectivity? How can we stop what Agamben calls the anthropological machine—an especially pointed challenge for an anthropologist? Agamben argues that the human/animal binary is "not just one question among many . . . but rather a fundamental metaphysico-political operation."[7] Similarly, for Ingold, both the mind/body binary that rends our self-imagination as humans and the associated rift between the human sciences and natural sciences in the academy ultimately are nonintuitive, problematic divisions that "derive from a single, master dichotomy that underpins the entire edifice of Western thought and science—namely, that between the 'two worlds' of humanity and nature. For this is what has given us the overriding academic division of labor between those disciplines that deal, on the one hand, with the human mind and its manifold linguistic, social, and cultural products, and, on the other, with the structures and composition of the material world."[8] Ingold's "master dichotomy" is nothing other than the product of Agamben's "anthropological machine."

Agamben turns to Walter Benjamin for assistance in deconstructing this long-enduring machine.[9] Ingold, circling similar terrain, finds in hunter-gatherers no anthropological machine to begin with and seeks to make available to his readers hunter-gatherers' own way of being immersed in an "active, practical and perceptual engagement with constituents of the dwelt-in world"—their own "enskillment" rather than enculturation.[10] Both Agamben and Ingold (who has recently engaged Agamben directly)[11] struggle to articulate an imagination of the kind of being "we" are without dividing ourselves and our world into human and animal, culture and nature, and so on.

As we will see, in hunter-gatherer traditions the anthropological machine is not only "out of play," as Agamben says of Benjamin's writings, but absurd. Ingold remarks, "What *we* [scholars] distinguish as humanity and nature merge, for [hunter-gatherers], into a single field of relationships. . . . We find nothing corresponding to the Western concept of nature in hunter-gatherers' representations, for they see no essential difference between the ways one relates to humans and to nonhuman constituents of the environment."[12] One cannot divide the human into human and animal because for hunter-gatherers the world is not split into human and animal any more than it is split, for example, into people biologically related to Aaron Gross and people not related to him.[13]

To repeat, Ingold is not suggesting hunter-gatherers have a different view of the animal, but rather that they have no view of "the animal" or anything else. "The contrast, I repeat, is not between alternative views of the world: it is rather between two ways of apprehending it, only one of which (the Western) may be characterized as the construction of a view, that is, as a process of mental representation. As for the other, apprehending the world is not a matter of construction but of engagement, not of building but of dwelling, not of making a view of the world but of taking up a view in it."[14]

Here Ingold draws, or attempts to draw, a subtle and decisive line between "views of the world," which apply only to nonhunter-gatherers, and "ways of apprehending the world," which he argues offer both a path grounded in a hunter-gatherer ontology and a more promising path for the comparative project. "Apprehending" as opposed to "viewing" grasps "our" condition as prior to the human/animal, culture/nature, and subject/object binaries, leaving open the possibility of communities apprehending the world by "constructing a view" or not. This is in sharp contrast to a Western hermeneutic in which all engagements are already from within a constructed view. In this apprehension the identities of the vital actors are established not through policing borders such as human/animal nor "by species membership but by relational accomplishment."[15] "As a locus of creative growth and development, each self differs from each and every other because of its position within an unbounded and all-embracing relational matrix."[16]

This difference between "viewing" and "apprehending" does some heavy lifting, and through it Ingold attempts to smooth a knotty difficulty of anthropological interpretation that must be addressed if we are to seriously consider hunter-gatherers: how are we to comprehend human communities like

hunter-gatherers whose ontology bars the most basic moves of scholarly interpretation, which are based on the assumption of a common natural world
that is perceived through diverse cultural lenses? An earlier generation of
scholars, such as Durkheim and Mauss, also noted the absence of the human/
animal binary among those whom they called primitives and addressed this
challenge by arguing that primitive peoples lack a fully developed capacity
for reason and thus (like animals) are afflicted by certain intellectual limitations.[17] A later generation, represented by Claude Lévi-Strauss, rejected
this, but, while critiquing the limitations of utilizing the nature/culture binary because of its historical and cultural specificity, nevertheless continued
to privilege the nature/culture—and thus animal/human—binary as a "scientific" hermeneutical tool.

Ingold finds Lévi-Strauss's solution insufficient since, he argues, it suf-
fers from the same basic problem as the view that hunter-gatherers are not
fully rational (which Lévi-Strauss, like Ingold, rejected): both privilege an
ontology in which the world is split into human/animal and culture/nature,
distorting those communities who lack this ontology. The result is a kind of
ethnocentrism, an insidious racial bias.

The insinuation of a certain ethnocentrism certainly needs our critical attention, but this cannot be done, Ingold's reflections suggest, by simply saying that we know better today—that we know that hunter-gatherers
are fully rational humans as far removed from animals as we are (which is
a tempting response to the legacy of Durkheim and Mauss in scholarship).
This response would certainly have advantages; however, to follow Ingold,
such an attempt continues to distort hunter-gatherer ways of enskilling
themselves and engaging constituents of their dwelt-in world. It would be
like fighting anti-Semitism by arguing that Jews are good Christians or com-
bating sexism by arguing that women too can be men. To address the interpretive wrong done to hunter-gatherers by granting them reason is to lose
an opportunity to confront the potentially fruitful alternative ontologies we
encounter among many hunter-gatherers. It is this confrontation that Ingold, and I following him, are advocating. Both Ingold and I wish to reverse
the hermeneutical hierarchy and give priority instead to the hunter-gatherer ontology (over our Western academic ontology)—attempting, even if
it remains in an important sense impossible, not simply to view the world
from their perspective but to dwell in the world differently and apprehend
the unified field of relations that constitutes us by enskilling ourselves more

as hunter-gatherers do. This would be something akin to learning another language, and it would be anything but simple.

Like learning a language etymologically unrelated to one's own, it proves extraordinarily difficult to get outside the human/animal binary because, as we will see more clearly in the next chapter, the presence of this binary does not mark a "view" or even a "worldview," but the world within which we dwell. At stake in the circling around the human/animal binary that the present study is pursuing is not an idea or complex of thoughts but the genesis of thinking.

In *one* sense Durkheim, Mauss, and others who denied hunter-gatherers the full repertoire of reason were correct. According to Ingold's analysis, and given the extent to which "reason" is bound together with the human/animal, culture/nature, mind/world binaries, hunter-gatherer ontologies lack "reason." For example, reason, as imagined by Francis Bacon, is a uniquely human instrument of mind that, in dialogue with secure facts, allows us to stand outside the world as the perceiving subject and to dissect the world (literally and metaphorically) for the sake of knowing what it "really" is.[18] If such is reason, hunter-gatherers are fairly said to be without it (as are some of us in the West).

However, if reason is not defined in this restrictive fashion, could we, returning to J. Z. Smith's question in the previous chapter, speak of hunter-gatherers as offering us "alternative standards of rationality"?[19] Drawing on a range of Western scholars who have challenged dominant conceptions of mind, including Irving Hallowell, Gregory Bateson, Andy Clark, and David Bohm, Ingold invites us to think of mind as "immanent in the entire system of organism-environment relations within which all human beings are necessarily enmeshed."[20] The "world" of mind "reaches out into the environment along the multiple and ever-extending sensory pathways of the human organism's involvement in its surroundings."[21] Mind, then, is not set apart from the world, but rather each mind is "a node or nexus within a universe of relations and processes which, as they unfold in the world, are developmentally enfolded into its very constitution."[22] Such a conception of mind, Ingold offers, while "hard for modern western thinkers to grasp," would be "self-evident, for example, to the Greenlandic Inuit, for who *sila*, equivalent to what we would call mind, intelligence or consciousness, while manifest in each and every person, 'is an all-pervading, life-giving force connecting a person with the rhythms of the universe, and integrating the self with the natural world.'"[23] To lack *sila*, for the Greenlandic Inuit, would be, Ingold concludes "to take leave of reason itself."[24]

WHAT IS AN ANIMAL?

PARADOX

As noted earlier, Ingold gives us entry to hunter-gatherers' ontologies by emphasizing that the entire concept of culture upon which so much of the human sciences rests is a paradox. This becomes especially lucid, he suggests, when we consider the observation, intended to deconstruct the nature/culture binary, that "'nature' is a cultural construct." In his seminal essay, "Hunting and Gathering as Ways of Perceiving the Environment," he writes, "That nature is a cultural construction is an easy claim to make, and it is one that figures prominently in recent anthropological literature. It is not so easy, however, to ascertain what might be meant by it. One of my principal objectives in this chapter is to demonstrate that this claim is incoherent."[25]

The idea that nature-too-is-a-cultural-product is a sophisticated version of a commonsense understanding that we have already touched upon: there are different ways of perceiving the world, different ways (and here is where the problem begins) of viewing the *same* natural phenomena. In this view "nature" (culturally constructed) is one way of perceiving (real) nature. Nature becomes double.[26] That is, there are different, culturally inflected kinds of humanity possible on the basis of a single animal-biological-natural body. In this critique, which Ingold is critiquing, "nature" becomes but one peculiar category that Western cultures in particular use to conceptualize the (real) world "out there." Ingold cites Richard Shweder and Marshall D. Sahlins as scholars who exemplify this optic.[27] Perhaps the most well-known articulation of this view is Franz Boas's famous articulation of culture as reading glasses (*Kulturbrille*).

The paradox Ingold is concerned with emerges because just as the categories humanity and animality are part of a single thought that always ties one immediately to the other, so also does the category "nature" imply the category "culture." Thus to say that nature is culturally constructed is also to say that culture is culturally constructed—a blatant paradox. Ingold explains:

The paradox may be represented as follows:

```
                          ┌─ Culture
          ┌─ Culture  ─┤
          │             └─ Nature (culturally perceived)
          │
          └─ Nature (really natural)
```

If the concept of nature is given within the intentional world of the Western scientist, the concept of culture must—by the same token—be given within the intentional world of the Western humanist. Each, indeed, presupposes the other. Not only, then, must the concept of nature be regarded as a cultural construct, but so also must that of culture.[28]

Oddly, scholars appear more comfortable with the idea that nature is a cultural construction than the idea that culture is a cultural construction, but both lead to the same paradox. There is, of course, no way out of the paradox while speaking any of the dominant languages of scholarship—or speaking in "commonsense" terms for that matter.[29] As Ingold points out, any attempt to adopt a culturally neutral *view* would itself be culturally constituted, and so on, in infinite regress.[30]

Neither Ingold nor I wish to deny that there is scholarly recognition of this paradox. While contemporary anthropology is self-critical enough that Ingold himself noted (decades ago) that he is attacking "something of . . . a 'straw man,'"[31] it remains the case that this fundamentally paradoxical idea of culture nonetheless is frequently deployed by scholars. Lévi-Strauss, whose thinking we will more carefully consider in the next chapter, could justly respond to this critique of the idea of culture as a paradox by saying "I know that already." This book argues that such is not an adequate reply. The challenge to scholarship today is not in recognizing this problematic paradox but in recognizing *how problematic the paradox really is*.

Ingold readily acknowledges the challenge in taking seriously the views of hunter-gatherers, which, he argues, play "havoc with the established Western dichotomies between animals and society, or nature and humanity."[32] He further argues, however, that anthropology can do more than merely "contain the damage" as it has in the past. Ingold proposes a more adequate and far-reaching response. In "From Trust to Domination" he calls for a rewriting of "the history of human/animal relations" taking the hunter-gatherer ontology as our starting point. "We might speak of it," he imagines "as a history of human *concern* with animals, insofar as this notion conveys a caring, attentive regard, a 'being with.'"[33] I will not pursue this rewriting of "history" here, but I would rather attend to what opens this potential re-write (which would be not so much an alternative history as an alternative to thinking historically): taking seriously the hunter-gatherer ontology in which we find animals, but not "the animal."

We cannot entirely displace this paradox at the heart of cultural rela-tivism, but we can—and this is Ingold's bold call—"follow the lead of hunt-er-gatherers in taking the human condition[34] to be that of a being immersed from the start, like other creatures,[35] in an active, practical and perceptual engagement with constituents of the dwelt-in world."[36] Instead of the dichot-omy of nature/culture we can imagine the holism of nature-culture. We can work through hunter-gatherer "ontolog[ies] of dwelling" and allow them to work through us.[37] It is through this imaginative, existentially significant work that scholarship may offer us a way of rethinking animals, which is ultimately to rethink or reject the entire idea of subjectivity. It is through this work that agencies, human and nonhuman, might cease to appear in our view as subjects and yet still be apprehended as persons. Or, to put it another way, it is through this work that we may discover a (religious) subject that is no longer a (human) subject: the subject after the subject.

HUNTER-GATHERER ONTOLOGIES

To review, Ingold argues that the binaries Western thought (and the present study) has wrung its hands over are often glaringly absent in hunter-gath-erer communities. "Hunter-gatherers do not, as a rule, approach their en-vironment as an external world of nature that has to be 'grasped' conceptu-ally and appropriated symbolically within the terms of an imposed cultural design, as a precondition for effective action. They do not see themselves as mindful subjects having to contend with an alien world of physical objects; indeed, the separation of mind and nature has no place in their thought and practice. I should add that they are not peculiar in this regard."[38] More spe-cifically, we can say that in such communities the category of personhood is not limited to the human species. Like the contention that "nature is a cul-tural construction," the contention that for hunter-gatherers "animals are persons too" is an easy claim to make and a difficult one to make meaningful and constructively relevant to scholarship.

I will be concerned especially with Ingold's consideration of the Cree and the critique he gives of the use of metaphor, the "as if," in (scholarly) thinking. My primary concern here will be to give a close reading of Ingold's thought and bring it into dialogue with the study of religion. I will then consider an important limitation of Ingold's work in relation to what I will call, following Derrida, "the question of pathos and compassion," which will lead us toward the next chapter and a further consideration of Derrida.

The Waswanipi Cree of northeastern Canada report that if they are successful in hunting and killing an animal it is because the animal has given itself to them. Since animals are denied the subjectivity required for such "giving" in Western thought, it is difficult to understand this statement in other than metaphorical terms. (This difficulty is persistent even among scholars who take a particular critical interest in animals.) Surely, we say, this is a myth used to express some kind of "solidarity" with life (the idea we found to play such a key role in Eliade and Cassirer) or perhaps a myth that eases the difficulty of what appears to be a widespread discomfort with the killing of larger mammals, what James Serpell has helpfully theorized as "zoo-ocentric sympathy."[39] It is easy for scholars to acknowledge that the practices that might go along with the Cree's understanding contain robust ethological, biological knowledge, but the idea of actual relations with animals that might be substantially (rather than metaphorically) equivalent with human social relations is ruled out without question. Ingold cites Adrian Tanner as representative of this approach. Tanner remarks that "facts about particular animals are reinterpreted [by the Cree] *as if* they had social relationships between themselves, and between them and . . . the hunters."[40]

Can we understand this statement by the Cree in other than metaphorical terms like those suggested by Tanner? Can we understand the Cree's statements as other than "contrary to fact"?[41] I want to suggest that we can and that Ingold offers us a compelling alternative that could be acceptable to both scholars and perhaps to the Cree themselves (whose relative absence from this inquiry is a point of shame). Our ability to do so hinges on the question of whether we can expand, displace, or hold differently our notions of subjectivity and sociality. Ingold's statement of the problem is masterful and worth quoting at length:

> Western thought, as is well known, drives an absolute division between the contrary conditions of humanity and animality, a division that is aligned with a series of others such as those between subjects and objects, persons and things, morality and physicality, reason and instinct, and above all, society and nature.[42] Underwriting the Western view of the uniqueness of the human

species is the fundamental axiom that personhood as a state of being is not open to nonhuman animal kinds. It is for this reason that we are able to conflate both the moral condition and the biological taxon (*Homo sapiens*) under the single rubric of "humanity." And for this reason too, we can countenance an enquiry into the animal nature of human beings while rejecting out of hand the possibility of an enquiry into the humanity of nonhuman animals. Human existence is conceived to be conducted simultaneously on two levels, the social level of interpersonal, intersubjective relations and the natural ecological level of organism-environment interactions, whereas animal existence is wholly confined within the natural domain. Humans are both persons and organisms, animals are all organism. This is a view, however, that Cree and other northern hunters categorically reject. Personhood, for them, is open equally to human and nonhuman animal (and even nonanimal) kinds.[43]

What can this mean? Are we, to again return to Smith, encountering an alternative standard of rationality?[44] Can we understand the Cree's "expansion" of personhood in nonmetaphorical terms? Is the understanding of peoples like the Cree that hunted animals are persons "understood in terms of sentience, compassion, memory and vocalization (thought of as a way of being rather than of communicating information)" any more fraught than our own endlessly debated understandings of personhood?[45]

Rather than making the case that we should take the Cree view seriously by assuming that we already know that humans are subjects and arguing that other animals *also* can be subjects (a line of argument perhaps doomed to failure from the start), I would ask some hard questions about what we think we already know. Can we really, since Freud's famous three traumas to human self-conception—the Copernican, the Darwinian, and the Freudian[46]—take seriously the idea that humans are self-conscious agents in the manner implied when we speak blithely of "subjects"? More than a century ago Friedrich Nietzsche already quipped that man "has become an *animal* . . . he who was . . . almost God."[47] Even cognitive science of religion, a recent inheritor of the evolutionary paradigm begun with Darwin, won't flinch from following Nietzsche in insisting that "humans are animals," but the radical implications of this assertion are rarely grasped. This has brought us a bizarre situation where scholars of religion eager to claim the authority of the natural sciences deny human exceptionalism only to then go on as if important corollaries to this worldview, such as the exclusion of animals from religion, are perfectly reasonable. Exactly what are we assigning to ourselves when we assume human-human relations that are not merely unique (of course they are unique) but *uniquely unique* in the world of the sentient and therefore can be only metaphorically similar to human-animal relations?

At least since Durkheim scholars have turned a critical glance to commonsense ideas about human sociality. Scholars today begin with a critical awareness that, whatever humans are, we are not simply self-conscious subjects that make rational decisions about how to form our social relations. This is no longer in question. Our classic notions of social relations, which presume a concept of the human as a self-conscious agent, have become "metaphorical" even when applied to humans.

By what right then do we say that the Cree's talk of animals who enter into social relationships are merely metaphorical, while our talk about humans entering into quite parallel interactions are not? Do we have any scholarly grounds to assume that the Cree understanding of sociality that makes a mess of the human/animal border is any more metaphorical than our own insistence on the reality of this binary?

"The problem hinges," Ingold explains, "on the question of whether, when the Cree hunter refers to animals or to the wind as he would to human persons, he does so within the compass of . . . a 'culturally constructed world.'"[48] We can only place them within that compass, Ingold points out, by assuming from the beginning and before any empirical investigation a Western, dualistic ontology that already dismisses one of the most basic assumptions of Cree ontology: reality is not split into cultural and natural pieces. Is this dismissal plausible, descriptively helpful, or desirable at this historical moment? Or, instead, can we say with Ingold that "it is not 'anthropomorphic' . . . to compare the animal to the human, any more than it is 'naturalistic' to compare the human to the animal"? (50). Can we follow the Cree in accepting other animal species as persons who can participate in the dramas of life that we label religious?

None of this would require, of course, that the Cree—or that we—merely collapse the category of the human with other animal species. Our aim here, perhaps in contrast to Nietzsche's provocation, is not to rhetorically lower the human to the status of the animal. "On the contrary," Ingold explains, "[the Cree] are acutely concerned about such differences" (49), as scholarship ought to be. I am not proposing simply a blurring of the human/animal binary but, at very least, constraining it with a logic of difference (I could say,

with Derrida, a logic of *différance*): neither a logic of degree nor of binary difference, but of multiplicity. Ingold suggests we might understand the Cree
as understanding the difference "between (say) a goose and a man [a]s not
between an organism and person, but between one kind of organism-person
and another. . . . Personhood is not the manifest form of humanity; rather
the human is one of many outward forms of personhood" (50).

How can we positively, rather than metaphorically, understand the Cree's
attribution of agency to animals, their spreading of personhood over what
to us seems a peculiarly expanded range of phenomena? "What humans and
nonhumans have in common, for Cree as for other hunter-gatherers," Ingold
explains, "is that they are *alive*. Ostensibly, and barring certain geophys-
ical phenomena that Cree would regard as animate but that we might not,
this is a conclusion with which Western thinkers would not disagree. Yet in
Western biology . . . life tends to be understood as a passive process, as the
reaction of organisms" (50). Here Ingold is pointing to our commonsense
resistance (and not without good reason) to including ourselves among the
natural phenomena with which certain dominant scientific understandings
are concerned. Yet, as Ingold also points out, we do not wish to deny that we
and animals (and plants and so on) are alive; thus the question of the "living" becomes a location of a possible reimagination of the animal, a point,
Ingold is suggesting, of contact between our commonsense views of animals
and those of the Cree.

To say this of course merely pushes back the question "what is an animal?" to "what is life?" So what for the Cree is "life?" Ingold interprets:

> To be alive is to be situated within a field of relations which, as it unfolds, ac-
> tively and ceaselessly brings forms into being: humans as humans, geese as
> geese, and so on. Far from revealing forms that are already specified, life is
> the process of their ongoing generation. Every living being, then, emerges as
> a particular, positioned embodiment of this generative potential. Hence per-
> sonhood, far from being "added on" to the living organism, is implicated in the
> very condition of being alive: the Cree word for "persons," according to Scott,
> "can itself be glossed as 'he lives.'" Organisms are not just *like* persons, they *are*
> persons. Likewise, consciousness is not supplementary to organic life but is, so
> to speak, its advance front.   (51)

Significantly, Ingold's prose here goes beyond description. Deploying powerful, abstract imagery—"field of relations," "positioned embodiment," "ad-

vance front"—Ingold works to invoke in his readers an alternative to our usual conception of personhood. "This is to think of a world not of finished entities, each of which can be attributed to a novel conception, but of processes that are *continually carrying on*, and of forms as the more or less durable envelopes or crystallisations of these processes."[49] This invocation of another kind of personhood—a subjectivity after the death of the subject—does not disprove our own perhaps anthropocentric ideas about personhood, but can open other ways of thinking about religious actors—especially the "religious subject" that is the primary subject of religious studies.

Ingold argues that there is "a corollary of capital importance" to the ontological common ground the Cree understand to exist between humans and other animate beings as organisms-persons, namely, that "for both the world exists as a meaningful place, constituted in relation to the purposes and capabilities of action of the being in question."[50] In Western ontologies such claims are generally denied. Animals may have a point of view, but not of the same order as humans. Nevertheless, I do not believe that the hunter-gatherers' understanding of animal personhood, at least in its simplest features, is a difficult way of thinking for most of us to appreciate. Many, if not most people readily attribute points of views to the animals they know most intimately, in particular companion animals. And empirical studies have suggested (I think unsurprisingly) that these commonsense attributions of perspectives and emotions to animals may map the same regularities that "hard" scientific studies illustrate. For example, Françoise Wemelsfelder has demonstrated in an "empirical" study involving pigs that "whether observers were students, scientists, pig farmers, veterinarians or animal rights activists, we persistently found high levels of agreement . . . in how they judged the pigs. With their personal terminologies, observers created coherent and meaningful semantic frameworks that they could use to characterize the expression of individual pigs in precise and repeatable ways."[51]

I do not bring up our relations with companion animals lightly. The growth of pet keeping has had important ramifications in Western life more generally and constitutes a serious platform from which to engage "the question of the animal."[52] As we will see in the next chapter, Derrida deploys his own relationship (is it a social relationship?) with his cat in his reflections on animals.

All this is simply to say that I think it is quite possible (for some it might actually be more intuitive) for us to follow Ingold and remove the "as if" involved in our understanding of the Cree's attribution of personhood to animals. And, once we do this, a door has been opened to imagining social and religious dimensions of nonhuman animals. In fact, once animal personhood is granted, we may no longer be able to close this door. Ingold is helpful in enriching our sense of what this might mean:

> A creature can have a point of view because its action in the world is, at the same time, a process of *attending* to it. Different creatures have different points of view because, given their capabilities of action and perception, they attend to the world in different ways. . . . What is certain, however, is that humans figure in the perceptual world of geese just as geese figure in that of humans. . . . And human hunters, for their part, attend to the presence of geese *in the knowledge that geese are attending to them.*[53]

As we will consider again in the next chapter, this issue of mutual attending, of a two-way gaze, is decisive for our understanding of the Cree, of animals, and of religion.

There is no scholarly or popular resistance to the idea that humans interact with animals, manipulate their bodies, sacrifice them, consume them, worship them, and so on, in ways that we consider not only part of social life but also of religious life. Animal sacrifice has in fact been a paradigmatic exemplum in the study of religion. Yet if we reverse the point of view and consider animals' interactions with humans—as Ingold tells us the Cree do—most scholars would insist that the possibility of robustly social or religious activity is foreclosed without further investigation. If humans interact with animals, that interaction is understood, to employ Martin Buber's evocative language in *I and You*, an "I-it" rather than an "I-you" relation. The very idea of mutual religious experience with an animal is absurd, according to the dominant understanding. And, as we would expect, Buber's description of his own I-you encounter with a cat was greeted suspiciously—so much so that it prompted him to defend this possibility in the 1957 afterword to *I and You*.[54] To speak of mutual social interactions—and mutual religious interactions—between humans and animals will continue to appear absurd so long as animal personhood is understood as metaphorical in a way that human personhood is not. One question hunter-gatherers present to us is whether this understanding of personhood, and by extension sociality and religiosity, as exclusively human is sufficient. I would argue that the encounter with hunter-gatherer ontology reveals this still dominant understanding to be paradoxical, narrow, and unhelpful.

Is it really so implausible to think of the Cree's (or our) relations with animals within an alternative, but still recognizable, understanding of personhood and sociality, thereby opening the door to the possibility that some aspects of these social relations are best described as religious—as much for animals as for humans? "Animals," Ingold writes, continuing his exposition of the Cree, "do not participate with humans qua persons only in a domain of virtual reality. . . . They participate as real-world creatures,[55] endowed with powers of feeling and autonomous action, whose characteristic behaviors, temperaments and sensibilities one gets to know in the very course of one's everyday practical dealings with them."[56] Could we perhaps take the knot Durkheim imagined in which the human, society, religion, and thought itself are constituted and constituting and imagine the actors who participate in it as not exclusively members of the human species? This is the direction in which Ingold presses us.[57] Continuing the earlier quote from Ingold:

> In this regard, dealing with nonhuman animals is not fundamentally different from dealing with fellow humans. Indeed the following definition of sociality, originally proposed by Alfred Schutz, could—with the insertions of indicated brackets—apply with equal force to the encounter between human hunters and their prey: "Sociality is constituted by communicative acts in which the I [the hunter] turns to the others [animals], apprehending them as persons who turn to him, and both know this fact." Humans may of course be unique in their capacity to *narrate* such encounters, but no one can construct a narrative . . . who is not already situated in the world and thus already caught up in a nexus of relations with both human and nonhuman constituents of the environment. The relations that Cree have with the latter are what we, outside observers, call hunting.[58]

This perhaps gives us a way to answer the question of how we might best imagine the phenomenon of hunting among peoples like the Cree: it is not *like* but rather *is* an interspecies social phenomenon and, depending on the purposes of the person asking the question, it could easily be understood as a religious phenomenon dealing with ultimate issues of life and death, violence and compassion.

A final point that Ingold brings to our attention is helpful in making this imagination plausible. Ingold turns a critical eye toward the fact that the dominant narratives of the West envision (and practice) hunting as an act of domination and that this consequently tends to be the way in which all hunting is viewed. Such a view, of course, is foreign to many hunter-gatherers, and thus perceiving the human-animal relationship as one of domination—or its opposite, protective benevolence—limits our ability to sympathetically consider hunter-gatherers' ontologies. For hunter-gatherers "animals are not regarded as strange, alien beings from another world but as participants in the same world to which the people also belong. They are not, moreover, conceived to be bent on escape, brought down only by the hunter's superior cunning, speed or force."[59] This leads to a conclusion that in our usual way of understanding hunting sounds quite strange: hunting becomes nonviolent.

> [Hunter-gatherers] are well-known for their abhorrence of violence in the con-
> text of human relations, and the same goes for their relations with animals: the
> encounter, at the moment of the kill, is—to them—essentially *non*violent. And
> so, too, hunting is not a failed enterprise, as it is so often depicted in the West
> . . . [if it ends in] pursuit that is not ultimately crowned by capture. It is rather a
> highly successful attempt to draw the animals in the hunters' environment into
> the familiar ambit of social being, and to establish a working basis for mutuality
> and coexistence.[60]

Hunting animals is founded on a relationship of trust with them. The successful hunt may or may not result in a kill, but a successful hunt is an experience of what Ingold calls, in a striking turn to religious vocabulary, a "revelation." Citing the Ojibwa as exemplary of many hunter-gatherers, he argues: "You get to know other human persons by sharing with them. . . . And if you are a hunter, you get to know animals by hunting . . . the hunter does not transform the world, rather the world opens itself up to him. Like words, the hunter's tools are caught up in chains of personal (not mechanical) causation, serving to reveal the otherwise hidden intentions of nonhuman agents. . . . In short, the hunter does not seek, and fail to achieve, control over animals; he seeks revelation."[61] Ingold's point is not that this is the only or best way to interpret these activities, but that it is closer to the apprehension of hunter-gatherers and no less plausible than the dominant view that would set human-human sharing in the category of personal relations and hunting in the category of manipulation or domination.

It is worth lingering over how and why, at this crucial moment in his interpretation, Ingold turns to *revelation,* a word that so directly evokes a biblical and Abrahamic heritage. His use of revelation is related to an analogy he draws between words in human relations and the weapons of hunting in human/animal relations. This poetic gesture sets human relations with nonhuman animals, I think helpfully, in the same category as human relationships with the divine. Both can be described through a language of revelation. And both involve a kind of "faith" or, to use Ingold's preferred word, "trust": "Trust presupposes an active, prior engagement with the agencies and entities of the environment on which we depend; it is an inherent quality of our relationships towards them. And my contention is that in this strict sense, trust rather than confidence characterizes the attitudes of hunters and gatherers towards their nonhuman environment, just as it characterizes their attitude towards one another."[62]

Without saying it in so many words, Ingold has asked us to take the concept we normally reserve for understanding a paradigmatic religious relation—revelation of the divine to the human—and apply it to human/animal relations—revelation of animals to humans. The holy word has as its counterpart the holy tool of hunting, both word and tool functioning to mediate a revelatory relation with nonhuman agencies. By suggesting that the relationship between human and nonhuman agents (usually animals) is in these cultures marked by a play of mutual revelation and concealment set in the context of personal bonds of trust, Ingold does more than help us understand particular peoples; he points us toward a way of thinking a religious actor that is no longer strictly a human (or divine) subject. In the usual sense of the word, there is no subject at all. The thought of persons as subjects is abandoned; persons are agencies, and they come in human and nonhuman forms. Here agents are those who see and are seen in a play of revelation that creates the world we live in and makes us what we are today. Such reimagination or deconstruciton of the (religious) subject, I am arguing, is salutary for the study of religion. It provides a more adequate poetic, so to speak, for the historian of religions as he follows the contours of the religious landscape, pursuing the strange to make it familiar (and vice versa) and using the theoretical tools of our discipline to capture the phenomenon of religion in the words of scholarly texts. Thus I agree with Ingold's suggestion that we should take these hunter-gatherer ontologies seriously, and I see a particular advantage to doing so in the study of religion.

A further point, however, must be made to fully appreciate why this shift is desirable: such a reimagination, I would argue, is at once more descriptively rigorous and more compassionate. These two qualities cannot be separated in this case. The move from confidence in our inherited dualistic ontologies toward an opening to hunter-gatherer ontologies of dwelling—a move that is most disruptive in its implications for what we call animals—is not just a change in scholarly method, but something of an existential leap. Ingold argues that doing so is not simply good for anthropology but moreover "provides us with a better way of coming to grips with the nature of human existence."[63] However atypical it may be to speak of a normative value like "compassion" to justify a theoretical shift in the scientific study of religion, it is unavoidable in the present case. Whether we choose to consider it or not, both resistance to and interest in considering the relevance to religious studies of animals and the parts of humans considered animal (for example, data from neurology, primatology, and ethology—to list the fields in an order from those that generate the least to the most resistance from scholars of religion) are manifestly bound to and complicated by ethical questions that loom in the background.

QUESTIONS OF PATHOS

Only by appealing to something I will call, following Derrida, "the question of pathos and . . . compassion" can we fully appreciate the importance of giving—or refusing to give—priority to an ontology that does not restrict personhood exclusively to human beings and its important corollary: some animals too can be loci of religious action and meaning (can be religious "subjects" in the sense of not being mere objects or unwitting participants, but agents within the phenomena of religion).[64] The study of religion has always and will always find its ground and authority by "taking sides" on issues of pathos and compassion that precede us. I am not proposing a new insertion of these normative values into scholarship, but rather a revaluation of the values that are already embedded in our scholarly work in and outside the study of religion. Ingold vividly recalls how the reality of this taking sides marred his experience as a student at Cambridge in the 1960s. He was driven to the study of anthropology, and presumably to many of the insights discussed in this chapter, after completing his first year in the natural sciences, only to have the realization dawn "that the scientific establishment was so heavily institutionalized, internally specialized, and oppressively hierarchical that the most one could achieve as a professional scientist would be to become a very small cog in a huge juggernaut of an enterprise—one moreover that seemed to have lost touch both with its sense of social responsibility and . . . to have become largely subservient to the military-industrial complex." Ingold thus understands his oeuvre as, among other things, a response to "an intellectual, political, and economic climate that has always tended to divorce human affairs from their bearing in the continuum of organic life."[65]

The study of religion has in recent years, at least in principle, accepted that the normative valuations of male/female, Christian/Jew, white/black, civilized/savage and so forth have distorted our scholarly vision. If we accept this, then we should also recognize that the valuation of human/animal and nature/culture, which is implied in all of these other binary oppositions, has similarly infected our theory and that both descriptive and normative issues are at stake in "the question of the animal and religion," just as they are at stake in relation to questions of sex and gender (especially sexual orientation), race, and so on. I would suggest that the persistence of camouflaged orientalist, sexist, heterosexist, racist, ableist and colonialist conceptions is unavoidable so long as the human/animal binary and the associated questions of pathos and compassion are not brought into critical awareness.

In sum, critical thinking—and critical thinking about religion above all—is not only an inquiry through logos but also pathos. In speaking of religion especially, we cannot avoid what Derrida calls "the immense question of pathos and the pathological, precisely, that is, of suffering, pity, and compassion" and the place of pride "that has to be accorded to the interpretation of this compassion, to the sharing of this suffering among the living."[66] The general existential question of who counts as a *who* rather than a *what*, like the more specific question of the kinds of subjectivities—or, perhaps better, the kinds of agencies—that scholars will consider appropriate candidates for participation in the phenomenon of religion, is underdetermined by data. This notion of underdetermination shares much with Smith's (now unshocking) quip that "*there is no data for religion*. Religion is solely the creation of the scholar's study." I am simply emphasizing one implication of Smith's insight: there is no pristine study of religion free of normative decisions. Particularly unavoidable is the normative investment inherent in deciding what or who a "subject" is and, indeed, in choosing to speak of "subjects" rather than from the start declining to bifurcate reality into subjects and objects in the classical manner. The foundational and unavoidable scholarly question of what beings are eligible to count as religious agents—however it is imagined—is always already bound with the question of pathos and compassion.

Ingold's efforts to help us understand hunter-gatherer ontologies can help us to see more vividly just how bizarre our own exclusion of animals from the spheres of personhood and religion can appear. While the scholarly study of religion has been eager to level critiques against other pretensions to speak objectively when in fact speaking from a particular historical-temporal-cultural vantage, except in marginal new subfields scholars of religion continue to ignore the manner in which our apprehensions of animals are often more Western than they are East Asian or South Asian, more modern than medieval,[67] more Protestant than Catholic or Eastern Orthodox, more Christian than rabbinic, and more associated with male than female. At the very least, we could say, our typical stances are more "civilizational" and less of the hunter-gatherer variety. Because of these biases, modern Christian understandings of animals' (lack of or impoverished participation in) subjectivity—which is to say modern Christian understandings of the subject as such—are taken as natural and become invisible.

It can therefore appear to scholars and religious practitioners themselves as if there is little significance to the material relationships religionists have with animals in, for example, contemporary Protestant Christianity; the highly particular views of these religionists (e.g., Protestant Christians), such as the denial of personhood to animals, can easily appear to scholars as factual rather than a community-specific value that needs explication. Moreover, the bias that implies animals are irrelevant to religion is not evenly applied to all religions: it is typical for scholars to acknowledge that the material relationships that *hunter-gatherers* have with animals shape their understandings of personhood and religion, but suggesting that there is similar religious significance to actual human relations with animals in Western cultures appears odd. Taking animals seriously as persons is flagged as a "religious" conception, and scholarship frets over explaining it (recall the red parrot discussed in chapter 3), but the act of denying animal personhood is "normal."

I am circling back to a point I have already made. Simply put, there is a leap of faith (perhaps of a Western, Protestant, Christian, biblical, Abrahamic, or modern kind) in the apparent secularity and objectivity of taking religion as a human—and only human—phenomenon. Moreover, while the leap of faith that sculpts our vision such that only humans can appear to be religious subjects is a problem, this is not simply because it involves a "leap" and normative judgment. Since no scholarship can escape a certain leap into the normative in relation to questions of ontology, the problem cannot be "the leap," but *this* leap—that is, the particular leap we have taken. We will always have to make normative leaps, and in this limited but important sense the nontheological study of religion is always as theological as theology proper. The question is only which theology, which normative leap, and when and where do we make the leap?

As philosopher Ralph Acampora has recently framed it in relation to the question of animal ethics, philosophers have tended to begin with the assumption of "a certain (and special) kind of separation" between humans and animals and therefore "the interspecies ethical theorist must bridge the gulf to and from other creatures."[68] Acampora argues "that this way of framing the issue has the experienced phenomena and the ethical problem entirely backward. . . . Where we begin . . . is always already caught up in the experience of being a live body thoroughly involved in a plethora of ecological and social interrelationships with other living bodies and people."[69] That is, Acampora attempts to transfer "the burden of proof from what has been denigrated as ethical 'extensionism' [extending moral regard from humans to animals] to, instead, what we should rightly refer to as ethical isolationism or contraction."[70] I am arguing for something similar in the realm of religion rather than ethics. The dissociation of animals from the sphere of the religious perhaps needs as much or more justification than including them in the phenomena of religion. As Acampora has it, "It is the movement toward dissociation and nonaffiliation that needs to be justified against a background of relatedness and interconnectivity. Put another way, it is relinquishment of disavowal of our aboriginally constituted bodily being with others, or our 'somatic sociability' if you will, that would require defense. . . . Leave it to the anthropocentrists to justify, if they can, why we ought to renounce, give up, or let go of that primordial experience."[71]

Do we leap into a science of religion that is,[72] first of all, about subjects and objects and preoccupied with human subjectivities in particular, or do we imagine a science of religion "whose overriding concern is to *follow what is going on*, within dynamic fields of relationships wherein the forms of beings and things are generated and held in place"?[73] This study is proposing a leap along the lines of the latter, a leap that, at a minimum, shifts our understanding of personhood not simply within the academy but specifically in the study of religion and at a historical moment when the denial or obfuscation of animal personhood is implicated in a violence against them that would appear, to quote Derrida, "monstrous" to most human communities in most times.[74] I refer here to the ubiquity of industrial animal farming, which, as we saw in chapter 2 and will see in the next chapter, casts its shadow not only on the exemplum of AgriProcessors in a direct way but also upon the entire question of the animal and religion.[75]

The stakes could not be higher. It is not only that the material conditions of scholars shape what we often imagine as pristine intellectual constructions, but that the constructs we deploy shape our material conditions. I do not think we can seriously doubt that if we granted animals the status of being potential participants in the phenomenon of religion it would raise some ethical and pragmatic-political questions. For example, it might trouble the complacency with which Americans accept that 99 percent of the farmed animals slaughtered in this country are slaughtered with no legal limits on the amount of suffering that can be inflicted upon them.[76] These questions would not be simple or reducible to a political concern for animal rights or vegetarianism. At the same time, the questions raised by the motley movements we point to when we invoke animal rights and vegetarianism would not be entirely external. Such concerns would, in fact, "lead us to the center of the subject," as Derrida put it.[77]

My point here is that whether we choose to *rethink* the religious subject—what Ingold calls a "complementarity" approach, insofar as it tries to synthesize different disciplinary approaches into a more satisfactory vision of the subject—or whether we choose to *challenge* the very division upon which the idea of subjectivity is based—what Ingold calls an "obviation" approach, insofar is it obviates the need to synthesize by not hewing the world in two in the first place—we make a decision that involves our capacity for empathy as much as our intellectual rigor.[78] Will we, following the Cree and Ingold, choose to apprehend religion so that it allows the (perhaps accusing) look of animals to reach us, or will we exclude animals from being able to look at us at all? Both choices are prior to any "data" that could arbitrate the matter. While unapproachable through strictly rational tools, this decision is capable of being weighed and considered with empathetic, or ethico-empathetic, ones (with "pathos and . . . compassion"). The faculties and intuitions involved in ethical decision making—in questions of pathos and compassion—are the same ones we must exercise in critically clarifying the question of the animal and religion. All these faculties are needed to ask if the study of religion should be the study of human religious subjectivities or of religious agencies that are not exclusively human.

Whom do we grant the ability to confront us in that most important mode we call religious? Who do we allow to confront us at all? Who counts as a "who"? Is the animal—in the study of religion or elsewhere—to be questioned under the mantle of "who" or "what"? These issues are the knottiest points in "the question of the animal and religion" and it is to the ethically charged inquiry that they raise that I now turn and to which we must perhaps endlessly turn and return.

5

Disavowal, War, Sacrifice

JACQUES DERRIDA AND THE
REIMAGINATION OF RELIGION

Derrida, in a similar direction to Ingold, challenges a cluster of ideas related as much to our actual relations with other species as our ideas about animality and humanity. He not only helps us attend to animals differently but also to the knot in which the animal is bound to other core concepts. Rather than leading us from animals to subjects of "greater importance" to which animals are connected (for example, looking at animals for the sake of understanding humanity), Derrida shows how we need to reconsider our own subjectivity to responsibly consider animals and how we must confront our own being-confronted-by animals—by individual animals in our lived-in world—to reconsider our own subjectivity.

Like Ingold, Derrida's critical engagement with the question of the animal both challenges our ideas about who might count as a subject and invites us to think beyond binary oppositions like human/animal, culture/nature, and subject/object. "For some time now I have been emphasizing the fragility and porosity of this limit between nature and culture," Derrida tells the audience of one of his seminars.[1] "The only rule that for the moment I believe we should give ourselves in this seminar," he continues, "is no more to rely on commonly accredited oppositional limits between what is called nature and culture . . . God, man, and animal or concerning what is 'proper to man.'"[2] Derrida, however, far more than Ingold, exposes the way that such binary oppositions insinuate themselves in our thinking even at the moments when we consciously try to move beyond them.

Whereas Ingold has called upon us to cease moving in a world imaginatively divided into subjects and objects—to *stop* what Agamben called the anthropological machine—Derrida is more focused on *exposing* and thus *troubling* the operations of this machine. Ingold's proposal is infused with optimism about our ability to cultivate alternatives to our present modes of apprehension. Derrida's deconstruction is warier. Ingold and his remarkable engagements with hunter-gatherer peoples offer us a vision of the proverbial mountaintop. Derrida equips us to endlessly climb the mountain.

To be specific, Derrida argues that the dominant Western relationship with animals in modernity has taken the form of a "disavowal" (*dénégation*), a "war" (*guerre*), and a "sacrifice." Each of these three words signals particular interpretive strategies, and following them provides entry into Derrida's reflections on animals at the point where his writings are particularly productive in the task of considering the question of the animal and religion.[3] To anticipate, we could say that *disavowal* brings to bear an existential and loosely psychoanalytic hermeneutic; *war* brings a pragmatic-political hermeneutic; and *sacrifice*, recasting structuralist themes, locates the human/animal relationship in the context of the Abrahamic traditions.

Extending and particularizing Derrida's critique, I argue that by limiting the religious subject to a human subject the study of religion has become implicated in both the "disavowal" of regard for animals and the "war" against them of which Derrida speaks. Rather than study the "sacrifice" of animals, religious studies participates in it. Both Derrida's and Ingold's critical insights converge in unsettling a simple exclusion of animals from the sphere of the social, the cultural, or—our present focus—the religious. Ingold, by imploring us to take seriously the hunter-gatherer ontologies he explicates, and Derrida, through his deconstructive analysis of "the animal" and his reflection on an encounter with a specific animal (an encounter that echoes, in some ways, the human-animal relation Ingold finds among hunter-gatherers),[4] both give us reason to think that the study of religion would do well to revise its self-understanding as the study of certain dimensions of human life. More specifically, following Ingold's and Derrida's critiques, we have good reason to, at very least, revise our understanding of the religious subject, making both nonhuman and human animals *eligible* for participation in the general phenomenon of religion. Or, going further, we have good reason to press beyond the idea of a religious subject entirely and begin to think about religion more along the lines of a dimension of depth within a field of relations involving various kinds of agencies.

PHILOSOPHY AND COMMON SENSE

The metaphor of the knot, which I have used throughout this book, is also frequently employed by Derrida. Derrida insists that to trouble the human/ animal binary is to challenge a knotty point where commonsense understandings are wound together with those of philosophy. Philosophy, Derrida argues, agrees with common sense that certain questions about animals need not be seriously entertained. As Derrida argues in a text that will be central for this chapter, *The Animal That Therefore I Am*,[5] "Philosophical right . . . presents itself as that of 'common sense.' This agreement concerning philosophical sense and common sense that allows one to speak blithely of the Animal in the general singular is perhaps one of the greatest and most symptomatic *asinanities* [*bêtises*] of those who call themselves humans."[6] As we will see, this agreement is also and in a particularly pointed way a barrier to critical reflection on religion. The word *animal* makes us forget that there is no such thing as "the animal" (only animals). To speak of "the animal" elides difference and particularity, making ideas about animality and associated concepts such as humanity appear more secure than they are. As Derrida asserts, "animal" is a "stupid word," a word that *makes* us stupid, forgetful.[7]

Faced with this alliance of philosophical and common sense, Derrida's strategy for theorizing animals will be to step away from the productive abstraction of metareflection and invite his readers to follow him down a rabbit hole of sorts,[8] toward an encounter with an animal, his cat. He begins *The Animal That Therefore I Am* by telling of this encounter through a story, an almost prosaic story of finding himself confronted (confronted "naked" Derrida tells us) by his cat as he prepares to enter the shower.[9] "[The cat] follows me when I wake up, into the bathroom, asking for her breakfast" and then, regretting her decision, "demands to leave that said bathroom as soon as it (or she) sees me naked . . . naked under the gaze of what they call 'animal.'"[10] Even if the experience is common, something disquieting and embarrassing has happened. I think it is easy for most readers to relate viscerally to Derrida when he goes on to confess "I have trouble repressing a reflex of shame. . . . Especially, I should make clear, if the cat observes me frontally naked, face to face."[11]

The cat that looks at Derrida "does not appear here to represent, like an ambassador, the immense symbolic responsibility with which our culture has always charged the feline race."[12] Faced with the cat looking at him, "Something happens there that should not take place—like everything that happens in the end, a lapsus, a fall, a failing; a fault, a symptom (and 'symptom,' as you know, also means 'fall': case, unfortunate event, coincidence, what falls due [*échéance*], mishap)."[13] Something happens that cannot be denied—something that Derrida did not choose, but rather fell or was thrown into. Derrida's embarrassment is a symptom of this falling—a response to the vertigo of shifting boundaries. Animals are supposed to see us, account for us in their way, but they are not to *look* upon us. When they do it "is as if, at that instant, I had said or were going to say the forbidden, something that should not be said."[14]

Derrida emphasizes that the conflict between those who would follow him in admitting being seen by an animal (acknowledge the "shame" and sense of the "forbidden") and those who would not follow him is sufficiently meaningful to become the basis for dividing Western thought into two groups of texts and signatories. Furthermore, he sees a conflict between these two groups—a conflict marked by an imbalance of power. "In the first place there are texts signed by people who have no doubt seen, observed, analyzed, reflected on the animal," Derrida proposes, "but who have never been *seen seen* by the animal.[15] Their gaze has never intersected with that of an animal directed at them. . . . That category of discourse, texts, and signatories . . . is by far the one that occurs most abundantly."[16] The question of which relation to animals is most abundant is important because of the constant insinuation of certain dominant conceptions in language and common sense. The denial of animals' gazes, Derrida writes, "is probably what brings together *all* philosophers and all theoreticians *as such.*"[17] This insinuation means that quite often even supposedly critical discourses are uncritical when it comes to the question of the animal and ethical responsibility to animals. This forgetfulness helps establish what Derrida calls "the agreement concerning philosophical sense and common sense."[18]

As will become clearer throughout this chapter, for Derrida, the rules of the dominant discourse have been fixed in such a manner that to avow compassion, to avow animals, one must *almost* by necessity have left behind the dominant language of philosophy, theory, law, and nation. These discourses are all but inextricably bound to disavowal. As soon as one attempts to avow the animal within them, the words of avowal will be greeted as a foreign discourse that Derrida has invited us to name "poetry" and "prophecy," which is to say these discourses will have no legal or national power and thus little ability to protect either animals or the human sentiment of compassion.

Aware of this trap, Derrida attempts to do more than simply side with the poets and prophets (which he certainly does do); he also, by laying bare the mechanics of this disavowal in his deconstruction, invites us to occupy a third space that would be outside the dialectic in which the voice of compassion can only be heard as poetry and prophecy and thus would always remain at the margins of the authority enjoyed by philosophical, theoretical, legal, and national discourses. He sides with the poets, but—and this is where he is most original—he further attempts to push the question of the animal into a space that is not simply poetry or philosophy (neither, for example, the discourse of Rilke or Heidegger)—a space in which "the animal" might fade, allowing something like "animals" to properly appear to us and us to them. As Matthew Calarco, a pioneer of animal studies, has argued, "If there are any properly philosophical stakes in the field of animal studies, I would argue that they lie precisely here, in the clearing of the space for the *event* of what we call animals."[19]

THE UNTHOUGHT

Derrida, in his encounter with the gaze of his cat, seeks a moment prior to this split in which the very meaning of poetry-prophecy and philosophy-theory-law (and thus the meaning of compassion, responsibility, ethics, and justice) might be grasped differently. It is from this space that one might, for example, imagine a law that would avow animals or a philosophy that would somehow remain philosophy while overcoming the disavowal of the animal that "brings together *all* philosophers and all theoreticians *as such*."[20] For Derrida, the *differánce* between avowing and disavowing, philosophy and poetry, animality and humanity opens up the possibility of truly originary thought—the "unthought" or thought-held-in-suspension—that makes all thinking possible.[21] If there is no encounter with the unthought and unrecognizable, there is no true thinking and no possibility of ethics:

The "unrecognizable" [méconnaissable], I shall say in a somewhat elliptical way, is the beginning of ethics, of the Law, and not of the human. So long as there is recognizability and fellow, ethics is dormant. It is sleeping a dogmatic slumber. So long as it remains human, among men, ethics remains dogmatic, narcissistic, and not yet thinking. Not even thinking the human that it talks so much about.

The "unrecognizable" is the awakening. It is what awakens, the very experience of being awake.[22]

This is why, beyond the more salient ethico-pragmatic concerns with disavowing animals' gazes, Derrida attributes such significance to the difference between those "who have never been *seen seen*" and those "who admit to taking upon themselves the address": the movement between one and the other traverses a space that encompasses and gathers diverse questions, even the very meaning of questioning. It encompasses, on the one hand, the question of thinking and, on the other hand, the question of compassion, responsibility, ethics, and justice. Derrida imagines those who have been "seen seen" and who deny animals' gazes as locked in "an unequal struggle, a war" that, on the one hand, is waged over a "sentiment of compassion . . . an irrefutable testimony to . . . pity" (and here he takes sides with compassion), but that also, on the other hand, "concerns what we call 'thinking'" (and here Derrida attempts to reimagine or rethink thinking itself).[23] "The animal looks at us, and we are naked before it. Thinking perhaps begins here."[24] The gift of thinking and the possibility of compassion, responsibility, ethics, and justice comes to us not from an encounter with the superhuman or human other—*not* from "the fellow," from the dogmatisms of "human rights," "social justice," or, for that matter, from "environmental protection" or "sustainability" or even "animal welfare" and "animal rights"—but from the reception of an animal's gaze.[25]

DISAVOWAL

I always place denial at the heart of all these discourses on the animal.

–JACQUES DERRIDA

It is a question of avowal and disavowal that creates the rupture between those who are "seen seen" and those who are not. We are all seen by animals. Individual animals with their own biographies and sufferings and desires, do, for Derrida, look at us. This is a basic datum, a naked fact, a fact shared among the sentient: we look at each other. We are naked, vulnerable, exposed, suffering, and we can communicate this to each other. "[T]he possibility of sharing the possibility of . . . nonpower," the possibility of compassion, precedes us, even as its completion recedes forever as we approach it, remaining "the possibility of [an] impossibility."[26]

VULNERABILITY AND ORIGINARY COMPASSION

For Derrida, we who call ourselves human (whether in a philosophical sense or common sense) are bound together within "the anguish of this vulnerability, and the vulnerability of this anguish."[27] We are divided in whether we avow this shared fate of the sentient or disavow it. As Derrida will argue, "we," our individuality and ethics, are constituted in a givenness, an irrefutable pity that is either (or in alternation) avowed and disavowed in infinite variations. "That's why I always place denial at the heart of all these discourses on the animal."[28]

At a certain level, the entire point of Derrida's elaborate discussion of being seen by an animal is not to convey something new but to prompt us to confession, to an acknowledgment of animal gazes as something we have already encountered. To do so, as we have seen, is to open a space for genuine thought and also to open one's heart. "I would like to choose words," Derrida says on the first page of *The Animal That Therefore I Am*, "that are, to begin with, naked, quite simply, words from the heart."[29]

Most of the time we scholars proceed as if we (individually or as an academy) had indeed investigated all animals, had each kind come before us like they did before Adam—"still without woman"—in Genesis.[30] We proceed as if we had determined that the violence—even violence "in the most morally neutral sense of the term"[31]—of our relations with them are just. Ultimately Derrida's suggestion is that the full force of the dominant Western intellectual and moral inheritances (philosophical and common) have asked us to forget "animals" in the generality of "the animal." The refusal to admit being "seen seen" denies animals our compassion in that it relieves us from obligations to respond when their gaze becomes a plea, but it also disavows the compassion and (critical) thinking that could call this disavowal into question. The generality of "the animal," insinuated in language, works silently to disavow impulses of pity and the often spontaneous tendency to place human and nonhuman animals in the same or proximate categories (for example, as Sigmund Freud observes in children).[32] As classics scholar and literary critic Mark Payne has it, instead of disavowing this pathos, "this moment of unwilled empathetic understanding," Derrida suggests that this moment "must become the active exercise of the imagination."[33] In sum, the disavowal of the animal gaze is a burdensome constraint on critical thinking and ultimately a disavowal of an originary compassion.

REMEMBERING ANIMALS

For Derrida both animal suffering and the possibility of compassion in the human response to it are undeniable: "No one can deny the suffering, fear, or panic, the terror or fright that can seize certain animals and that we humans can witness. (Descartes himself . . . was not able to claim that animals were insensitive to suffering)."[34] It is not simply that the suffering of animals is "obvious" (which it surely is) or that humans are "obviously" capable of compassion. The recognition of a suffering other is a particularly searing kind of perception fundamentally different but no less real than sense perception. The suffering animal other, we might say, is more revelation than fact. When we face a suffering animal, we have not simply acquired a bit of information; rather, we have been seized by a foreign being, a fellow subject or agent. And, as Levinas says of the human, the "subjectivity of [this] subject is vulnerability."[35] "The response to the question 'Can they suffer?' leaves no room for doubt," Derrida concludes, "In fact, it has never left any room for doubt; that is why the experience that we have of it is not even indubitable; it precedes the indubitable, it is older than it."[36] Compassion precedes us. The very nature of our being depends upon a compassion (of mothers, parents, society, and the larger sentient world) into which we are not so much thrown as born and reborn, always already pulsating in a dynamic field of relations.

Significantly, what Derrida and I call compassion can also be explored in dialogue with certain relatively new scholarship in the life sciences. Here compassion can appear as a higher-order function based on the "building blocks" of basic capacities for empathy shared by social mammals (and surely other animals).[37] Frans de Waal and Sarah Hrdy are leading figures among a larger group of scientists who argue out of an evolutionary paradigm that basic capacities (what I have called building blocks) that are essential to the working of more complex behavioral patterns, including ethics, are present in animals that are closely related to humans genetically and likely emerge out of the unique bonds between parents and offspring, particularly the mother-child bond. Based on studies in both human children and nonhuman primates, de Waal persuasively argues that empathy and sympathy are already robust in nonhuman apes and almost certainly other social mammals.[38] Hrdy, too, argues that the special development of parental care in mammals allowed empathy to grow in extraordinary ways.[39] We can think of these scientists as subversively admitting to having been "seen seen" by animals.

To be clear, the life sciences do not have the resources to exhaustively explain what we are calling compassion, nor do they necessarily hew any closer to the "real," than, say, literary explorations of compassion. They are, however, extraordinary valuable discourses. Consider de Waal's discussion of a 1992 Italian study that showed that when a monkey reaches for an object a certain configuration of brain cells fire and that the same cells fire when it only *sees* someone reach for an object.[40] What makes the "mirror neurons" that may explain these neural patterns so special, de Waal explains, "is the lack of distinction between 'monkey see' and 'monkey do.' They erase the line between self and other."[41] The upshot of this and other studies is that when we "guess" at another human or nonhuman animal's mental state, we do more than simply deduce the other's mental state. Rather, de Waal explains, "seeing someone in pain activates pain circuits to the point that we clench our jaws, close our eyes, even yell 'Aw!' if we see a child scrape its knee. Our behavior fits the other's situation, *because it has become ours*."[42] We are not, for de Waal, anthropomorphizing in a problematic way when we imagine we know something of the mental state of other animals, especially other mammals. What J. M. Coetzee, through his character Elizabeth Costello, has called the "sympathetic imagination," a faculty that allows humans to think their "way into the existence of a bat or a chimpanzee or an oyster, any being with whom [we] share the substrate of life," may be, more or less, a biological fact in addition to an ethical one.[43] Per Derrida, this awareness of other animals is undeniable. When Derrida argues that our awareness of the pain of others, whether human or nonhuman, "has never left any room for doubt,"[44] he is speaking in a manner proximate to a poet or prophet and emphasizing precisely that we do not *require* any studies to know something of the reality of compassion. What studies such as those of de Waal and Hrdy offer us, however, is a possible path toward speaking such truths—tentatively and incompletely—within the discourses of contemporary life science, that is, within dominant discourses that overall seek to suppress such speech.

The self as we know it arises both responding to a shared vulnerability that propels it toward consciousness and held in a compassion that makes life possible. We are born into our own vulnerability among vulnerable others, and a basic restraint—the seed of what we are here calling compassion—must be present for the world to continue. "No doubt either, then, of there being within us the possibility of giving vent to a surge of compassion. . . . (yes, they suffer, like us who suffer for them and with them) . . . that precedes all other questions."[45] The realization that "yes, they suffer" cannot be doubted because it is prior to the subject who asks questions—it is in a sense the origin of questioning. Prior to the question "why is there something and not nothing," prior to the certainty of "I think therefore I am," Derrida encounters suffering, vulnerability, and compassion.

The undeniability of compassion is what makes our relations with animals a *disavowal* rather than a denial and what opens the possibility of a kind of ethically-charged remembering. We cannot *simply* deny compassion any more than we can deny that we think. And when one cannot acknowledge the undeniable, one can only endlessly endeavor to forget it. Such a disavowal cannot by definition be acknowledged publicly; such a secret cannot "even appear to one alone except in starting to be lost, to divulge itself, hence to dissimulate itself, as secret, in showing itself: dissimulating its dissimulation."[46] This dissimulating of dissimulation—this revelation *via negativa*—is the very movement of what Derrida calls deconstruction, and its manifestation is compassion.

Derrida does not *argue* for the inclusion of animals in the sphere of moral concern, but rather appeals to the irrefutability of their suffering and our compassion. He does so quite simply by pointing to the "terrifying and intolerable" conditions to which we subject them, first and foremost in contemporary animal agriculture, which for Derrida is marked by an "industrial, mechanical, chemical, hormonal, and genetic violence" against animals.[47] He makes this appeal, however, in the abstract, for Derrida's understanding is that we know more than we admit to ourselves. This leads Derrida to eschew a detailed description of the violence in favor of a plea to remember, "I do not wish to abuse the ease with which one can overload with pathos the self-evidences I am drawing attention to here. Everybody knows what terrifying and intolerable pictures a realist painting could give to the . . . violence to which man has been submitting animal life for the past two centuries. Everybody knows what the production, breeding, transport, and slaughter of these animals has become."[48] Practically no one is exempted from the guilt of participating in this disavowal, but neither is anyone barred from the possibility of remembering.

Derrida chooses to end his first chapter of *The Animal That Therefore I Am* with a barrage of open-ended questions instead of a conventional conclusion. "The animal in general, what is it? What does that mean? Who is it? To what does that 'it' correspond? To whom? Who responds to whom? Who responds in and to the common, general and singular name of what they thus blithely call the 'animal?' Who is it that responds?"[49] This barrage of questions turn circularly on themselves, questioning themselves. If Derrida is successful, we his readers find ourselves not so much asking the questions as letting the questions work through us. Derrida's questions pile into and upon one another with a prayerlike urgency. The questions and the responsibility they recall summon us, perhaps exposing the wound of a disavowed pity. They invoke a "surplus of responsibility that summons the deconstructive gesture or that the deconstructive gesture . . . calls forth."[50] To engage the questions of the animal and religion, I do not see how we can avoid confronting this disavowal, a confrontation that inexorably draws us into—or, rather, reveals to us our involvement in—a larger conflict, a war.

WAR

[A] war [is] being waged between, on the one hand, those who violate not only animal life but even and also this sentiment of compassion, and, on the other hand, those who appeal for an irrefutable testimony to this pity.

—JACQUES DERRIDA

If Derrida's questions succeed and the gazes of animals are acknowledged, then the undeniable violence of our relations with animals flashes before us. As the disavowal is exposed, Derrida argues, these relations are revealed to be a war between those who avow and disavow animals—a war in which those who disavow animals have the upper hand but "whose inequality could one day be reversed."[51]

A NEW AND OLD WAR

It would be a mistake to take Derrida's use of the word *war* as strictly metaphorical. Like the conventional use of the term *war*, it signals an immense mobilization of resources, social (local, regional, national, global) planning, an intensified use of technologies, destruction of environments, and mass killing. And just as war has become intensified in modernity—sword to gun, bomb to nuclear bomb—so has the war against animals.

At one level, Derrida wants to mark something new that has emerged in contemporary human-animal relations, an intensification of violence that amounts to war; at another level, however, the language of war is used to emphasize a continuity with what is most ancient. In suggesting that the war against animals may be ancient in origin, Derrida follows Hobbes. As cited by Derrida, Hobbes explains that "one may at discretion reduce to one's service any animals that can be tamed or made useful, and wage continual war against the rest," a right of man that Hobbes locates not with a divinely ordained right but "natural right."[52]

For Derrida, while it is useful to consider the war against animals as "modern" in order to make ourselves heard (stemming from the last two hundred years, he suggests),[53] in saying so we implicate ourselves in a structure of thought in which the animal is already disavowed. That is, because the very idea of modernity—modernity as the epoch in which reason begins to prevail, the epoch in which humans rise out of an animality in which premoderns were allegedly trapped—tends to shore up the idea of the animal that Derrida is trying to deconstruct. As is the case with his use of the term *animal,* Derrida speaks of this modern period only "in order to recall, for convenience to begin with and without laying claim to being exact, certain preexisting indices that *allow us to be heard and understood* and to say 'us' here today."[54]

UNPRECEDENTED SCALE

In the West today 98 percent of our interactions with land animals are the animals we eat,[55] and it is the war against these animals that appears most visible and imposing when disavowal gives way to the acknowledgment of inconvenient truths. It is in this domain too that the intensification of the war against animals is most evident. "Limiting ourselves to the most imposing of these indices we can refer to those that go well beyond the animal sacrifices of the Bible or of ancient Greece . . . beyond the hunting, fishing, domestication, training, or traditional exploitation of animal energy. . . . It is all too evident that in the course of the last two centuries these traditional forms of treatment of the animal have been turned upside down."[56] While insisting on a basic comparability of the classical animal sacrifice of ancient Greece and Israel with modern animal slaughter, Derrida attempts to mark a change of decisive significance: a change that takes us "well beyond" these earlier forms.[57] Derrida describes modern industrial animal agriculture (in which I would include industrial fishing, cattle feedlots, and factory farming) in terms Michel Foucault applied strictly to the human sphere. Industrial animal agriculture, for Derrida, is a product of intensive regimentalization and the deployment of new forms of knowledge:

> This has occurred by means of farming and regimentalization at a demographic level unknown in the past, by means of genetic experimentation, the industrialization of what can be called the production for consumption of animal meat, artificial insemination on a massive scale, more and more audacious manipulations of the genome, the reduction of the animal not only to production and overactive reproduction (hormones, genetic crossbreeding, cloning, and so on) of meat for consumption but also of all sorts of other end products.[58]

Derrida himself does not undertake the task of describing what this regimentalization looks likes in actual application, even emphasizing he will not explore these details because all this, he asserts, "is all too well known; we have no need to dwell on it."[59] Derrida is well aware that common knowledge of modern agricultural methods is quite limited—his discussion of disavowal makes this clear—so in what sense is this regimentalization "well known"? It is "well known" only in the sense of being well-documented: the details are readily available to anyone who cares to know.

Filling in some of the well-documented but rarely publicly discussed details to which Derrida only alludes will help give a fuller picture of the decidedly nonmetaphorical aspects of this war and of why Derrida wants to mark the last two hundred years as a period of intensification. Consider contemporary industrial fishing, where a number of scientists have, uncharacteristically, also taken to using the language of war. For example, research scientists at the Fisheries Centre of the University of British Columbia argue that "our interactions with fisheries resources have come to resemble . . . wars of extermination."[60] Since World War II, wartime technologies have been systematically applied to commercial fishing,[61] increasing the weight of sea animals brought to market globally 350 percent from 1948 to 1970.[62] Radar now allows fishers to move with more precision through fog and the dark of night. Echosounders once used to locate enemy submarines now allow fishers to identify schools of fish underwater. Navy-developed electronic navigations systems and, in the last decade of the twentieth century, satellite-based global positioning systems give fishers unprecedented abilities to identify and return to fish hot spots. Satellite-generated images of ocean temperatures are used to identify fish schools. The combined force of these changes is so significant that some studies suggest that all sea animals presently fished will experience population collapse by 2048.[63] These changes in fishing technology have occurred in tandem with many others in every area of animal agriculture. I will, like Derrida, leave further details to other texts, but it is important to keep this context constantly in mind to appreciate the force of Derrida's writings on animals. Like the events at AgriProcessors to which we will return in the final chapter, Derrida's work on animals occurs in the "long shadow" of the factory farm.[64]

It is details like the ones that I have just reviewed regarding contemporary fishing that provoke Derrida to assert in response to this new factory fishing and farming that "however one interprets it, whatever practical, technical, scientific, juridical, ethical, or political consequences one draws from it, no one can deny this event any more, no one can deny the unprecedented proportions of this subjection of the animal."[65] This "subjection" is both a subjugation and subduing, on the one hand, and, on the other, a process of subject formation: we humans are the subjectivity that subjects. According to a certain reading of Genesis—a text with which Derrida is in constant dialogue concerning the question of the animal and to which this study will return in chapter 6—to become human is to become master, the one who wields dominion.

"Neither," Derrida proposes, "can one seriously deny the disavowal that this involves. No one can deny seriously, or for very long, that men do all they can in order to dissimulate this cruelty or to hide it from themselves, in order to organize on a global scale the forgetting or misunderstanding of this violence that some would compare to the worst cases of genocide (there are also animal genocides)."[66] The invocation of genocide, attributed to animals only in the safety of parentheses and spoken in the name of an anonymous "some," gives us a fuller picture of the kind of war Derrida imagines having emerged between humans and animals in modernity.[67] It also leaves no room for neutrality or inaction.

TAKING SIDES

Derrida does not level violence to humans and animals. His point in speaking of genocide is rather to highlight a *structurally* similar engagement with humans we exterminate and animals we endlessly breed for slaughter. As I will discuss, Derrida argues that there is a similar structure—a "sacrificial structure"[68]—linking both forms of violence. There are also more obvious similarities: the scale, the coordination, the application of technology, the writhing bodies, the willing perpetrators, the disavowals.

Derrida recognizes the danger of comparing the systematic animal abuse of industrial farming to genocide, but he equally fears the danger of assuming these two forms of violence are unrelated. "One should neither abuse the figure of genocide nor consider it explained away," he writes. The real if also complex and upsetting interlacing of these forms of violence demands acknowledgment. Derrida continues, "For it gets more complicated here: the annihilation of certain species is indeed in process, but it is occurring through the organization and exploitation of an artificial, infernal, virtually interminable survival, in conditions that previous generations would have judged monstrous, outside of every supposed norm of a life proper to animals that are thus exterminated by means of their continued existence or even their overpopulation."[69]

The "monstrous" signals a taboo border crossing, something new and, in this case, something disturbing. Again, some "empirical" details are helpful. The "monstrous, outside of every supposed norm" might, for example, call to mind the condition of virtually all modern turkeys, who through the use of intensive ("hybrid") breeding techniques have been made incapable of sexual reproduction (the male is no longer physically capable of mounting the female). Females must be artificially inseminated en masse in an astonishingly violent process[70] that has sometimes led the turkey industry to pursue exemptions from state antibestiality laws. Or we might think of today's "hybrid" methods of breeding chickens—used to produce more than 99 percent of chickens raised in the U.S.—which require the maintenance of specialized breeding flocks who carry a genetic mutation that, while conferring certain economic advantages, leaves birds *incapable of experiencing satiety*. This is the industry's own conclusion, not an outside description by activists or critics.[71] What kind of evil is involved in creating billions of animals incapable of copulation or experiencing even the modest comfort of a full stomach?

Derrida's reference to "animal genocides" suggests that such forms of violence are structurally similar to genocidal violence, despite the fact that the living beings that are violated are nonhuman. In both cases the goal is annihilation, but in the case of animals, this "annihilation . . . occur[s] through

... virtually interminable survival."[72] He continues, "As if, for example [*par exemple*], instead of throwing people into ovens or gas chambers (let's say [*par exemple*] Nazi) doctors and geneticists had decided to organize the overproduction and overgeneration of Jews, gypsies, and homosexuals by means of artificial insemination, so that, being more numerous and better fed, they could be destined in always increasing numbers for the same hell, that of the imposition of genetic experimentation or extermination by gas or by fire. In the same abattoirs."[73] Derrida thus calls our relations with animals war to point to the similarities this war has with the more familiar use of *war* in reference to human conflicts, but he also deploys this language of war and genocide to incite us to respond. By calling our relations with animals a war, Derrida calls upon us to take sides.

Building upon Derrida, I argue that this war pervades the entire academy and is waged as much in the study of religion as it is individual religious traditions themselves, such as the Abrahamic traditions, which Derrida engages. The war Derrida invokes against animals is not conducted by rogue ranchers without social consent. The academy has been profoundly involved in the execution of this war, something abundantly documented in any history of modern farming. As animal husbandry departments were abandoned in favor of animal science departments in the 1960s, the institution of the academy, especially the life sciences, were leveraged in crucial ways to produce the "event" of the factory farm. Large faculties worked and continue to work specifically on advancing kinds of agriculture in which the idea that animals are machines is the disavowed premise.

Departments of human sciences may not execute the war on the front lines as do departments of animal science, but Derrida's idea of a disavowed war is an apt description of the role that the human sciences have played here. Even as the university—marshaling its resources from every possible direction—has radically altered the human relationship with other animals by ushering in the event of factory farming, the human sciences, like the life sciences, except for a few growing but still marginalized protests, have failed to critically consider these transformations and the attendant violence. The human sciences—the institutions given a certain authority to decide matters of *history* and *knowledge* and therefore to guide the development of *technology* (an important trio for Derrida)—have watched this war unfold with little critical consideration of animals, and, in the case of the study of religion, I would link this with the field's failure to critically consider the theoretical significance of "the animal" for its own self-conception. As writer Jonathan Safran Foer articulates it in his book *Eating Animals*, "There is a war not only between us and them [animals], but between us and us. It is a war as old as story and more unbalanced than at any point in history." [74] This failure to develop an "animal turn," a hermeneutics to gain critical purchase on animal agribusiness among other institutions, does not constitute neutrality but complicity. This is what makes me say, following Derrida, that the study of religion has participated in the war against animals and why attending to this participation is an urgent mater.

SACRIFICE

At the heart of all these discourses *sacrifice* beats like a vital impulse.

—JACQUES DERRIDA

Derrida argues for the existence of a "sacrificial structure" that can equally apply to the practices of industrial farming or the discourse of the modern academy. Two thoughts, fundamentally different in their logic, are stitched together here. First, Derrida is arguing ahistorically for persistent associations and alliances in which the human/animal binary is knotted up with other binaries. For example, male/female is "structurally" linked with ruler/ruled and human/animal. These associations and alliances do not so much occur within historical time as at the "genesis of time [*la genèse même du temps*]"[75]—at the very moment of the institution of "what is proper to man [*le proper de l'homme*],"[76] at the moment the subject becomes subject. Second, Derrida is suggesting that these structural links have contributed to a *historical* form of violence: so-called factory farming.

In describing our relationship with animals, especially animals that are eaten, as governed by a "sacrificial structure," Derrida is also making a fundamentally ethical point: our relations with animals unfold within a "space" where violence to the point of putting to death is not merely a fact of life, but socially authorized.[77] Paradoxically, this violent space is opened as the result of a gesture of restraint. What Derrida calls a "sacrificial structure" does not, at least in theory, authorize violence to animals as such. Rather it authorizes (or even celebrates) this violence in the name of protecting the human: protecting human livelihood (jobs, "the economy" and so on); satisfying human desires (craving for meat, the sport of the hunt, and so on); extending human life (animal research, for example); and an almost limitless array of human "rights" or mere preferences. Ultimately, as we will see, Derrida argues that both the structure of religiosity—that is, *Abrahamic* religiosity (for when Derrida speaks of religion he is speaking of the Abrahamic)—and the structure of the subject are such that they open this "sacrificial" space in which the supreme value of the human leads to the sanctioning of violence to animals. Religion and the subject—and in particular the religious subject thought as human—are sacrificial structures for Derrida. He argues that both Abrahamic religion and the structure of subjectivity, in transforming the animal *homo sapiens* into "the human," *require* the violability of the animal—in theory, all animals. This is why the very conception of subjectivity may need to be displaced if we are to imagine a religious subjectivity open to nonhuman animals.

THE SACRIFICE OF SACRIFICE

For Derrida, even the most innovative thinkers of the subject, including Martin Heidegger and Levinas, fail to escape this sacrificial structure. In his critique of Heidegger, Derrida suggests that we "venture . . . a few questions" to illumine this sacrificial quality: "For example, does the animal hear the call that originates responsibility? Does it question?"[78] Can we be "seen seen" by animals; can an animal's gaze confront us and demand our concern? Derrida argues that both Heidegger and Levinas would answer "no."[79] This brings us to a further question Derrida poses: "Do we have a responsibility toward the living in general? The answer is still 'no,' and this may be because the question is formed,[80] asked in such a way, that the answer must necessarily be 'no' according to the whole canonized or hegemonic discourse of Western metaphysics *or religions*, including the most original forms."[81] Neither Heidegger nor Levinas created this "sacrificial structure" (they simply inherit it), but they do, for Derrida, fail to "sacrifice sacrifice." That is, Heidegger and Levinas fail to turn the sacrificial gesture on itself in a manner that might weaken its hold and shrink the space it carves out for authorized violence.

Derrida's task, in the face of an urgent call "that summons the deconstructive gesture or that the deconstructive gesture of which I am speaking calls forth,"[82] is precisely to push toward the sacrifice of this sacrificial gesture. His wager is that "a certain kind of question"—a new kind of questioning that has avowed the undeniability of a compassion that reaches beyond the human fold—may yet be possible. If possible, this would amount to nothing less than the beginning or renewal of questioning itself: a question that is not secretly already an answer—a break with sacrifice. This questioning of the question is bound with the sacrificing of sacrifice and is, to put it simply, Derrida's way of imagining a critical discourse on animals.

Significantly, Derrida explains that he does not draw attention to this sacrificial structure that ultimately disavows responsibility to animals and to the living "to start a support group for vegetarianism, ecologism, or for the societies for the protection of animals," thus both calling attention to the close proximity of his arguments with these political movements and demarcating his gesture as distinct from the perspectives of such advocates. This proximity is emphasized even further when Derrida adds that such tasks are "something I might also want to do, and something which would lead us to the center of the subject."[83] "Activism" too would lead us to both the center of our "subject" in the sense of the "topic" of the animal and the center of the "subject" in the sense of the subjectivity that subjects the animal. Derrida seems to suggest that "taking sides" on the pragmatic questions raised by critical attention to animals itself can produce a kind of insight parallel to deconstruction.

Whatever its merits and proximity, this activist path is not Derrida's. Rather, Derrida wants to do something more basic: identify the mechanism, structure, or gesture of sacrifice. He finds this sacrificial structure not only in Heidegger and Levinas but also in "Descartes, Kant . . . and Lacan, as a single living body at bottom, indeed, as single *corpus delic-iti*,[84] the mobile system of a single discursive organization with several tentacles."[85] Ultimately this sacrificial structure is "a matter of discerning a place left open, in the very structure of these discourses (which are also 'cultures') for noncriminal putting to death."[86] This place functions as a machine, a mechanism by which other beings—in a sense *any* other being—can be subjected to the most extreme violence without the perpetrator becoming guilty. "Sacrifice" here comes to name a procedure, milieu, and ultimately a mode of being in the world—a mode of being a subject—that both necessitates a "nonviolence" synonymous with the inviolability of the human and, in the name of this restraint, justifies violence of potentially unlimited scale, making war against the nonhuman possible and perhaps inevitable.

SACRIFICE AS ABRAHAMIC

This space in which violence becomes permitted is opened by energy built up through a dialectical or point-counterpoint movement between nonviolence and violence, between the inviolable and eminently violable. It is the infinite inviolability of the human—the "absolute imperative, holy law, law of salvation: saving the intact, the unscathed, the safe and sound (*heilig*) that has the right to absolute respect, restraint, modesty"—that casts a shadow, creating a dark place where violence is considered justified or, even more, necessary. This procedure, Derrida further hypothesizes, is a "universal structure of religiosity."[87] Various articulations, justifications, accommodations, and proliferations of violence and inviolability follow this pattern. "The poles, themes, causes are not the same (the law, sacredness, holiness, the good to come, and so on), but the movements appear quite analogous in the way they relate to them, *suspending* themselves, and *in truth interrupting themselves*. All of them involve or mark a restraint <*halte*>."[88] This restraint is interrupted, even constituted, by a space of nonrestraint, where one can do what one pleases.

In exploring the manner in which Abrahamic traditions are knotted up with sacrifice, Derrida in no way means to deny the presence of complementary and contrary institutions. Rather Derrida finds a constant struggle between respect for life and sacrifice of it (an unequal struggle):

> On the one hand, the absolute respect of life the "Thou shalt not kill" (at least the neighbor, if not the living in general, the "fundamentalist" prohibition of abortion, of artificial insemination, of performative intervention in the genetic potential, even to the ends of gene therapy, etc.); and on the other . . . the no less universal sacrificial vocation. It was not so long ago that this still involved, here and there, human sacrifice. . . . It always involves sacrifice of the living, more than ever in large-scale breeding and slaughtering, in the fishing or hunting industries, in animal experimentation.[89]

Here Derrida provides us with what almost amounts to a method for exposing sacrificial structures: attending to these oscillations between nonviolence and justified violence, their mutual interruptions.

In his discussion of Levinas, Derrida explains that in the very moment Levinas establishes the origin of the subject (which for Levinas is the responsible subject—the subject held hostage by the demand of the other that initiates our being: "Thou shalt not kill") animals and all nonhuman life are sacrificed. "The other, the neighbor, the friend . . . is no doubt in the infinite distance of transcendence. But the 'Thou shalt not kill' is addressed to the other and presupposes him. It is destined to the very thing that it institutes, the other as man."[90] The restraint of "Thou shalt not kill"—the prohibition of murder of the human—does not, Derrida argues, come to apply to the already extant creature we know as "man." Rather, "man" flashes forth with this prohibition: the subject as we know it arrives together with human vulnerability and a demand not to violate the human, and this inviolability arrives together with the "sacrificability" of the animal.

The inviolability of man might be extended—say to woman or even to certain animals such as the dog—but the very concepts of "human" and "animal" are forged in a sacrificial fire. "It is by him [the other man] that the subject is first of all held hostage. The 'Thou shalt not kill'—with all its consequences, which are limitless—has never been understood within the Judeo-Christian tradition, nor apparently by Levinas,[91] as a 'Thou shalt not put to death the living in general.' It has become meaningful in religious cultures for which carnivorous sacrifice is essential, as being-flesh."[92]

Eating flesh, then, or at least the right to eat flesh—the legitimacy of sacrificing not merely vegetable or mineral (as Cain did and God rejected) but flesh (as Abel did and pleased God)—is not one feature among others that might be removed while leaving the basic concept of the human subject as expounded in the Abrahamic traditions intact. For Derrida, it is no accident that the first act of Noah after the flood is the sacrifice of animals and that the Noahide covenant is a complex blend of inclusion and exclusion of animals within the fold of covenant: animal sacrifice is the act that founds the world we live in and, in a sense, founds the subjects we continue to be. From Genesis to Levinas, Derrida argues, the space of human inviolability, the genesis of time, and the subjects we are originate in and with animal sacrifice.

SACRIFICE AND THE CARNOPHALLOGOCENTRIC SUBJECT

Following this line of thought, Derrida exposes a sacrificial structure that operates in the everyday workings of Western society and links together a wide range of discourses and activities. Derrida invites us to consider "the virile strength of the adult male, the father, the husband, or brother. . . . [These] belong to the schema that dominates the concept of the subject. The subject does not want just to master and possess nature actively. In our cultures, he accepts sacrifice and eats flesh."[93] Here Derrida distinguishes himself in a decisive manner from the more simplistic observation that "the subject" is articulated as one who dominates. This is true, he would agree, but too generalized an observation; stopping there might even function to mask more than it reveals. The domination that "dominates the concept of the subject," Derrida argues, is not merely that of the active, free master; the subject must consume flesh, usually literally, but at least symbolically. Since truly defending such a thesis is the work of a lifetime, Derrida illustrates this point in part by asking his readers to imagine a vegetarian head of state:

> Since we have not much time or space here, and at the risk of provoking some loud protests, . . . I would ask you: in our [Western] countries, who would stand any chance of become a *chef d'Etat* (a head of state), and thereby acceding "to the head," by publicly, and therefore exemplarily, declaring him- or herself to be a vegetarian? The *chef* must be an eater of flesh. . . . To say nothing of celibacy, of homosexuality, and even of femininity. . . .
>
> In answering these questions, you will have not only a schema of the *dominant*, of the common denominator of the dominant, which is still today of the order of the political, the State, right, or morality, you will have the dominant schema of subjectivity itself. It's the same.[94]

When Derrida asks us to imagine a vegetarian *chef d'Etat* and we cannot, he helps alert us to the significance of the act of sacrifice as practiced today in the act of meat eating. He insists, and this seems decisive to me, that with such questions we do not simply probe a "schema of the dominant" but "the dominant schema of subjectivity itself."

Ultimately Derrida explains his intention to expand his well-known argument that the schema of the subject has a "phallogocentric" (*phal* for phallus, *logo* for logos) structure by demonstrating that "this *schema* implies carnivorous virility. I would want to explain *carnophallogocentrism*."[95] This carnophallogocentric structure, Derrida emphasizes, not only has dictated the shape of the idealized subject as represented in Jewish and Christian discourses or in contemporary national politics but also has silently shaped discourses like Heidegger's that have sought to avoid an assumption of this subject,

> Heidegger's obstinate critique of vitalism and of the philosophies of life, but also of any consideration of life in the structure of *Dasein*, is not unrelated to what I

am calling here a "sacrificial structure." This "sacrificial structure" . . . defines
the invisible contour of all these reflections, whatever the distance taken with
regard to ontology in Lévinas's thinking . . . or in Heidegger's with regard to the
onto-theological metaphysics. Going much too quickly here, I would still try to
link the question of the "who" to the question of "sacrifice."

It would be a matter not only of recalling the concept of the subject as phallogocentric structure, at least according to its dominant *schema*: one day I hope
to demonstrate that this *schema* implies carnivorous virility. I would want to
explain *carno-phallogocentrism*.[96]

Thus Derrida concludes "that in spite of many denegations [disavowals],
Heidegger was a Judeo-Christian thinker."[97] Heidegger, like "Kant . . . Lévinas, and Lacan—let's say, the signatory subjects who carry or are borne by
those names,"[98] all follow Descartes in theorizing our being and ethics within
a sacrificial space. In Derrida's estimation,

At the heart of all these discourses *sacrifice* beats like a vital impulse. They
represent four varieties of thinking sacrificial experience, four varieties of
thinking that would not gather together around themselves in such a systematic and consequential way were it not for their reaffirmation of the necessity
of sacrifice. Not necessarily of sacrifice as ritual sacrifice of the animal—even
though, to my knowledge, none of them has ever denounced the same—but of
sacrifice as fundamental, indeed, of a founding sacrifice . . . exercising power
over the animal to the point of being able to put it to death when necessary is
not forbidden.[99]

Derrida suggests there is something symptomatic in the fact that Western
philosophical discourses have never condemned animal sacrifice. Animal sacrifice in the restricted sense of ritual sacrifice (for example, biblical sacrifice)
is never condemned in these discourses because, despite appearances, to do so
would be to condemn something fundamental about the Abrahamic subject.

The sacrificial structure of subjectivity, Derrida further argues, may be
paradigmatically related to the sacrifice of animals, but it hardly "stays put,"
affecting "only" nonhuman animal species. Rather, sacrifice overflows—has
always already overflowed—into the human sphere. Theodor Adorno, Derrida, points out,

takes things much further: for an idealist system, he says, animals virtually
play the same role as Jews did for a fascist system. Animals would be the Jews of

the idealists, who would thus be nothing but virtual fascists. And such fascism begins whenever one insults an animal, even the animal in man. . . .

How far can one take this reference to Judaism, to idealist hatred of the animal as hatred of the Jew, which one could easily extend, according to the now-familiar outlines of the same logic, to a certain hatred of femininity, even childhood . . . from hunt to bullfight, from mythologies to abattoirs, except for rare exceptions it is the male that goes after the animal, just as it was Adam whom God charged with establishing this dominion over the beasts.[100]

Some of the kinds of links between hatred of Jews and hatred of animals that Adorno and Derrida gesture at here have been more carefully traced by Andrew Benjamin in his book *Of Jews and Animals.*

Benjamin links together what he theorizes as the "figure" of animal and Jew—and other "others" in a wide range of European sources starting with Hegel.[101] He defines the figuration to which both Jew and animal are subjected "as the constitution of an identity in which the construction has a specific function that is predominantly external to the concerns of identity itself,"[102] for example functioning to render particular beings the legitimate target of violence. Benjamin further argues that Jews and animals are linked together in being marked by what he calls the *"without relation"*—a disavowal of relationship. In sum, Benjamin traces the usually unseen threads connecting the processes of othering animals and Jews.

Here we catch a glimpse of what Lévi-Strauss called an "invisible thread" that unites multiple registers of meaning; Jew/gentile and animal/human— not to mention female/male, child/adult, and so on—are strung together. The invisible thread that constitutes the structure of the subject, which is also perhaps the structure of (Abrahamic) religiosity, has been soaked in the blood of sacrifice.

Derrida's move from a critique of logocentrism to phallogocentrism and ultimately to carnophallogocentrism is merely the tracing of this thread. The centrality of the male in relation to the female and the logos in relation to pathos is organically connected with the centrality of the human in relation to the animal. "The deconstruction of 'logocentrism' had, for necessary reasons, to be developed over the years as deconstruction of 'phallogocentrism,' then of 'carnophallogocentrism,' its very first substitution of the concept of the trace or mark or those of speech, sign, or signifier was destined in advance, and quite deliberately, to cross the frontiers of anthropocentrism, the limits of a language confined to human words and discourse."[103]

EATING ANIMALS AS SACRIFICE

The sacrificial gesture that Derrida and I have in mind, as should now be clear, is not limited to what has been classically called sacrifice—for example, sacrifice as it has often been theorized in the study of religion. The sacrificial structure does appear in classical exempla of sacrifice (ancient Israelite or Grecian, for example), but, for Derrida, it is still part of our everyday world. A sacrificial structure, marked by warlike violence, governs our relationships with numerous others. Crucially for our present purposes, the sacrificial gesture regulates in particular what we call consumption or eating.

> Such are the executions of ingestion, incorporation, or introjection of the corpse. An operation as real as it is symbolic when the corpse is "animal" (and who can be made to believe that our cultures are carnivorous because animal proteins are irreplaceable?), a symbolic operation when the corpse is "human." But the "symbolic" is very difficult, truly impossible to delimit in this case, hence the enormity of the task, its essential excessiveness, a certain unclassifiability or the monstrosity of that *for which* we have to answer here, or *before* which (whom? what?) we have to answer.[104]

The actual practice of eating animals—sacrificing them to our needs and wants—is here imagined as a material manifestation or location in which a politics and ethics of "eating"—both real and symbolic—is constructed. The question of eating animals is a question about the meaning of eating and "eating well" (*bien manger*)—both good eating and eating the good. The practice of eating animals (or not) is practice for eating—a paradigm of what consumption should look like. And the question of eating well will always "come back to determining the best, most respectful, most grateful, and also most giving way of relating to the other and of relating the other to the self."[105]

Eating is about more than eating: "For everything that happens on the edge of the orifices . . . the metonymy of 'eating well' would always be the rule."[106] And eating animals is more than eating animals: it is arguably the most literal form of sacrifice today. Eating animals is, in any case, a charged location through which, drawing on the tools given to us by Ingold and Derrida, we can learn a great deal about Western culture in general and the various specific forms it takes.

This brings us back to the incidents at AgriProcessors, which we are now in a position to interpret as religious events—events that emanate from and work through the deeper, recessed folds of living that shape our subjectivity and bind us in community. As we will see, the incidents at AgriProcessors are not "religious" simply because they occurred at a plant that calls itself kosher or in a community that calls itself Jewish—which is not fundamentally different than what may be occurring in a plant that calls itself USDA certified and in a community that calls itself American.[107] They are religious because the charge of the incidents comes from the way in which they exposed and put into play long-standing structures—what in the history of religions we consider under the name of *myth*—that define what it means to be a subject, a human, ethical, and a part of the Jewish community.

6

Sacrificing Animals and Being a Mensch

DOMINION, REVERENCE, AND THE
MEANING OF MODERN MEAT

THE HUMANE SUBJECT

The crisis situation represented by the AgriProcessors animal abuse scandals made manifest an often invisible structure of meaning implicit within the consumption of kosher meat. This structure, which I will call the *humane subject*, makes meaning by way of implied anthropologies and taxonomies embedded in the act of eating (or refusing to eat) animals. The humane subject ritually welds together words about animals and interactions with them to produce and reproduce both explicit ideologies and unconscious ways of being.

The differing responses to the animal abuse at AgriProcessors reveal different usually implicit imaginations of human beings and their relationship with other living beings that all accord with the various structures of this humane subject—or, to suggest these structures' Jewish accent, the *menschlich* subject, the mensch.[1] Both the lives of animals and a lived compassion are at stake in the production of these different subjectivities. In the responsibility we share for the living beings within our power and our actual responsiveness to their suffering when it confronts us, as it did in the case of AgriProcessors, ethics itself emerges.[2] The dimension of depth in the controversy at AgriProcessors is a clash between different embodied conceptions of animality, humanity, and divinity that ultimately represent different modes

of subjectivity and ethics. What unites the disparate responses to AgriProcessors—from those who urged vegetarianism to those who defended the
dismemberment of conscious cattle—is the shared structure of the humane
subject. What divides the responses to AgriProcessors is the variations on
this theme, the different accents and emphases, underlinings and erasures
that constitute different kinds of humane subjects.

The anthropologies and taxonomies that the humane subject embeds in
eating animals are not simply projected symbolically onto the neutral acts
of raising, killing, and consuming animals, as if these acts were a tabula rasa
upon which any story could be written. Animals who are eaten as kosher
méat are given symbolic meanings, but they are never simply symbolic. They
are also always individuals whose lives and deaths have inherent meaning.
Does, for example, the actual act of mechanically immobilizing, inverting,
standing over, looking down upon, cutting, killing, and butchering an animal (or paying someone to do the same) constitute a symbol of the important
biblical theme of human dominion over creation, or do such actions actually
constitute dominion? This study suggests they do both.

The AgriProcessors events are significant on both an economic and symbolic plane, and it is not always possible to tell one plane of meaning from the
other. On one level the act of obtaining and eating food is a basic ecological
and economic activity that has significance as a brute material act. On another level the act of eating animals according to kosher law amplifies, modi-
fies, supplements, or otherwise manipulates the significance of these actions
so that they do not simply impact the world directly but propel individuals
and communities into the world with particular sensitivities, dispositions,
and ethics. While articulated explicitly only on occasion, the daily repetition
of eating kosher meat works silently, inscribing words in the expansion and
contraction of muscle, embedding ideas in gestures, and shaping how Jews
who participate in the practice categorize, perceive, and experience both
their selves and others.

THE MEANINGS OF EATING ANIMALS

It is not that kosher practitioners—or anyone eating animals—first form a
view of the world around them and then begins to eat in a certain way in response to it. Before we eat animals, we are already, as the (Jewish) novelist
Jonathan Safran Foer has expressed it, "eating animals"—that is, we are an-

imals defined in part by how we eat. We are eating before we are ourselves—we are born into the world eating, constituted by eating. Foer describes the experience of watching his first child's first meal:

> Perhaps the first desire my son had, worldlessly and before reason, was the desire to eat. Seconds after being born, he was breastfeeding. I watched him with an awe that had no precedent in my life. Without explanation or experience, he knew what to do. Millions of years of evolution had wound the knowledge into him, as it had encoded beating into his tiny heart, and expansion and contraction into his newly dry lungs. The awe had no precedent in my life, but it bound me, across generations, to others. I saw the rings of my tree: my parents watching me eat, my grandmother watching my mother eat, my great grandparents watching my grandmother . . . He was eating as had the children of cave painters.[3]

The ways in which "a human being is what he eats,"[4] as Ludwig Feuerbach put it, are more numerous and layered than usually thought. Feuerbach had in mind the way in which the material conditions of life drive the rest of culture, an idea that influenced his Jewish contemporary, Karl Marx, but the material and ideational ultimately cannot be separated in this manner.

How we eat animals may even help determine, as our consideration of hunter-gatherers in chapter 5 helps make visible, whether we will apprehend the world as divided between subjects and objects, culture and nature, humans and animals in the first place. It helps determine whether we imagine humans as coming to know the world "by virtue of first [having] removed themselves from it"[5] (the path of science and its promise of ever expanding objective knowledge) or whether, more along the lines Ingold calls forth, we imagine humans "knowing" the world "through the very processes of living and making their ways in it."[6]

There is ample precedent for the idea that dietary practices contain multiple layers of meaning in Jewish studies.[7] For example, Gillian Feely-Harnik's important study of the meaning of food in early Judaism and Christianity opens with the helpful observation that food provides "a powerfully concentrated 'language' for debating moral-legal issues and transforming social relations."[8] Jordan Rosenblum's studies of food in the earliest strata of rabbinic Judaism, the tannaitic Judaism of the first two centuries (*Tannaim* refers to the rabbis of this period), similarly show how culinary regulations are wielded to address commensal concerns in general, and commensal concerns about women specifically, thus constructing social and gender relations.[9] Rosenblum's analysis of the Babylonian Talmud's tractate Hullin 1:1 further brings us the important insight that in the ancient rules surrounding animal slaughter the distinction between Jew and Gentile is linked to a distinction between the human and the ape—between man and animal. Rosenblum explains, "In order for slaughter to be tannaitically valid for Jewish ingestion, the butcher must be a Jew. Butchery—a cultural practice that separates humans from animals—is now marked by the Tannaim as a distinctly Jewish practice. Gentile slaughter is . . . equated with slaughter by an ape. . . . The Gentile's slaughter is likened to the action of an animal; it is a natural, not human, act."[10] Jonathan Brumberg-Kraus—who gives animal food considerable attention—has similarly argued that rabbinic dietary practices related to the consumption of meat encode a larger system of meaning that elevates "rational, imaginative humans over brute animals, men over women, Torah scholars over those unschooled in Torah, and ethnic/kinship ties over ties based on shared faith or shared charismatic experiences."[11]

The pairing together of views towards "those unschooled in Torah" and animals that Brumberg-Kraus alludes to is part of a larger trope in rabbinic texts in which non-Jews and animals are imaginatively linked. For example, one of the more persistent tropes regarding the status of non-Jews in Talmudic literature links the uniqueness of Israel among the nations with the uniqueness of humans among animals. Elliot Wolfson has documented this phenomenon with some care.[12] A pervasive rabbinic trope that Wolfson finds persistent in later kabbalistic texts denies the full humanity of *certain* non-Jews: as it appears, for instance, in Bava Metzia 114a, "You are called '*adam*,' but idolaters are not called '*adam*.'"[13] The borders between human and animal, Jew and non-Jew, the faithful and the idolatrous, eater and eaten are porous, interpenetrating and mutually constituting. Still today the production, certification, and consumption of meat from kosher animals remains an ever evolving symbolic "language" that shapes Jewish attitudes not only toward animal others but non-Jewish human others.[14]

The consumption of animals, whether regulated by kashrut or not, lies at the intersection of multiple tectonic plates of meaning: human/animal, ruler/ruled, Jew/gentile, male/female, and so on. It is a paradigmatic example of what Pierre Bourdieu has called "enacted belief, instilled by the childhood learning that treats the body as a living memory pad, an automaton that 'leads the mind unconsciously along with it.'"[15] Such symbolically invested activities function as "a repository for the most precious values. . . . Practical sense, social necessity turned into nature, converted into motor schemes and body automatism, is what causes practices, in and through what makes them obscure to the eyes of their producers, to be *sensible*, that is, informed by a common sense. It is because agents never know completely what they are doing that what they do has more sense than they know."[16]

ASCENDANCY AND KINDNESS

What I am calling the humane subject presents to us, first of all, a tool, a rubric, an analytic, and a methodology for making sense of the complicated ways in which animals in general, and in particular animals that are eaten, are pressed into the service of creating human subjects of a particular kind. In its most basic terms a humane subject is one of several modes of human subjectivity that becomes intelligible through its opposition to the animal. This opposition marks the subject as distinctly human (as opposed to animal) and—at the same moment—as ethical, as *menschlich* (as opposed to inhumane and brutish). The human and the humane are co-constituted through an ultimately unresolved tension between two countervailing movements: one sacrificial in the sense Derrida gives to the word, which I will call *ascendancy*, and the other antisacrificial in the sense that Derrida speaks of the "sacrifice of sacrifice," which I will call *kindness*.[17] Humans' ascendancy over animals (their use as resource, exploitation, domination) and humans' kindness and kindredness to animals (shared vulnerability, embodiment, mortality, creatureliness) are pitted against each other to such an extent that one cannot be thought without the other.

I choose the word *ascendancy* in part because of the metaphor of height it suggests; in numerous ways throughout Jewish traditions humans are understood as elevated above animals. At the same time, eating animals with particular restraints can encode kindness. I choose the word *kindness* because it implies both a simple similarity in kind (kindness, or kindredness) and the proper affections and concerns that may arise from this similarity in kind (kindness or, perhaps, compassion, in Hebrew, *rachamim*). While human beings are understood in Jewish traditions to be ascendant in creation, they are bound to behave toward the rest of creation under certain rules that recognize, in a limited measure, kindness in one or the other sense of this word.

At particular moments in particular places the tension between ascendancy and kindness may be temporarily fixed to produce particular instantiations of human subjectivity and an associated ethics, that is, instantiations of the general structure I am calling the humane subject. To clarify, the *humane subject* refers primarily to the *structure* that provides the mechanism through which potentially infinite instantiations of subjectivity and ethics can be articulated and reproduced. Recalling my discussion of Agamben in chapter 3, the humane subject can be thought as both subsystem of and product of Agamben's "anthropological machine."[18] Communities in particular times and places, like American Orthodox or Conservative Jewish communities responding to the AgriProcessors event in 2004, utilize this structure to invoke and articulate specific modes of subjectivity and associated ethical orientations.

From another angle the humane subject can be understood as a myth or family of myths—myths that tell how "we humans" are both ascendant over animals, similar in kind to animals, and kind to animals. However, as J. Z. Smith has insisted, "there is no pristine myth; there is only application."[19] A rigorous analysis requires, as Wendy Doniger has articulated it, both the contextualization of myths diachronically "by showing how each narrative is a reaction to narratives that came before it within its own tradition" and discerning how a given instantiation of a myth was "configured by the events of the times, how it responded to what was happening on the political and economic scene."[20] The humane subject I theorize here does not, for example, necessarily foster environmental abuse or respect for the living. Rather, the humane subject is the *gatekeeper of intelligibility*. Its practical implications must be discerned by a contextualized analysis each time it is deployed.

The "structure" or "myth" of the humane subject first became evident to me prior to the AgriProcessors incidents while examining the ethical tropes of kosher certification companies reviewed in chapter 1. I was struck by the constant repetition of themes of compassion for animals, on the one hand, and elevation above them, on the other, in the literature of the big four kosher certification companies and the *dynamic tension* that the simultaneous, one might say dialectical, articulation of these sentiments created. It was as if there was an unwritten rule in Jewish discourses about animal food (and surely other discourses on eating animals) that there must always be—at least rhetorically—an assertion of both responsibility to and superiority over animals and that the actual physical relation with the animals we eat must be explicable in terms of both these claims. When I later came to the work of Derrida, discussed in the previous chapter, in which he too discovers a point-counterpoint, or dialectical, structure—"sacrifice" and the "sacrifice of sacrifice"—embedded in the consumption of animals, I began to see the larger utility of exploring the meaning of kosher practice through the analytic of the *humane subject*. This analytic would illumine the events at AgriProcessors as moves in a larger dance—not aberrations but innovations that simultaneously altered kosher practices and the meanings embedded in these practices. The ultimate meaning of the kinds of humane subjects that were articulated by and in response to the incidents at AgriProcessors become most vivid when set against other historically important instantiations of humane subjects (diachronic contextualization), and it is to several of these instantiations that I now turn.

MENSCHLICH SUBJECTS FROM GENESIS TO AGRIPROCESSORS

At the center of this chapter is an attempt to characterize the particular manner in which the humane subject was deployed by AgriProcessors, its largely Orthodox defenders, and its largely Conservative critics. I argue that those who fought for the plant's right to do what it did to animals and those who used the occasion to call for a heightening of concern for the Jewish principle of compassion for animals, *tza'ar ba'ale chayyim* (צער בעלי חיים), were responding not only to the particularity of the moment but also to an older and less conscious conflict—what Derrida has called war.

Let us consider how the humane subject illumines one of the most canonical articulations of the meaning of eating animals: the one given by the Priestly (P) source in Genesis 1 and 9. I will then go on to consider a representative range of sources: rabbinic interpretations of the Genesis creation narrative by Rashi and Joseph Albo; the Talmudic tale of Judah ha-Nasi's encounter with a calf en route to slaughter in the Babylonian Talmud tractate Bava Metzia; and, finally, the articulation of the meaning of kashrut by Samuel Dresner in *Keeping Kosher: A Diet for the Soul* (1959), a modern classic highly influential among Conservative rabbis.

Genesis, in particular 1:26–30 and 9:1–7, will be given special attention in my analysis because of its immense authority within Jewish traditions. I will demonstrate that the structure I have called the humane subject is not only visible in these verses but is a long-noted and particularly salient feature of the text. I suggest not only that the humane subject *can* be read in the biblical text but that it in fact has been found repeatedly by scholars for more than a century, even if not critically interrogated. To this end, I will not only offer a close reading of these verses, but I will do so in dialogue with a handful of the most influential Genesis commentaries produced by English, French, and German-speaking scholars of biblical studies in the last hundred or so years (more technical or repetitive parts of this discussion are consigned to the notes). The essential features of the humane subject that I will highlight in my analysis are

1   the assertion of a human ascendancy over animals that articulates a special ontological and ethical status for the human within creation;

2   the assertion of limits on this ascendancy that recognizes certain commonalities between humans and other animals and that highlights human responsibilities to animals; and

3   the juxtaposition of these two assertions such that they are set in a tension that functions to define a human subject or, more precisely, an ethical human subject that is, ideally, "humane."

Together these three markers indicate the operations of the humane subject and, by identifying this common structure, allow us to productively compare different instantiations of the more basic phenomena of subject formation in Jewish texts.

PRIESTLY SOURCE: GENESIS 1:26–30 AND 9:1–7

GENESIS 1   In the same biblical verse that reports the creation of the human, Genesis 1:26, humans are set in relation to God and animals, as if the human would be unintelligible without these two horizons. In this verse humans are created by God and then immediately marked as rulers over animals of the sea, sky, and land. In 1:28 humans are given the further command to "fill the earth and master it."[21] These bold assertions of dominion are the upward swing of what I have termed ascendancy. Yet even as 1:28 marks humans as distinct from animals through their dominion over creation, it links them with animals by conferring upon humans the same blessing previously given to animals of the sea and sky (not land), "be fertile and increase," פרו ורבו. The repeated phrase suggests that the divine valuation of fertility and reproduction includes both humanity and animality. Thus humans are produced in a tension between their divinelike rule over animals, on the one hand, and the common capacity and charge to reproduce shared with animals, on the other. Indeed, the history of exegesis on 1:28, as Jeremy Cohen has shown in his comprehensive survey, is *predominately* the history of "how to resolve this seeming contradiction in human nature, between animal-like sexuality and God-like rulership."[22] For the moment, however, let us bracket consideration of the postbiblical interpretive tradition.

The next verses, Genesis 1:29–30, makes the tension between human rule and limitation explicit. These verses work in part to constrain the ascendancy of the immediately preceding ones. Significantly, verses 1:29–30 are about food; they command both humans and animals to be strictly herbivorous: "And God said: 'See, I give you every seed-bearing plant that is upon all the earth, and every tree that has seed-bearing fruit; they shall be yours for food. [30] And to all the animals on land, to all the birds of the sky, and to everything that creeps on earth, in which there is the breath of life, [I give] all the green plants for food.' And it was so." Scholars have long noted that this vegetarian command is surprising in light of the "harsh" connotations of rule, רדה, and master or subdue, כבש—verbs that elsewhere refer to rule over subjugated peoples and slaves.[23]

John Skinner notes that Richard Kraetschmar argued more than a century ago that "the prohibition of animal food to man nullifies the dominion promised to him in vv. 26, 28," but Skinner himself rejects this extreme conclusion.[24] Hermann Gunkel approvingly cites Kraetzschmar's observation that "the vegetarian diet of humans (v 29) does not fit well with their dominion over animals (v 28)" and concludes therefore that P is working with "two, originally allogenous traditions."[25] Claus Westermann reaches the same conclusion.[26]

Interestingly, even within Genesis 1:29–30, where humans and animals are brought closer together, P distinguishes their now vegetable diets. Humans receive the seed-bearing and thus cultivatable plants and fruit trees while animals receive the leafy plants or leafy parts of plants. P maintains, as this source is always careful to do, the crucial boundary between humans and animals even as it emphasizes "kindness"—that is, constraints upon human rule. Still, this difference in foods given to humans and animals is minor compared to the striking fact that both humans and animals are similarly restricted to vegetarian food.[27] Thus, while these verses maintain the tension between ascendancy and kindness, they underscore kindness.

The constraint the P source makes explicit in 1:29 is already anticipated in the attention lavished on creation and the sixfold description of creation as "good" in 1:1–25 before humans are created. Walter Brueggemann observes that "though expository attention tends to concentrate on the subsequent verses 26–31, verses 3–25 protest against an exclusively anthropocentric view of the world. The creator God is not totally preoccupied with human creatures. God has his own relation with the rest of creation."[28] Moreover, the restriction to vegetarian food is intelligible only as a result of the common divine concern for the sanctity of all life and as a marker of the paradisiacal nature of God's original creation. Thus a principle of kindness—an ethical concern related to a similarity in kind—is expressed here.[29]

A softer piece of evidence that supports this reading is the closure of the creation narrative immediately after it puts into tension the traditions of ascendancy and kindness. This arrangement prohibits us from reading the human rule and mastery of verses 1:26–28 as "very good" except in light of the limitation that follows it in verses 1:29–30. Verse 1:31 concludes the narrative by declaring "all that he had made" as "very good," מאד טוב; the modifier "very" (literally "mightiness"), מאד, is added only to this final of seven assertions that creation "is good," טוב. It has long been observed that the "very" is added to the appellation "good" in verse 31 because the entire sweep of creation is being surveyed rather than the specific creations on an individual day. This is well established and should not distract us from the further observation that this stylized closing device also places emphasis on the already striking final command that precedes it, for the appellation "very good" describes the entire sweep of creation that is given its final shape precisely in 1:29–30.[30] As Skinner observes, verses 29–30 regulate "in broad and general terms the relation of men and animals to the vegetable world."[31] Gerhard von Rad helpfully emphasizes that *very good* "refers more to the wonderful purposefulness and harmony than to the beauty of the entire cosmos."[32]

GENESIS 9   The question of animal food continues in Genesis 9:1–7 in a lucid example of inner-biblical exegesis or what Michael Fishbane has more specifically identified as an example of inner-biblical "aggadic exegesis."[33] Genesis 9:1–7 is delimited as a single semantic unit by the *inclusio* formed by the blessing to "be fertile and increase" in lines 9:1 and 9:7:

> God blessed Noah and his sons, and said to them, 'Be fertile and increase, and
> fill the earth. [2] The fear and the dread of you shall be upon all the beasts of

the earth and upon all the birds of the sky—everything with which the earth is astir—and upon all the fish of the sea; they are given into your hand. [3] Every creature that lives shall be yours to eat; as with the green grasses, I give you all these. [4] You must not, however, eat flesh with its life-blood in it. [5] But for your own life-blood I will require a reckoning: I will require it of every beast; of man, too, will I require a reckoning for human life, of every man for that of his fellow man! [6] Whoever sheds the blood of man, by man shall his blood be shed; For in His image did God make man. [7] Be fertile, then, and increase; abound on the earth and increase on it.'

As in Genesis 1, the assertion of human ascendancy is linked with a countervailing principle of kindness. This time, however, the terms of ascendancy have a less benevolent tone and animals are given to humans as food. The upward swing of ascendancy once again asserts itself marking out the unique territory of the human, and indeed, as Fishbane emphasizes, also *explaining* this ascendancy. The phrase "for he created man in the image of God" now signals an explanation that links rule over animals with proximity to the divine. Moreover, in 9:1 the recast commands of Genesis 1 are now given specifically to men, "Noah and his sons," rather than to all of humanity—an amplification of the dominance of male over female that is so intimately linked with the dominance of human over animal.[34] Moreover, the new terms of ascendancy are harsher, involving "fear and the dread of you."[35] In 9:2–3 humanity's restriction to a vegetarian diet is repealed and fish, formally unmentioned in the divine allotment of food in 1:29–30, are explicitly designated as possible food for man, along with "all the beasts of the earth" and "all the birds of the sky." Thus verses 9:1–3 constitute a reiteration and amplification of the ascendancy in verses 1:26–28 and a transformation of the subject of this mastery from humanity to men. However, the subsequent verses 9:4–6, like 1:29–30, limit this amplification with a qualified reassertion of kindness.

Genesis 9:4 and 9:5 both begin with the restrictive particle אך, "however" or "only," which explicitly marks their contents as a counterpoint or limitation to verses 9:2–3.[36] Flesh must not be eaten "with its life-blood in it" (9:4) and "a reckoning" will be required if man or animal sheds human blood (9:5). 9:6 specifies the nature of this reckoning as death and provides explanation for this special punishment by recalling that man is created "in His image."[37] There are, in fact, two tensions between ascendancy and kindness articulated here: one between the overall impact of 1:26–31 and 9:1–7 (Genesis 1 emphasizing kindness and Genesis 9 ascendancy) and the other between 9:2–3 and 9:4–6 (the permission to eat animals emphasizing ascendancy and the blood prohibition emphasizing kindness). Like the present analysis, Westermann emphasizes that 9:2 "is meant to express the tension that now exists" with what was previously said about human ascendancy over animals in Genesis 1.[38] "On the one hand the animals are delivered into the hands of humans with the consequent 'fear and dread,' on the other there is the good will of the creator toward every living being."[39] Commenting on 9:3, Westermann continues, "Again the tension is evident. . . . It is this tension that calls for the restriction that is now to follow [in 9:4]."[40]

The manner in which 9:4 emphasizes kindness is most clearly seen only after the ethical overtones of the blood prohibition have been critically recovered in light of other P source texts. However, even before considering the contextual meaning of this verse within the larger P source we can note that both 9:4 and 9:5–6 present explicit limitations on the privileges granted in 9:2–3, which underscore blood as the kindred life-force of both animal (9:4) and human (9:5–6).[41] The ethical overtones of the blood prohibition are dealt with extensively in the work of biblicist and Conservative rabbi Jacob Milgrom and anthropologist Mary Douglas.[42] Both scholars describe the prohibition as embodying the central ethical principle of P's sacrificial system, which they respectively characterize as a principle of "reverence for life" and "sanctity of life."[43] Notably, much of their argument was already established a century ago by Delitzsch and Dillmann, who describe the meaning of the blood prohibition as "a sacred reverence for that principle of life flowing in the blood" and as demanding "respect for the divineness of life."[44] Westermann does not employ the language of "reverence" or "sanctity," but he concludes much the same when he comments on 9:4–5: "One's conduct toward other people is not to be separate from one's conduct toward animals."[45]

Milgrom explains that the P source itself provides a rationale for the blood prohibition in Leviticus 17:11, which Milgrom translates, "For the life of the flesh is in the blood, and I have assigned it to you on the altar to ransom your lives; for it is the blood that ransoms by means of life."[46] Blood is to be offered on the altar "to ransom" (לכפר) or, as JPS translates it, as "expiation." Why is this ransom or expiation necessary? The answer is stated just a few verses before in Leviticus 17:3–4, which Milgrom translates: "If anyone of the house of Israel slaughters an ox or a sheep or a goat in the camp, or does so outside the camp, [4] and has not brought it to the entrance of the Tent of Meeting to present (it as) an offering to YHWH, before YHWH's Tabernacle, bloodguilt shall be imputed to that person: he has shed blood; that person shall be cut off from among his kinspeople."[47] To slaughter an animal without the proper regard for its life as shown in the special handling of blood, Milgrom argues, is here presented as a serious crime ultimately tantamount to murder. The blood prohibition and related cultic and dietary practices work to mitigate the problem inherent in killing and causing death while affirming the goodness of creation and life. Milgrom summarizes the ethical force of the blood prohibition as follows: "The human being must never lose sight of the fundamental tenet for a viable human society. Life is inviolable; it may not be treated lightly. Mankind has a right to nourishment, not to life. Hence the blood, the symbol of life, must be drained, returned to the universe, to God."[48]

Continuing with the present analysis, just as in Genesis 1:29–30 humans and animals are given similar but differentiated food, the principle of kindness in Genesis 9:4–6 does not establish a thoroughgoing equivalency between humans and animals, even though it constrains human ascendancy. Animal "flesh with its life-blood in it" cannot be consumed, but human blood may not even be shed. Once again, even as humans are reminded of the common basis of life and constrained by the blood prohibition in how they can eat animals, the P source is careful to pair these sentiments with others that emphasize ascendancy.[49] Thus the P source presents a humane subject in Genesis 1 in which the principle of ascendancy is paired with what strikes most careful readers of the biblical text itself as an exceptionally strong countervailing principle of kindness; the humane subject of Genesis 1, we could say, gives priority to kindness. The P source then replaces this humane subject with another version of the humane subject in Genesis 9 in which the principle of ascendancy is given far greater priority.

RASHI AND JOSEPH ALBO

Let us continue this identification of previous instantiations of the humane subject by briefly considering a pair of medieval thinkers, Rashi (Shlomo Yitzhaki, 1040–1105) and Joseph Albo (1380–1444), who interpret the Genesis text. Before starting with Rashi, some stage setting is needed.

The ascendancy articulated by the P source was frequently amplified by the rabbinic tradition to discuss humanity's and Israel's God-like rule.[50]

Cohen identifies Saadya Gaon (d. 942), as offering the most amplified articulation of human ascendancy over animals found in authoritative Jewish texts. "No other ancient or medieval writer, Jewish or Christian, interpreted the primordial blessing of dominion to incorporate quite as much as Saadya did,"[51] Cohen explains. Not only does Saadya amplify the dominion decreed in 1:28, but he "virtually ignored the blessing of fertility"—the part of 1:28 that emphasizes the common capacity of humans and animals to reproduce. Saadya argues:

> The word "they shall rule" includes the entire range of devices with which man rules over the animals: over some with fetters and bridles, over some with ropes and reins, over some with enclosures and chains, over some with weapons of the hunt, over some with cages and towers, and so on. . . . And the word "the fish" includes the stratagems for catching fish from the bottom of the sea and rivers. . . . And he added the word "of the sea" to include man's subjugation of the water as well; for he finds it within the ground and raises out with pulleys and with . . . [lacuna in Saadya's text] or with containers or with a machine utilizing force and pressure. . . . And his word "and the birds" corresponds to the various snares for hunting birds . . . [and] the process of taming some in order to hunt others. . . . And with the word "the cattle" he gave him the authority to lead and the power to make use of them all, to eat the flesh of those fit for consumption . . . to heal from that which is medicinal, to ride on those suited for riding. . . . And with the word "and all the creeping things" he hinted at the understanding which he gave man to confine bees in hives to make honey for him.[52]

A striking part of Saadya's amplification of human ascendancy is the prominent role he allots to technology (fetters and bridles . . . ropes and reins . . . enclosures and chains . . . weapons of the hunt . . . cages and towers. . . . well[s] . . . containers . . . a machine utilizing force and pressure. . . . snares. . . . hives). This is of special interest for at least two reasons: first, had we more time, we could consider how the technological is another important torsion in the knot that we are tracing here in which ideas about humanity and animality (and divinity) are woven together.[53] The question of the animal is, as we see here in Saadya, not only a question about humanity, animality, and religion (the focus of this book) but also a question about technology.[54] The humane subject is always a technological subject. Second, this appearance of a "technologized" dominion in Saadya's (and broader Jewish) conceptions of humanity seems to anticipate the technologically advanced slaughter practiced at AgriProcessors. The welfare problems at AgriProcessors can be understood as in part the result of the way in which technology was wielded against animal bodies, and one can imagine how sentiments like Saadya's would encourage the conviction that technologically intensified violence to animals is permissible.

In his review of interpretations of Genesis 1:28, Cohen notes that Nachmanides (Moses ben Nachman Gerondi or RaMBaN, 1194–1270) and Obadiah ben Jacob Sforno (1475–1550) also refer to technological devices used to subdue animals in their commentaries on 1:28 and that David Kimchi (ReDaK, 1160–1235) and Levi Gersonides (Levi ben Gershon or RaLBaG, 1288–1344) achieve a similar effect by championing the human capacity for reason. However Maimonides (Moses ben Maimon or RaMBaM, 1134–1204) and Abraham ibn Ezra (1092–1093) explicitly reject "the view that God created the entire world expressly for human benefit."[55] If Saadya's commentary on Genesis presents an unusually intensified account of ascendancy, Rashi's and Albo's readings of Genesis present more modest rabbinic modifications of the P source's instantiation of the humane subject. Nevertheless, the humane subjects deployed by both Rashi and Albo in their interpretations of Genesis do amplify the scope of ascendancy and diminish the importance of kindness. Whatever measure of anthropocentrism one finds in the P narrative, I think it is fair to conclude that Rashi, Albo, and a range of other medieval rabbis intensify it.

RASHI: RULE OR BE RULED   Rashi glosses "master it" in Genesis 1:28, which is generally taken to refer to human mastery of the earth and its animals, as "'master her' to teach you that the male masters [כובש] the female."[56] Here Rashi extends the notion of ascendancy beyond the human/animal relationship to the intrahuman relationship of the sexes, reinforcing a link between the human/animal and male/female binaries. However, as in the biblical text, for Rashi too the permission to rule the earth and animals is constrained in the next verses 1:29–30, where Rashi declares, "He made cattle and animals equal to them [humans] with regard to food and did not permit Adam and his wife to kill a creature and eat its flesh." Even more interesting for our purposes, Rashi, echoing the influential midrashic compilation, *Genesis Rabbah* (8:12), offers a similar interpretation of וירדו, "and they will rule" (1:26); playing on the proximity of the Hebrew root ירד (to descend) to רדה (to rule), Rashi argues that וירד means *both* to descend and to rule. Rashi thus interprets 1:26 to suggest that "if worthy, he rules [רודה] over animals and cattle, if not worthy, he becomes lower than them [נעשה ירדו לפניהם] and the animal rules him [החיה מושלת בו]."[57]

In his commentary on Genesis 9:5 where God states that animals will be punished for shedding human blood, Rashi continues the myth of the human struggle to properly separate male from female, ruler from ruled, man from animal, and, the one who eats from the eaten. Rashi, perhaps drawing on a Talmudic interpretation of Psalms 49:13 (Shabbat 151b), explains: "Since the generation of the flood went wrong, they were allowed to become food for wild animals—to be ruled by them. As it says, 'He is ruled because they are comparable to cattle.' Therefore it was necessary to caution the animals regarding [the status of humans]." Rashi thus suggests that God allowed the "natural" order to be reversed, for animals to make humans food, because humans were insufficiently different from animals—because humans' ascendancy, we might say, did not reach the heights God intended.

If Rashi emphasizes the theme of ascendancy in the biblical text in these ways, he is also sensitive to the limitations God places upon this rule. As we have seen, Rashi notes that in 1:29–30 God "made cattle and animals equal to them" even if this equality is only "with regard to food." Following the Talmud (Sanhedrin 59b), Rashi further sees the permission to eat meat restricted not only by a prohibition against consuming blood but by a prohibition against אבר מן החי, eating a limb detached from a living creature. In sum, Rashi amplifies the tradition of ascendancy, but does not ignore the countervailing principle of kindness.

JOSEPH ALBO: A CASE AGAINST/FOR VEGETARIANISM   J. David Bleich has noted that Rabbis Joseph Albo, Isaac Abarbanel (1437–1508), and Abraham Isaac Kook (1864–1935) are all exceptional in the rabbinic tradition for emphasizing and to some extent practicing vegetarianism as a moral ideal. What is more interesting for our purposes is that, while maintaining this positive stance toward vegetarianism, all three thinkers also tell a very similar horror story of the nightmare that might follow improperly motivated vegetarianism. Improperly motivated vegetarianism, they argue, will lead to murder, even cannibalism![58] Consider Albo's classic and beloved work *Sefer Ha-'Ikkarim,* or *Book of Principles.*

Albo's interpretation in *Sefer Ha-'Ikkarim* is embedded, not surprisingly, in a commentary that serves on the surface to explain that the change in dietary laws from Genesis 1 to 9 is the result of the human failure to properly distinguish humans and animals. To explain this properly, Albo maintains, he must begin by describing the nature of the sins of Cain and Abel, which also surround issues of food. Cain's first sin, Albo tells us, is that he did not recognize the significance of the difference in vegetable food given to humans and animals in Genesis 1:29–30, the purpose of which "was to show the superiority of the human species to the other animals."[59] But the more serious sin, the עיקר החטא, the root sin, was that "he did not think that man's superiority to the animals amounted to anything. Also he thought that he was forbidden to kill the animals because they were like him and were subject to death like him" (131).[60] Abel, by contrast, recognized human superiority to animals, but his transgression was that "he did not think that man was authorized to kill the animals. So far human superiority did not reach, according to his opinion. . . . This is why Abel was killed, because his opinion was close to that of Cain, and more calculated to mislead men" (132).[61] Through his own interpretation of Genesis 4:6, in which God calls to Cain asking why his countenance has fallen, Albo offers a clear articulation of the workings of the anthropological machine that generates the humane subject. The meaning of the divine speech to Cain in Genesis 4:6–7, Albo explains, is that "man is born a wild ass, and has no superiority over the animal in actuality when he comes into the world, but he has superiority potentially if he practices goodness and realizes his potentialities and recognizes the greatness of the Lord. If he does well, he will be lifted up above the animals" (133).[62] Neither Cain nor Abel understands this properly, according to Albo. Cain's error, his failure even to begin to initiate the anthropological machine that demarcates humans from animals, ultimately leads him to murder. God does not intervene on Abel's behalf because Abel does not, as it were, keep the engine of the anthropological machine running long enough to recognize the human right to kill animals—not only for God but also for human purposes. (Significantly, throughout Albo's discussion the act of distinguishing humans from animals is equivalent to recognizing that humans are created in the image of God—the divine and animal horizon work in perfect symmetry to define the human. Failure to distance oneself from animals, to kill them, is also a failure to recognize God.)

Albo continues his narrative by arguing that it was precisely the spread of Cain's error, the failure to distinguish humans from animals, that led to the necessity of the flood. Albo further explains that this generation was "corrupt and lived like animals" (135). It was to eradicate this error that God permitted humans to eat animals after the flood! Albo seems to agree with anthropologist Nick Fiddes, who argues that "consuming the muscle flesh of other highly evolved animals is a potent statement of our supreme power."[63] For Fiddes, in part following Douglas, eating meat is a "natural symbol"—a symbol that is predisposed to tangibly represent "human control of the natural world."[64] In Albo's understanding, nothing could better teach the uniqueness of humanity and establish the postdiluvian era on its proper ethical basis than killing and eating animals.[65] Only when human superiority was beyond question would God even institute the kosher laws, and this in turn, in Albo's reading, provided the basis for exceptional individuals to return to the ideal vegetarian diet. Since the reason to eat animals is to know the difference between human and animal, once that difference is entrenched in the heart of an exceptional individual, vegetarianism no longer poses the same danger.

In sum Albo, like Rashi, amplifies the biblical tradition of ascendancy, but also gives some weight to the countervailing principle of kindness. Had we more time to examine their historical context and to look at other texts contemporary with, respectively, those of Albo and Rashi, we might be able to say more about how their respective emphases on ascendancy and kindness would have appeared to their contemporaries, a desideratum that must be left for another study if such is recoverable at all. For our purposes, however, this is not essential. What is most important to see is that what I have called the humane subject is visible not only within the text of Genesis, but, with different accents, within highly influential medieval rabbinic traditions that are explicitly in dialogue with this biblical text. This long-standing rabbinic reproduction of the humane subject, which I have only hinted at here, helps fill in the background within which the contemporary responses to animals at AgriProcessors can be best understood.

BAVA METZIA 85A

We already encountered another striking instance of the humane subject in canonical Jewish texts that can help further fill in this background—and that resonates strongly with the AgriProcessors incidents: the Talmudic story of Judah ha-Nasi's encounter with a calf being led to slaughter.[66] I will read this story as a literary and "didactic . . . rather than [a] reliable historical account"[67] and interpret it, as it has often been interpreted, primarily as closed unit that generates its own internal logic rather than engage in the also desirable task of trying to more deeply contextualize the tale within the larger *sugya* (passage).[68] The story juxtaposes two sentiments: on the one hand, the idea that animals were created for human use and, on the other, the idea that God's concern extends to all creatures, human and animal. I choose to highlight this story not only because of the stature of its protagonist, but because of the manner in which it underscores and amplifies the significance of kindness. If we take the book of Genesis as our starting place, this Talmudic incarnation of the humane subject works to elevate compassion for animals and reinforces a sense of common creatureliness; in this regard, it can be contrasted to the perspective in Genesis 9, Rashi, and Albo. This emphasis on the principle of kindness is heightened by the fact that earlier in Bava Metzia (32a–33a) we encounter what is arguably the most important legal discussion of animal life in the Talmud: a debate about whether tza'ar ba'ale chayyim is a "Torah law," that is, a law from the "Written Torah," what Christians know as the Old Testament, rather than a "Rabbinic Law" from the "Oral Torah" (that is, the Talmud and other rabbinic texts that in Jewish tradition are also considered "Torah").[69] Though "it is the virtually unanimous opinion of rabbinic decisors" that this principle of minimizing pain to animals is a Torah law—and thus resides in the most authoritative stratum of Jewish law—the debate in the Talmud itself is left unresolved.[70]

The debate about the status of tza'ar ba'ale chayyim is engaged through the question of why one is obligated, with certain exceptions, to help unload a burden on a pack animal. A striking feature of the discussion is that the debate is not about what one is allowed to do to animals oneself but is rather about the question of whether one is obligated to intervene in the affairs of other people to relieve the suffering of animals. It is a question about "animal activism" that the Babylonian Talmud here chooses to think through the status of the principle of tza'ar ba'ale chayyim. That one should personally strive to reduce tza'ar ba'ale chayyim seems assumed. This is not a debate about how we should propel ourselves into an ideal world but rather about how to respond to this broken one. At the opening of the debate (the very end of Bava Metzia 32a), Rava asserts that the interpretation of both "the Rabbis" (that is, the collective rabbinic judgment) and the interpretation of Rabbi Shimon regarding the requirement of a passer-by to unload an overburdened animal proves that tza'ar ba'ale chayyim is a Torah law, and the text then considers a series of challenges to this claim. Immediately prior to this point in the text there is a discussion of the relatively greater obligation to unload an animal as opposed to loading an animal, and Rava appears to claim that the relatively greater obligation to unload an animal can be explained only if the principle of tza'ar ba'ale chayyim has the status of a law based in the Written Torah. There is no dispute that tza'ar ba'ale chayyim is obligatory, but just how obligatory is it?

All of the challenges to Rava hinge on one of two possibilities. One type of challenge argues that what appears to be a Torah obligation to relieve the suffering of an animal by unloading its burden is in fact explicable as a Torah obligation to human beings. For example, the text asks if it is not possible that, rather than regard for the animal, the obligation to unload is motivated by a concern to prevent the financial loss incurred by the owner if the animal is "damaged." The other type of challenge argues that there are circumstances under which there would be no obligation to relieve such a burdened animal and that these would not arise if tza'ar ba'ale chayyim were the motivation for the law. For example, there is speculation that there might not be any obligation to unload if the owner of the animal refuses to assist in the unloading, which could suggest that the motivation for the command to unload is not primarily tza'ar ba'ale chayyim. These challenges highlight a major seam in Jewish animal ethics that reappears throughout Jewish history: in some texts and in some thinkers compassion for animals is primarily for the animals' own sake or for what animals means to God, but in other texts and thinkers compassion for animals is configured as more centrally about human virtue.[71]

Utilizing the theoretical apparatus of earlier chapters, let us ask what motivates this resistance to granting tza'ar ba'ale chayyim the status of a Torah law.[72] The structure I have called the humane subject is not being challenged—some degree of human "ascendancy" and some degree of "kindness" are both taken for granted in the text. The question is one of relative priority (which is, in a sense, *eternally* the question). As I read it, one of the implicit worries of the rabbis who resist giving tza'ar ba'ale chayyim the status of a Torah law is the possibility that if tza'ar ba'ale chayyim is the reason for this obligation to unload, then by the same logic tza'ar ba'ale chayyim could lead to many additional restrictions and obligations to the point of being burdensome. There perhaps was concern about restrictions upon other permitted actions that if done in excess or improperly might cause animal suffering. Imagine, for example, a rabbi who reasoned more like Saadya and wanted to defend the right of humans to use "all the devices with which man rules over the animals."[73] What about animals beaten for training purposes, mutilations to animals for the purposes of identification, castration, or a variety of other ancient (and ongoing) ubiquitous husbandry practices that involve animal suffering and that we can assume the rabbis of the Talmud would have at least heard about, if not seen? What about nonsacrificial slaughter itself? Is anyone not trained in the laws of Torah even capable of killing an animal without violating tza'ar ba'ale chayyim or some other principle?[74] If the view prevailed that tza'ar ba'ale chayyim is rooted only in Oral Torah (and thus rabbinically ordained) and not from the Written Torah, the potential scope of the mandate would be dramatically curtailed. If the obligation to help an animal in distress, however, is a divinely revealed law of the highest order—a Torah law—then those who worry more about limiting human power over animals (kindness) than about possible infringements on the human right to use animals (ascendancy) can more easily invoke this divinely ordained commandment in support of their concerns. Although this is not recorded in so many words, I read the objections to giving tza'ar ba'ale chayyim the status of Torah law as, among other things, expressive of an anxiety about the significant restraints on commonplace uses of animals that might result.

Even more, we might ask, if tza'ar ba'ale chayyim is a Torah law and provides sufficient grounds for compelling someone to unload an animal merely *seen*—perhaps from some distance away, according to certain rabbinic authorities—what obligation would be incurred when one is less tangentially connected to the animal's suffering? What if, to take the worry to an extreme, we not merely *saw the animal*, but the *animal saw us*? What if the animal pleaded with us—what obligation then? This last scenario is in fact precisely what is imagined in the Talmud some fifty odd folios later in the Talmudic story of Judah ha-Nasi and the calf. This evocative narrative, in which Rabbi Judah is punished with sufferings for thirteen years due to his indifference (not any act of violence on his part) to a calf being led to slaughter (*shechitah*), revisits the theological, existential issues raised in the debate about the status of tza'ar ba'ale chayyim in a narrative mode.

The Talmud divides the story into two instances, the first of which marks the onset of Judah ha-Nasi's sufferings: "For a calf which they were bringing to slaughter went [and] hung its head in the corner of Rabbi's garment and cried. He said to it: 'Go. For this you were created.' They said: 'Since he shows no compassion, let sufferings come upon him.'"[75] The second instance marks the departure of his sufferings: "One day Rabbi's maid was sweeping the house. Some young rats were scattered there and she swept them up. He said to her: 'Let them go. It is written: "And His mercies are over all His works" [Psalms 145]. They said: 'Since he shows compassion, we will have compassion on him.'"[76] The text emphasizes that the animal who approaches Judah ha-Nasi is not mature; it is specifically a calf, which means this bovine would have been taken from its mother relatively recently. (Heifers and calves have strong, easily recognizable bonds and vocalize in distress when separated.) The calf, the story continues, leaves those leading him to slaughter and hangs his head in the garment or lap of Rabbi (דרבי בכנפיה לרישיה תליא).[77] At this moment the Talmud adds a striking detail flagged with the particle קא, which perhaps indicates emphasis: and the calf wept (בכי וקא).

Before we continue with the story, it is worth attending to the fact there is cross-cultural evidence for a widespread discomfort with a sacrificial animal showing resistance to slaughter. I noted in chapter 3 that Eliade goes so far as to consider the ancient hunter's sympathy with his victim and the hunter's worry over the violence of killing as one of a small handful of features of Paleolithic humanity that are foundational for religion. Eliade calls this sympathy "mystical solidarity" and argues that its influence is "still active—altered, revalorized, camouflaged" today.[78] Similarly, we saw that Cassirer put forward a parallel thesis that a sense of "solidarity" with life is a root feature of religion that never wholly disappears.[79] Moreover, some evidence suggests that ancient Jews, like so many of the peoples around them, stressed, as Saul Lieberman puts it, "the apparent voluntary submission of the [animal] victim to its fate."[80] For example, in Midrash Tanhuma, a canonical compilation of rabbinic midrashim, we encounter a midrash explaining that the bull Elijah brought to sacrifice in First Kings went willingly, while those of Ba'al's resisted so fiercely that they could not be moved at all.[81] Perhaps the most prominent example of this sentiment in rabbinic literature is the Mishnaic principle that the red heifer sacrificed to atone for Israel's sins must not show resistance on its way to sacrifice.[82]

Returning to our story, Judah ha-Nasi, despite these traditions, is not moved to pity and says to the calf, "Go. For this you were created [זיל, לכך נוצרת]." The heavenly court, citing his lack of "compassion," or his lack of "mother love" (the Hebrew root here, רחם, can mean womb), condemns Judah ha-Nasi to suffer. In the second incident, which removes Judah ha-Nasi's sufferings, some small, young animals are scattered on the rabbi's floor. While the species of the animals is unclear, the text makes explicit that these animals are, like the calf, young animals (בני כרכושתא) and thus perhaps moth-erless.[83] When the rabbi sees his servant about to sweep them up, he stops her and, citing Psalm 145, declares "Let them go [שבקינהו]. It is written: 'And His mercies are over all His works' [מעשיו כל על ורחמיו]." The heavenly court then concludes that, since Judah ha-Nasi showed compassion, they will show compassion to him and they remove his suffering (עליה נרחם ומרחם, האיל הואיל).

Several features of the story highlight the vulnerability of bodies—a vul-nerability that both animals and humans face. First, the story is framed by an inquiry into what brought about the thirteen years of suffering Judah ha-Nasi endured and follows an evocative description of the extreme pain he experienced, which is described as so great that the groans the rabbi made after entering the bathroom (Rashi clarifies that he is suffering from a stone in the urinary tract) drowned out all other noises and was heard even by sailors at sea. Second, as I have noted, the text flags both the ani-mal Judah ha-Nasi sends to slaughter in the first incident and the animals he saves in the second incident as young animals still dependent on moth-erly care. Third, the central use of the root רחם in the passage and the fact that its noun form can mean womb also suggests vulnerability—the extreme vulnerability of the newly born. Finally, although it begins to take us be-yond the scope of what we can explicate at present, we can read the Talmu-dic passages that immediately follow our story as examining the theme of vulnerability. These subsequent passages explain that while Judah ha-Nasi suffered there was no rain. Rain here is configured as a dangerous, albeit necessary force, and the text seems to suggest that the rabbi's sufferings, because of his greatness, had a vicarious atonement effect, and thus while he suffered his people were spared exposure to dangerous rains. In this con-nection the story shades into a vulnerability not only of the animals and of Judah ha-Nasi but also of the entire people, who are vulnerable to extreme weather. This reading is supported by the fact that, as Jonathan Schofer has shown, rain and vulnerability are regularly associated in several areas of the Talmud, although often the rabbis in question emphasize vulnerability by a lack rather than an overabundance of rain. In a study of the pedagogical significance of rain-making narratives, Schofer concludes that "rabbinic rituals surrounding rain are prominent aspects of rabbinic culture that re-veal a strong sense of connection with their environment. Humans as em-bodied need food, and this need sets them in relation to their surrounding in concrete ways: [namely,] people are vulnerable to changes in climate and weather."[84]

With this theme of bodily vulnerability surrounding and cutting through it, the story juxtaposes two statements, both put in the mouth of Judah ha-Nasi: "Go. For this you were created" and "His mercies are over all His works." In this juxtaposition the story fits the pattern we have seen in other texts in which two countervailing sentiments—what I have called *ascendancy* and *kindness*—are set in tension. The idea that animals are created for the sake of humans is never denied. In fact, in the earlier passage (Bava Metzia 32a–33a) where the legal status of tza'ar ba'ale chayyim was debated, the actual act of relieving suffering is explicitly made subordinate to the mandate to subdue the evil inclination. Nevertheless, the most salient features of the story of Judah ha-Nasi and the calf work to elevate concern for tza'ar ba'ale chayyim. Most obviously, the fact that an act of indifference or coldness to a pleading animal would impact God's dispensation of compassion to the human actor immediately gives the question of tza'ar ba'ale chayyim significant moral weight. This is especially so since the animal in question is pleading not because it is suffering any unusual fate but merely because it wants to live, a right animals are explicitly denied by rabbinic tradition. That it is an action motivated by tza'ar ba'ale chayyim that saves the rabbi from his suffering also adds to the moral weightiness of tza'ar ba'ale chayyim. Finally, the story is centrally concerned with the development of the rabbi's own compassion. This is a story not only about a compassionate act but also about how a particular sage learned compassion. Tza'ar ba'ale chayyim, then, in addition to its inherent value, seems to have a value in the moral formation of humans—even that of a great sage. The explicit tension articulated between the idea that animals are created for human use and Psalm 145 ("And His mercies are over all His works"), and the story's depiction of a sage learning to privilege the sentiment of the psalm (kindness) at the expense of the idea that animals are intended for human use (ascendancy), makes our story an excellent example of a deployment of a humane subject that champions the principle of kindness.

This is not to deny that there is much in the larger sugya in which this story appears that configures the human/animal binary so as to shore up a more "carnophallogocentric" vision of the subject.[85] As Talmud scholar and rabbi Julia Watts Belser has demonstrated in her analysis of the full sugya, the text "begins with strong assertion of human-animal difference, using the species-binary as part of a complex cultural matrix that distinguishes between the righteous and the wicked, the Jewish and the Roman, the rabbinic and the wife, the sage and the unlearned man."[86] I merely insist that the details of the discrete episode of Judah ha-Nasi and the calf (an episode frequently isolated from its larger textual context in Jewish thought) can be read, quite appropriately, as a tale in which compassion and kindness are emphasized.

Conveniently, Watts Belser concludes that while the sugya explicitly "champions the suffering and heroism of Rabbi Elazar, who affirms a sharp dichotomy between righteous rabbinic masculinity and the wickedness of the bestial," the dialectic force of it "poses a subtle countervoice that ultimately valorizes the compassion of Rabbi Yehudah [Judah haNasi], affirming his eventual awareness of the shared capacity for suffering that unites rabbis and other animals."[87] Watts Belser's reading of much of the larger sugya thus conforms with my reading of this small episode within it. If Watts Belser's reading is correct, it is not only the story of Judah ha-Nasi and the calf, but the larger passage in which it appears that presents to us a humane subject emphasizing kindness.

SAMUEL DRESNER'S DIET FOR THE SOUL

Before turning to the AgriProcessors event itself, I want to move from identifying instantiations of the humane subject in canonical texts to a contemporary classic of the Conservative movement, Rabbi Samuel Dresner's small book *Keeping Kosher: A Diet for the Soul*. This text has been influential among Conservative rabbis and was recently reprinted by the movement's press. Beyond its significance for the Conservative movement, Dresner's book is of particular interest because he marshals some of the precise passages we have examined—in particular, Genesis: 1:26–30 and 9:1–7 and the story of Judah ha-Nasi and the calf—among other canonical texts in order to argue for a long-standing Jewish imagination of the humane subject that puts special emphasis on kindness. Dresner's text is a strong example of a sophisticated contemporary attempt to construct a particular instantiation of the humane subject *through the vehicle of kosher practice* and, in addition, to argue that the vision of the human and ethics he puts forth is part of an ancient lineage.[88]

In the same unmistakable way that the passage we considered from Saadya is an amplification of ascendancy, Dresner's text functions to elevate the status of kindness. For Dresner, kosher practice is founded upon "reverence for the life we take."[89] Dresner's text is a polemic against the forgetting of this "reverence for life"—a forgetting that he argues finds expression in both the Reform dismissal of kashrut as meaningless ritual, on the one hand,

and the Orthodox defense of it as a suprarational commandment whose meaning cannot be known, on the other hand.[90] As a student and friend of Abraham Joshua Heschel, Dresner's use of the word *reverence* cannot help but resonate with the usage given it by his teacher, for whom it was also an important word. In Heschel's writings, however, *reverence* is almost always associated with the unique status of human beings as images of the divine. Although Heschel did use the phrase "reverence for life," reverence is associated most obviously in his writings with human uniqueness. Nonetheless, Dresner cites Heschel specifically as transmitting to him a principle of reverence for life and uses this principle as the central organizing idea of his book.[91] "Jews are permitted to eat meat," he writes, "but they must learn to have reverence for the life they take. Reverence for life is an awareness of what we are about when we engage in the simple act of eating flesh. It is a constant lesson of the laws of *kashrut*."[92]

As mentioned earlier, Dresner's book expresses the understanding of the human and ethics implicit in his call for reverence through the structure of the humane subject. Note that Dresner's understanding of reverence, quoted previously, includes not only a stance toward life, but an "awareness of what we are about." For Dresner, reverence for life is about heightened concern for the suffering of life as well as a practice of self-cultivation. Moreover, Dresner finds the same tension between a principle of ascendancy and kindness in Genesis 1 and 9 that I have outlined in the present study and similarly links this tension to the tension between a vegetarian ideal and meat eating. Dresner interprets: "Human consumption of meat, requiring the taking of an animal life, *has constantly posed a religious problem to Judaism.* The Rabbis of the Talmud were aware of the distinction in the matter of food between man's ideal [vegetarianism] and his real condition [in which he is permitted meat]."[93] The constant "religious problem"—as Dresner names it—is what I have described as a generative tension between a principle of kindness and ascendancy. As in our analysis of the humane subject, for Dresner it is this tension that generates ethical Jewish subjects. "[The dietary laws] have helped to achieve Judaism's goal of hallowing the act of eating by reminding the Jews that the life of the animal is sacred and may be taken for food only under prescribed conditions. From this one learns reverence for life, both animal and human. Eating, then, is not simply a matter of replenishing one's nutrients . . . but first and foremost a process of moral education. . . . Israel has created a diet for the soul."[94] Eating animals with reverence for their lives is about more than the ethics of eating animals: it is a means of propagating a kind of person, a mensch. Kashrut generally, and kosher practice regarding eating animals in particular, is a technology of ethical self-reproduction.

LINEAGES OF JEWISH REVERENCE FOR LIFE

Where Dresner's reading of Jewish texts differs from—though by no means contradicts—my own analysis here is in his linking together of these diverse textual moments to argue that they constitute a coherent tradition of "reverence for life," which Dresner understands himself to be transmitting as it was transmitted to him. Dresner provides a variety of specific examples in which he finds the principle of reverence for life expressed and maintained in Jewish practice. For example, he considers *shechitah* as a humane method of slaughter.[95] While he does not attempt to do a rigorous tracing, he does make it clear that he sees this "tradition" of reverence for life coming to him from Eastern European Yiddish-speaking Jewry, and Hasidism in particular. "Even those distant from religious observance retained an aversion to cruelty to living creatures," he writes, citing as evidence Albert Einstein's alleged response when asked to define the spirit of the Jewish tradition: "If a Jew says he enjoys hunting, know that he is lying."[96] Dresner also invokes as bearers of this tradition an unnamed Polish survivor; the great Yiddish writer Sholom Aleichem; the sixteenth-century Talmudist, *posek*, and author of an influential commentary on the *Shulchan Arukh* (*HaMapah*), Rabbi Moses Isserles; and the Nobel prize–winning Hebrew writer Shmuel Yosef Agnon.[97]

A limited study such as the present one cannot answer in any definitive way whether Dresner is correct to argue that his articulation of the humane subject is part of a much older *lineage* (namely a *continuous* tradition) that has been transmitted to him as an ethical inheritance (rather than, for example, an idea that reoccurs but has multiple, distinct origins). We can say, however, that such seems possible enough given what we know from medieval sources.

The medievalist Kalman Bland argues that a "heterodox terrain in medieval Jewish thought" frequently disputed the idea of human superiority and radical difference from the rest of creation, for example as we encountered it in Rashi.[98] Among the medieval thinkers that challenged this "prevailing dualism," he includes, as Derrida anticipated,[99] not legal decisors acting in their official capacity but *poets* and *storytellers* including Shmuel ha-Nagid, Berakhiah ha-Naqdan, Judah al-Harizi, and Qalonymus ben Qalonymus.[100]

Bland calls the ideology associated with the dominant medieval articulation of the human/animal binary "brutism," which he defines as an "anthropocentric speciesism" that marks human difference so as to justify subordination of animals and defend the status quo.[101] Bland's "brutism" can be understood as yet another instantiation of the dominant articulation of the humane subject that one could argue appears at least as early as Genesis 9. Like all instantiations—or myths—of the humane subject, "brutism is utterly political in motivation and intent" (166). And like particular articulations of the humane subject that we could associate with those found in Rashi and Albo: "It defends the status quo. It denies to animals individuality, voice, political culture, and history" (166).

"Venerable in history," argues Bland, in a penetrating observation that deserves more attention, "Brutism is perhaps the primal template for any ideology that dialectically licenses and restrains both self and the Other" (166). Here Bland anticipates a central point of this chapter, namely that we encounter in diverse Jewish texts something like a "primal template" for an ideology that, on the one hand, "dialectically licenses" violence to animals—that is, marks humans as ascendant and superior to the point of being able to kill the animal—and, on the other hand, "restrains" this violence—that is, that limits ascendancy through a countervailing movement emphasizing kindness. "Brutism therefore," Bland continues, "precedes and complements the knot of exclusionary systems. Throughout modernity, for example, Brutism, sexism, racism, and colonialism have worked in tandem, validating and reinforcing one another" (167). As Bland observes, "The modern phase of revolt against medieval dualism, featuring the comparison of humans with animals, is well known," but "the medieval phase of the revolt against dualism remains something of a terra incognita in the history of Jewish ideas" (167), a lacunae Bland's scholarship on medieval Jewish understandings of animals has begun to address.

In any case, whether or not we can follow Dresner's intriguing self-understanding as the recipient of an ancient Jewish lineage that inculcates reverence for life, we can follow him in naming different historical instantiations of the humane subject, noting that some do indeed seem to inculcate greater regard for the living. Such naming of different instantiations of the humane subject would allow us to note resemblances between chronologically arranged humane subjects such that we can, as data accumulates, begin to speak of "lineages" that transmit and defend different humane subjects. So far I have insisted only that the structure of the humane subject occurs repeatedly and that it is deployed to generate diverse *understandings* of the human being and ethics *and* diverse modes of *being* human and ethical. I have also looked at particular texts and attempted to explicate the particular humane subjects they articulate. It is logical to assume that if this analysis were expanded to more texts, patterns would begin to emerge; we would find certain family resemblances among various articulations of the humane subject. In a sense I have already begun this in that I have crudely classified some of the humane subjects I have explicated as amplifications of ascendancy and others as amplifications of kindness.

Whether the various instantiations of the humane subject that lay emphasis on ascendancy or, alternatively, the various instantiations that lay emphasis on kindness cohere sufficiently that we can, like Dresner, speak of particular lineages is beyond the scope of this study. I will, however, for the sake of expediency, follow Milgrom, Douglas, and Dresner and characterize contemporary articulations of the humane subject that appear to increase the status of kindness as expressing a "reverence for life ethic." I will likewise characterize articulations of the humane subject that appear to be increasing the status of ascendancy as expressing a "dominionist ethic." In calling this concatenation of ideas embodied in practices an ethic I mean to emphasize its broad scope and the manner in which views about species, gender, and race are not simply related (as if by accident) but are *necessarily* related by countless, if also invisible, threads, for they are rooted in common constructions of sacrificial and nonsacrificial subjectivities. Both "ethics" are, for the present purpose, constituted by a basic family resemblance between various instantiations of the humane subject: on the one hand, those that (through their internal construction, psychological effect, political context, etc.) trumpet human ascendancy (among other things), and, on the other, those that emphasize the kinship of life and the regard for life that this kinship demands (among other things). With the benefit of these labels, we are now in a position to return to the AgriProcessors case.

THE AGRIPROCESSORS' CONTROVERSY

THE DEPTH DIMENSION OF A SCANDAL

We can better understand the incidents at AgriProcessors and the diverse Jewish responses to them if we see both *within* and *behind* the implementation of kosher meat production something like a war in the sense Derrida gives the term.[102] I say *within* the implementation to insist that, at one level, it is within the brute violence to animals or the protection of them that the war is waged; this is a war of deeds. I say *behind* the implementation to insist that the domination or compassion inherent in or "undetachable" from the actual treatment of animals was supplemented by *discourses* that further advanced either a dominionist or a reverence for life ethic; this is a war of words. Ultimately, it is a conflict of deed-words—*devarim*—and in this landscape dietary choice and theology cannot be distinguished.[103]

This war, of course, did not begin or end with AgriProcessors, so we must ask what has caused the conflict to flash forth with such vividness: some people defending the dismembering of live animals as the highest form of kashrut and others seizing on the occasion to urge abstinence from all meat in the name of Jewish values. In the episode of Judah ha-Nasi and the calf, the incident that initiates the story is an animal that shows considerable agency by breaking away from the person leading it to slaughter, burying its head in the rabbi's lap, and weeping. There is no animal rights group, no equivalent to PETA that dramatizes the wordless protests of the calf. The calf in this Talmudic story is a subject. It faces the rabbi and says with gestures and tears, "don't kill me."[104] It is the calf himself who destabilizes the balance between ascendancy and kindness. The calf, we might say, challenges the plausibility of the kind of humane subject that would say to it, "for this you were created." Judah ha-Nasi's response to the calf reveals a failure to give sufficient attention to the principle of kindness, and, since kindness is in part what defines humanity, this failure threatens the full humanity of Judah ha-Nasi. The calf interrupts a certain deployment of the humane subject that occurs silently every time an animal is led to slaughter for human consumption. The undercover video of AgriProcessors—which allows animals to "testify" themselves through their sounds and bodily movements—accomplishes something similar to what the calf does in the story of Judah ha-Nasi: all of these animals confront us, face us, and demand response.

The undercover video made and continues to make present what is normally hidden from view and disavowed—namely, the fact that in contemporary industrial slaughterhouses animals are regularly treated in ways most people would deem monstrous. The video functions as a kind of conduit for the charge that has always adhered to a suffering animal fighting for its life. The video makes the force of that charge present, collapsing what is normally a carefully guarded distance between the eater of meat and the slaughterhouse. We could argue, in fact, that bridging this distance—taking its viewers virtually into the slaughterhouse and in front of suffering animals—is the video's most salient function.

Political scientist Timothy Pachirat recently conducted a remarkable ethnography in an industrial slaughterhouse in the Great Plains of the United States, a (nonkosher) slaughterhouse using much of the same technology and methodology as AgriProcessors, by going undercover as an employee for roughly six months. The book Pachirat produced about this work, *Every Twelve Seconds* (a reference to the speed of the slaughter line at this plant), aims "to provoke reflection on how distance and concealment operate as mechanisms of power in modern society. . . . taking the contemporary slaughterhouse as an exemplary instance."[105] Pachirat's study, like this book, aims to make visible the manner in which the modern slaughterhouse represents, reinforces, and reproduces particular systems of meaning.

> Like its more self-evidently political analogues—the prison, the hospital, the nursing home, the psychiatric ward, the refugee camp, the detention center, the interrogation room, the execution chamber, the extermination camp—the modern industrialized slaughterhouse is a "zone of confinement," a "segregated and isolated territory," in the words of sociologist Zygmunt Bauman, "invisible" and "on the whole inaccessible to ordinary members of society." Close attention to how the work of industrialized killing is performed might thus illuminate not only how the realities of industrialized animal slaughter are made tolerable but the ways distance and concealment operate in analogous social processes. . . . Such scrutiny makes it possible, as social theorist Pierre Bourdieu puts it, "to think in a completely astonished and disconcerted way about things [we] thought [we] had always understood."[106]

The technologically achieved distance and concealment of the slaughterhouse make it possible to do what would otherwise be too dissonant with our understanding of humanity, of our "nature." "Once armed with sophisticated technical and conceptual products of modern civilization," argues Zygmunt Bauman, "men can do things their nature would otherwise prevent them from doing."[107] Or perhaps distance and concealment play an essential role in a plausibility structure that allows us to hold that our "nature" is one thing even while our behavior would suggest (even to ourselves, were we to look) that it is another. By federal law, the Humane Methods of Slaughter Act, all cattle slaughter in the U.S. must be "humane." We the people are humane, says the law, *precisely when we eat meat*. This is a myth of particular power for American Jews and surely other communities as well.

What happens, however, when the myth can no longer be plausibly narrated—when structures of distancing and concealment fail and the "forbidden, something that should not be said" is uttered?[108] In the bridging of the distance between the Jewish public and industrial kosher slaughter, the undercover video made untenable the idea that those who consume kosher meat are both ascendant *and* kind. For Jews all over the United States and in Israel, the video exposed a "public secret" that cut to the very meaning of their humanity.[109] Animal cries and grimaces and attempts to escape communicate. Their suffering and the surge of compassion that their suffering can elicit are, as Derrida has argued (perhaps here following a longer lineage of subversive Jewish thinkers), paradigmatically undeniable.

RESPONDING WITH A REVERENCE FOR LIFE ETHIC   Faced with the implausibility of the humane subject that kosher slaughter was supposed to embed in the act of eating, many Jews expressed feelings of shame, shock, or discomfort and responded by attempting to reestablish the plausibility of the humane subject they had thought was operative. *Stop AgriProcessors from doing these horrible deeds*, they insisted. *Institute measures to ensure humane slaughter and therefore ensure that we can be humane while continuing to eat meat.* They issued a call to emphasize reverence for life—at least for now, at least a bit more. In this regard I think especially of the response of a large part of the Conservative movement's leadership (although by no means the whole of it). I think, for example, of the statement issued by the president of the Conservative movement's Rabbinical Assembly, quoted earlier, that argued PETA had provided a "welcome, though unfortunate service to the Jewish community" and that AgriProcessors "must answer to the Jewish community, and ultimately, to God."[110] I think of Conservative rabbi Adam Frank, who, responding to the AgriProcessors abuses, editorialized in the *Jerusalem Post,* "Judaism is characterized by many laws that give humanity dominion over animals while, at the same time, protecting defenseless living creatures from needless cruelty at the hands of people. It would be ironic if kashrut, which historically represented a breathtaking ethical advance in the relationship between people and animals, were to be seen as indifferent to calls to become as ethical as it can and must be." Or, more institutionally, we could consider the entire creation of the movement's ethical certification program, Magen Tzedek.

Other voices were more radical and suggested that a viable humane subject could only be restored by a vegetarian diet—that is, an even more intensified ethic of reverence for life. Here we might consider the responses of the maverick Orthodox rabbi Irving Greenberg; Rabbi David Wolpe, the senior rabbi at Temple Sinai, one of the largest Conservative synagogues in the country; and National Jewish Book Award winner Jonathan Safran Foer. All three proposed vegetarianism as a response to AgriProcessors in a video released by Foer.[111] My own personal (rather than the present scholarly) response is quite close to Foer, Greenberg, and Wolpe.[112]

RESPONDING WITH A HYPERDOMINIONIST ETHIC   Whether one agrees with either of these responses (an argument for improving the regulation of meat consumption, on the one hand, or vegetarianism, on the other), they are, I think, the easier positions to understand. At least for people likely to be reading this book, it is the position of those who defended AgriProcessors that will look strange and demand analysis. Why, as detailed in chapter 2, did so many and *do* so many Orthodox leaders defend AgriProcessors, given the now undeniable documentation of its wrongdoings? Why is Shlomo Rubashkin, barely having made a dent in his twenty-seven-year prison sentence, being made a hero? Songs and videos have been composed about the tragedy of his downfall, and he has literally been put on posters alongside historically important Jews in some Orthodox day schools (not as a great penitent, but simply as a great man).[113] Oddly, it appears that PETA and their vegan ways actually continue to figure as an important cause of Rubashkin's downfall in the minds of at least some Haredi American Jews, perhaps the majority. In this Haredi narrative PETA, motivated by anti-Semitism, brings down the just Rubashkin, who, if he did do anything inappropriate (which some will readily acknowledge), surely did not do anything more than was common in such circumstances. PETA, its calls for better regulation of the slaughterhouse under the auspices of Temple Grandin and for vegetarianism, is figured as the enemy; Rubashkin is figured as the righteous Jew. If the humane subject is, as I have argued, a common structure, what kind of humane subject is being embraced?

There are many complex factors that figured into the defense of AgriProcessors by the vast majority of institutional Orthodox leadership, including historically well-grounded (if also unfounded) fears of anti-Semitic motivation, the considerable political clout of AgriProcessors, the very significant economic interests at stake, and fears of an interruption in the kosher meat

supply. However, this study is concerned with a deeper current of influence.[114] Put simply, this deeper influence is the manner in which kosher law
and Orthodox Jewish views of animals more generally are bound to particular visions of humanity and ethics—bound to particular humane subjects.

The rules of discourse propagated by the structure of this humane subject
require constant assertion of both human superiority over and obligations
to animals, thus different value systems will be articulated not by denying
human obligations to animals or dominion over them, but in the nuances
of emphasis. Attending to the humane subject helps to better understand
the implications of the various discourses on kashrut by focusing us on the
variations that appear within the relatively stable structure of the humane
subject.

The vast majority of Orthodox leaders, in their defense of AgriProcessors, both devalued the relevance of ethics to kashrut in general and amplified ascendancy.[115] In numerous popular press articles and official statements, we saw that Orthodox leadership professed their commitment to the
Jewish value of treating animals with compassion as well as reasserting the
moral gulf between humans and animals. We would now expect to find both
sentiments, and the mere fact that both are affirmed is so common that it
alone tells us almost nothing about the particular stance Orthodox leadership expresses. For our purposes, the meaning inheres not in the assertion
of ascendancy or of kindness but in whether the discourse *heightens or di-
minishes* ascendancy or kindness in the context in which it is deployed. In
the institutional Orthodox response to the 2004 undercover video detailed
in chapter 2, the right of AgriProcessors to treat animals the way it did was
almost beyond question. After all, the responses of the dominant Orthodox leadership suggested, *is this not the end for which animals are created?*
Moreover, public calls for a *more* merciful approach to God's creatures in the
form of improved slaughter processes (or any other concrete recommen-
dations) were, as we saw, all but totally absent in institutional Orthodoxy.
Quite plainly, institutional Orthodox leadership advanced what I have called
a dominionist ethic.

Much more important, this dominionist ethic is being advocated at a
moment in time when the subordination of food animals to human power
has reached a height unprecedented in agricultural history. Recall that the
strongest rebuke for the mistreatment of animals was the unofficial, oral observation made by the OU's executive vice president, Rabbi Tzvi Hersh Wein-

reb, that the second cut was "especially inhumane."[116] Animals languishing for minutes and being shocked in the face with electric prods earned no direct comment. In contrast, Grandin, whom no one could accuse of being unfamiliar with the imperfect operations of slaughterhouses, used perhaps the strongest language of her thirty-year career to condemn what she saw on PETA's video.[117] A spokesperson from Shechita UK, a British group that defends religious slaughter, said to the *New York Times* after watching the video with a rabbi and a British *shochet* "that he 'felt queasy,' and added, 'I do not know what that is, but it's not *shechita.*'"[118] Both the *New York Times* and the *Washington Post* chose the word *grisly* for the headline description of the video. Amidst responses of this vigor and strength, Rabbi Weinreb's belated suggestion that the second cut was "especially inhumane," which under different circumstances might have been a strong rebuke, is barely audible as a criticism. Weinreb's statement, in fact—and this is the counterintuitive conclusion that attending to the humane subject helps us see—functions in this context precisely as part of the defense of AgriProcessors. (A conclusion that I suspect would alarm Weinreb, who I have no doubt was personally sincere in his distaste for this cruelty.) His weak acknowledgment was a move forced by the discourse structured by the humane subject; it is analogous to the scripted statements of thanks or apology that all of us have become used to having read to us by paid employees of corporations. I am not claiming any knowledge of what was going on inside Weinreb's conscience, but merely arguing that, within its context, his statement did not inspire contrition but complacency.

To advance a dominionist ethic is one thing; to do so in the context of the contemporary American kosher slaughter industry is another thing. Despite the documentation that AgriProcessors was systematically dismembering conscious animals, despite the exceptionally rare fact that their procedures received enormous critical public exposure, despite the USDA's own conclusion that the Humane Methods of Slaughter Act was violated, despite the USDA's further conclusion that its employees received inappropriate gifts from AgriProcessors, and despite the legal pressure of a well-funded animal protection group, *nothing was ever done to penalize AgriProcessors for its treatment of animals*. It is in a social context where the systematic dismemberment of animals for years on end (during the watch of government and religious authorities) does not require *any* sanctions that a dominionist ethic has been championed. What does this mean?

Part of the answer lies in the fact that some Orthodox groups correctly perceived that, even though the actual changes PETA and other animal protection groups sought in the slaughterhouse were minor, PETA exposed the abuses at the slaughterhouse in part to raise bigger social questions about the treatment of animals. PETA had pragmatic aims for reforming AgriProcessors that ultimately were acceptable to many in the Orthodox community. (For example, as mentioned earlier, Rabbi Genack actively worked in the end to bring Grandin to AgriProcessors, which was PETA's suggestion years before they conducted their investigation.) However, the exposure of AgriProcessors was motivated by more than the modest aims animal protection advocates attempted to achieve in the short term for animals; the exposure of AgriProcessors was also a defense of the human capacity to show compassion for all life and a call to remember it. PETA and many of the other (frequently Jewish) animal advocates involved were deploying a radically different understanding of the humane subject. AgriProcessors, Agudath Israel of America, and, to a lesser extent, the OU ultimately defended what we might name a *hyperdominionist* ethic in which—at the moment when animal agriculture has magnified the intensity and scale of animal suffering in unprecedented ways—the Jewish legal tradition of compassion for animals is functionally nullified even as it is professed.

This defense of AgriProcessors is helpfully understood as part of a larger commitment to the construction of a particular instantiation of the humane subject. The defense of AgriProcessors was experienced as (and indeed was) a defense of an identity. An important consequence of this insight is that the domination of animals, even to the point of causing animals agonizing deaths, is less an unwanted side effect of a desire for tasty flesh or economic gain than it is a ritual support for a particular way of being human. Although couched in rather different terms, and with obviously different intent, I think the same basic understanding I am advocating here—that is, that PETA's video was experienced as an existential threat, a salvo in a *war*—is articulated by a prominent Haredi Orthodox defender of AgriProcessors, Rabbi Avi Shafran, the director of public affairs for Agudath Israel of America. In an article entitled "The PETA Principle," Rabbi Shafran suggests that the real conflict is not about better treatment of animals but a broader clash between animal rights activists who espouse what he calls "the PETA principle" and rabbinic authorities.[119] Shafran's characterization of PETA in "The PETA Principle" is not accurate, but, like any good solider in wartime, I doubt mischaracterizing the enemy troubles him very much.[120] However inaccurate, Shafran's understanding of PETA is a telling depiction of the fears that many Orthodox Jewish voices seem to have, fears that Shafran deftly cultivates. Sounding as if he has just read over Albo's midrash on Cain's murder of Abel, Rabbi Shafran explains that "the folks at People for the Ethical Treatment of Animals . . . object to all killing of animals . . . because of their belief . . . that animals are no different from humans. . . . Indeed, the 'PETA Principle,' the moral equating of animals and humans, is an affront to the very essence of Jewish belief, which exalts the human being, alone among G-d's creations. . . . That distinction is introduced in Genesis, where the first man is commanded to 'rule over' the animal world."[121] This statement by Rabbi Shafran is both representative of the popular attitude of Orthodox Jews toward PETA and an excellent illustration of my basic point. Shafran articulates *explicitly* what is always present more subtly in the debates around AgriProcessors's abuse: the fear that acknowledging the legitimacy of AgriProcessors' critics will uproot the foundations of particular Orthodox Jewish understandings of humanity and ethics. Shafran strikes back accordingly with a series of maneuvers: (1) emphasizing further the already robust denial of the relevance of ethics to kashrut, (2) obfuscating and misrepresenting those asking for different treatment of animals, (3) ominously warning of an existential threat to "the very essence of Jewish belief," and (4) emphasizing the absolute right of "man" (the lack of gender-inclusive language in Shafran's statement is symptomatic) to use the nonhuman as he sees fit.

In recognizing that these maneuvers are confrontations in a larger war, the charge of AgriProcessors and the peculiar defenses of the indefensible that it enjoined become legible. At stake in this theater is not only the humanity of our treatment of animals, but the very production of a gendered, racialized humanity.[122] In fact, we can go further than this: the final force of this analysis is to highlight the limits of analyzing situations like the AgriProcessors controversies, as did the popular press, under the assumption that the human is a fixed entity and that these scandals are about how this said human should behave. Rather, the scandals at AgriProcessors, powered by a video that allowed animals a voice when they were supposed to be silent, menaced the very machine that produces "the human." The Orthodox sensitivity to and concern with this menace (voiced explicitly by Shafran) helps make intelligible why AgriProcessors had to, for so many in the Orthodox world, be defended despite its improprieties.

HUMANE SUBJECTS AND THE STUDY OF RELIGION

As the analysis of AgriProcessors reaches completion, let us ask how the sort of inquiry into the humane subject that I have conducted here might be valuable in the larger task of understanding religion. One of this study's aims has been to make the familiar strange. By redescribing familiar Jewish texts and practices as vehicles for reproducing the humane subject (as subsystems of Agamben's anthropological machine), I have attempted to illumine unexpected features of them, such as the important role that animals play in human self-conception. At the same time, while I have not sought to make them more palatable, I have sought to make certain features of the discourse surrounding AgriProcessors and the ethics of eating animals that many experience as strange more familiar—for example, the idea that vegetarianism leads to murder, the defense of what appears as indefensible animal abuse, the making of "Saint" Rubashkin, and the insistence that animal advocates see no difference between humans and animals. More pointedly, however, I wish to suggest three reasons that the structure of the humane subject, whatever it is called, deserves our attention in and perhaps outside of Jewish traditions.

First, attention to the structure of the humane subject helps clarify *how* Jewish texts and dietary practices can function in tandem to construct and perpetuate particular visions of the human and ethics, thus allowing better understanding of the meaning-making functions of these religious activities. It is widely acknowledged in Jewish studies and food studies that *food practices* reveal social dynamics, but the important role that *animal lives* play in this process is often forgotten. The animal is often the hidden generator that produces the meanings that are passed along in kosher practice, and the analytic of the humane subject helps make this visible. Second, attention to these constructions of the humane subject highlights how addressing questions about the kind of being we are inevitably is bound up with ethical questions and, conversely, how confronting ethical dilemmas often raises questions about subjectivity and identity. All are torsions in the same knot. The question of being and the question of being ethical are coprimordial. The third point, which is also of special interest to animal studies, relates to the manner in which attention to the humane subject exposes the intimate interconnections between our constructions of gender, race, animality, and otherness—something this book has only begun to trace, but that the analysis presented here invites. In sum, first point: animals, especially those we eat, are integral to human self-imagination; second point: ethics and subjectivity are coimagined and coprimordial aspects of self; third point: the question of the animal is also and inherently a question about gender, race, and otherness (not to mention technology, the machine, modernity, and so on). It is in connection with these last two points that I wish in closing to return to Derrida and, by way of him, to Genesis.

In Derrida's reading of Genesis in *The Animal That Therefore I Am*, man is called into being in his act of calling out the names of animals—an act he performs without woman. "God lets *Ish* call the other living things all on his own,[123] give them their names in his own name, these animals that are older and younger than him, these living things that came into the world before him but were named after him, on his initiative according to the second narrative. In both cases, man is in both senses of the world after the animal. He follows him. This 'after,' that determines a sequence, a consequence, or a persecution, is not in time, nor is it temporal; it is the very genesis of time [la genèse même du temps]" (17[268])."[124] There is something, Derrida confesses, that has "always made me dizzy" about the primordial event of naming between man and the animal. There is a circularity here in which human and animal co-construct each other—a dizzying circularity. We follow the animal not just in the sense of hunting the animal, but we follow the animal ontologically. This ontological sense in which the human follows the animal is "not in time, nor is it temporal" because we are dealing here with "the very genesis of time"—that is to say, the moment that the human subject is born. Yet this moment of birth is also a moment of despotic naming; it not only hews the world into subjects and objects but also articulates a taxonomy that constitutes, to use the phrasing of Bruce Lincoln, a tyranny.[125]

The construct of the humane subject can be used to condition a type of ethical absentmindedness toward animals that reinforces or even helps constitute other forms of prejudice such as racism, sexism, and homophobia. The presence of actual animals and the reality of their suffering recede before us to become the monstrosity of "the animal"—that is, the animal-in-general, the animal-as-construct. Thus, as I have emphasized, AgriProcessors and its defenders almost invariably asserted a commitment to compassion for the animal, effectively turning our gaze away from the reality of how animals were actually being treated and toward a well-entrenched story where the imagination of "the animal" and concern for animals are pressed into the service of defining a humane subject, a mensch. When the reality of animals becomes "the animal"—that is, a foil and shadow of the human—an opportunity arises, which may or may not be actualized, to forget animals themselves.[126] This type of violence by way of generalizations, I would emphasize, is made as often in regard to nonhuman animals as it is made in regard to oppressed human groups, particularly groups marginalized through the construction of race and gender.[127]

This last observation about the way in which indifference to human and nonhuman animal others is bound together opens an entire additional subject of inquiry—an intensely uncomfortable inquiry. While it is commonplace in discussions of animal protection to link, albeit insufficiently and often naively, animal abuse with mistreatment of vulnerable human populations, and while the pragmatic value of the connection is commonly used by law enforcement and social service agencies to identify child abuse, spousal abuse, violent pathology, and organized crime,[128] the post-2004 documentation of systematic human rights abuses perpetrated by AgriProcessors against non-Jews has been discussed as if it were totally unrelated to their mistreatment of animals. For example, as the Conservative movement articulated its standards for its nascent Magen Tzedek program, the point was frequently made that the focus would be first on human rights abuses and only secondarily on animal protection—as if the two concerns were competing interests rather than torsions in the same knot, as if being forced to cause or watch animals suffer unnecessarily had nothing to do with the unpleasantness of the slaughterhouse for workers, and as if we did not know that attitudes toward the superiority of humans over animals have been from the rabbinic period forward consistently associated with parallel attitudes toward the superiority of men over women ("'master her' to teach you that the male masters the female") and of Jews over non-Jews ("You are called '*adam*,' but idolaters are not called '*adam*'").[129] Can it really be a coincidence, for example, that of the three Jewish constituencies in which we can trace a clear institutional response to the 2004 video—Haredi Orthodoxy, Modern Orthodoxy, and Conservative Judaism—Haredi Orthodoxy, which is the community that is most insular and most resistant to feminist ideas of the three, was also the most indifferent to the violence perpetrated against animals while the Conservative movement, which is the least insular and the most progressive on women's issues of the three, was the swiftest to condemn it? Proving this link beyond any doubt may be impossible (at least if the question is asked in a certain manner), but the alternative proposition that views of humanity, animality, race, and gender are totally unrelated leads to absurdity.

These are questions that call for further analysis, and it is in opening these questions that I conclude the present study. In arguing that the responses to the incidents at AgriProcessors recorded in 2004 are best understood through a consideration of the "humane subjects" they instantiate, I suggest that we give greater attentiveness to the symbolic and more-than-symbolic ways in which attitudes toward and treatment of animals, women, and other Others are linked in the depths of Jewish religiosity (and perhaps Abrahamic religiosity as such). We would do well to ask if a structure of subjectivity that makes it acceptable to kill animals while understanding oneself as kind to them may also enable men to dominate women and Jews to demean non-Jews while understanding themselves as equally kind. As Agamben has argued, the "ceaseless divisions and caesurae" between human and animal are "the decisive political conflict, which governs every other conflict" and even the human relation with the divine might depend "on that darker one which separates us from the animal."[130] "It is more urgent to work on these divisions," advises Agamben, "than it is to take positions on the great issues of so called human rights and values."[131] Agamben's advice resounds as much in a philosophical and scholarly register as it does in a political one, for in Agamben's work, as in the present one, the point of understanding is not *simply* understanding but pragmatic change.

It is worth pausing over the biographical and historical context of Agamben's striking analysis: Agamben's oeuvre has intended to and in fact been widely used to interrogate the intellectual mechanics of the Nazi death camps, the American government's use of torture, and other atrocities. Yet Agamben here directs us away from such attention to the human, and what he almost disdainfully calls "human rights and values," *if* it elides attention to the animal. "Perhaps concentration and extermination camps are," Agamben ventures "an extreme and monstrous attempt to decide between the human and the inhuman, which has ended up dragging the very possibility of the distinction to its ruin."[132]

Agamben is not the first to note the uncomfortable link between how we think and treat animals and how the modern death camp was envisioned and executed. In a largely overlooked passage in one of the most famous analyses of the Shoah, Zygmunt Bauman's chapter, "The Uniqueness and Normality of the Holocaust," Bauman observes that, "through the spectacles of modern power 'mankind' seems so omnipotent and its individual members so 'incomplete,' inept and submissive, and so much in need of improvement, that treating people as . . . cattle to be bred does not look fanciful or morally odious. One of the earliest and principal ideologists of German National Socialism, R. W. Darré, took the practices of animal husbandry as the pattern of 'population policy' to be implemented by the future *volkish* government."[133] In J. M. Coetzee's novel *Elisabeth Costello*, the heroine of the title, who often seems to speak for Coetzee himself, points to the imaginal rather than practical-policy dimension of National Socialism's animalization of the Jew and other others:

> The question to ask should not be: do we have something in common—reason, self-consciousness, a soul—with other animals? (With the corollary that, if we do not, then we are entitled to treat them as we like, imprisoning them, killing them, dishonouring their corpses.) I return to the death camps. The particular horror of the death camps, the horror that convinces us that what went on their was a crime against humanity, is not that despite a humanity shared with their victims, the killers treated them like lice. That is too abstract. The horror is that the killers refused to think themselves into the place of their victims, as did everyone else. They said, 'it is *they* in those cattle cars rattling past.' They did not say, 'How would it be if it were I in that cattle car?'"[134]

For Coetzee, like Agamben, the true horror of the camp is not, as often thought, that humans were treated like animals and that the line between the violable animal and inviolable human broke down. Rather the true horror is rooted precisely in the drawing of this line "between the human and the inhuman," a line that despite its scientific veneer is more fundamentally a "practical and political mystery" separating those beings for whom (whether they differ by species or human community) we will have empathy and those beings for whom we will not.[135]

If we find there are profound limits to our ability to change the deeper structures of sexism and racism, this study suggests that it is because we sometimes focus on the tip of an iceberg. The broader religious structuring of the human relationship with the rest of creation—a relationship worked out today vividly in the question of animal food—constrains our ability to reimagine gender and race, us and them. If we actively defend something like the present articulation of the human/animal binary, we constrain our ability to rethink the other binaries to which it is linked. Trimming back the relatively small part of a weed that is above ground will not eliminate it if one is simultaneously fertilizing its roots.

Perhaps we should "no longer . . . seek new—more effective or more authentic—articulations" of the human in contrast to "the animal" and instead confront what Agamben characterizes as "the central emptiness, the hiatus that—within man—separates man and animal, and to risk ourselves in this emptiness: the suspension of the suspension, Shabbat of both animal and man."[136] What would happen if we entered this darkness that stands before an infinitely deferred dawn, a darkness that precedes the division of the world into human and animal?

What would it mean if we paused, put to rest, or let go of the categories animal and human? As Calarco maintains, "any genuine encounter with what we call animals will occur only from within the space of this surrender."[137] The question of eating animals—both whether we should and, if so, how—matters and matters profoundly in and of itself because animals matter in and of themselves. The question of eating animals also matters because it simultaneously shapes the gendered and racialized world in which we live in pragmatic, macroeconomic, and symbolic ways. In the depths of the religious dimension of existence, who *we* are is bound to who *they* are: who animals are.

It is not a matter of doing away with differences and taxonomies, as if that were even possible, but rather a matter of taking diversely differing differentiations into account within experiential fields and "a world of life forms, and of doing that without reducing this differentiated and multiple difference."[138] I do not suggest that we pay less attention to the differences between the "vast heterogeneity of presences"[139] with whom we share the substrate of life, but rather more—enough attention so that the hierarchical binaries human and animal, male and female, white and black, civilized and primitive, and us and them fade before the demands of the undeniable that proceeds them all: the "possibility of giving vent to a surge of compassion, even if it is then misunderstood, repressed or denied, held at bay."[140]

Impossible though it may be, the final hope of this book is to return to the clearing that precedes the animal. If we are patient, if we can slip past the gears of the anthropological machine, if we can sacrifice sacrifice, we may sense ourselves seen by Others we cannot yet name. In this surrender, the phenomena we name religion in the academy and in the public square will not look the same and the face of the religious actor may no longer be a human face.

Epilogue

"The first decision I made had no direct bearing on religion, but to me it represented a religious decision" explains Joseph Shapiro, a character in Isaac Bashevis Singer's novel, *The Penitent*.[1] In the world of the novel, Joseph is a penitent—a *baal teshuvah*, the Hebrew phrase for a nonreligious Jew who becomes observant of traditional Jewish law. Joseph is telling his life story to what is presented to us as Singer himself, whom Joseph meets at the Wailing Wall, the only surviving remnant of the ancient Jerusalem temple and its once constant rhythm of animal sacrifice. Joseph's ambiguously religious decision is "to eat no more meat or fish, nothing that had ever lived and been killed for food."[2] Joseph's vegetarian practice rejects the more common way to observe a kosher diet in which, following rabbinic teaching, eating animals slaughtered according to Jewish law harks back to ancient blood sacrifice. For Singer's Joseph, this decision to eschew meat is, on the one hand, a response to his compassion for the vulnerable and oppressed, and, on the other, part of his return to Orthodox Judaism. "*Baal teshuvah* means one who returns [to Judaism]," Joseph explains, "I came home."[3]

Why does Singer conjure this character, who, in his heart, believes his refusal to eat meat is essentially religious—"to me it represented a religious decision"—but concedes that, as far as other people are concerned, his decision "had no direct bearing on religion"? Anyone familiar with Singer's real-life commitment to a vegetarian diet will realize that Joseph seems in part to voice Singer's own sentiments.[4] Joseph continues,

> Everything that had to do with slaughtering, skinning, and hunting always evoked disgust within me and guilt feelings that words cannot describe. I sometimes thought that even if a voice from Heaven decreed the slaughter of animals and the shedding of their blood to be a virtue, I would respond like that *Tanna* [early Rabbi] who said, "We don't care about voices from Heaven." As you can see, I've turned back to Jewishness, but even among the pious I live with, I've remained a kind of misfit.[5]

Joseph's coreligionists, he tells us, issue a rather curious rebuke to his chosen diet: "They often reproach me, 'You needn't be more saintly than the saints. You must not pity creatures more than the Almighty does.'"[6] It's a rebuke that simultaneously critiques and elevates Joseph's abstinence from animal food, a rebuke configured as contorted praise. What does it mean to be "more saintly" and why is that bad? Exactly what is the nature of the disagreement between Joseph and his detractors? These questions raised by Singer's literary imagination echo questions this book has raised in responding to the AgriProcessors events and their aftermath. *Just what is the nature of the tension between those who, on the one hand, defend or obfuscate an interwoven violence against both animals and animalized humans and those who, on the other hand, oppose such violence?* This question is as resonant in the Jewish community as it is in American, indeed Western, culture more generally. In the microcosm of Joseph Shapiro and the tension between his compassion and the religious mainstream, Singer presents to us no less than a figuration of the religious dimension of animal-human relations in modernity.

Joseph tells his story at the site of ancient blood sacrifice, sacrifices that traditional Jews pray will return in the daily Hebrew liturgy.[7] Joseph, by contrast, laments that killing and consuming animals remains, long after these formal sacrifices have ceased, a kind of religious obligation. Joseph finds his religion in refusing to do what dominant voices—even a certain anticipated divine voice—present as essential: eating animals. In this scene Singer suggests that the conflict between omnivore and vegetarian is a long-standing tension in Jewish traditions.[8] From the ancient temple whose ruins lay before Joseph to the modern state of Israel in which he recounts his tale, there is one kind of Jewish practitioner who sacrifices and eats animals and there is another, rarer kind that does not. We might say that there are those that feel accused by animals ("guilt feelings that words cannot describe") and those that do not. There are those who allow themselves to be confronted by animal suffering and those that malign such concern as excessive: "You must not pity creatures more than the Almighty does."[9] And, of course, there are those that fit somewhere between these two poles.

Note that Singer's character does not say "The first decision I made had no direct bearing on *Judaism*," but rather "The first decision I made had no direct bearing on *religion*." He does not say "but to me it represented a *Jewish* decision," but "to me it represented a *religious* decision." The text intimates that the conflict between an ethos that demands the consumption of animals, on the one hand, and another "misfit" ethical stance that refuses to sacrifice animals in this way is not only a Jewish conflict, but a larger religious conflict.

In doing so, Singer traces the same seam as Derrida when Derrida suggests that sacrifice is "a universal structure of [Abrahamic] religiosity."[10] For Derrida, we can recall, sacrifice and thus something fundamental about Abrahamic religion is rooted, first of all and paradoxically, in a move of *restraint*. The first gesture of sacrifice is to say "*we* must not be violated"—that is, we humans, or at least a certain kind of human (above all the virile, unblemished adult male) must not be violated. This restraint has a corollary: since *we* cannot be violated, *they* can be (more or less) violated to protect and sustain *us*. In this sacrificial logic, to eat meat is to assert the human's (or a certain kind of human's) inviolability. The dignity of the human is nourished by the shedding of animal blood.

As this book has argued, the line between meat eating and vegetarianism as well as the related line between defending modern industrial kosher meat production and critiquing it—both of which were sharpened in response to AgriProcessors—are battle lines separating different visions of the kind of being Jewish tradition asks Jews to be. I have described these different visions as various configurations of the *humane subject*—that is, different imaginations of an ethical human subject that is both ascendant over and similar in kind to animals (and other others). The humane subject can also be described as a tripartite structure within which *animal, human*, and *divine* serve as the main points of orientation. Like the plotting of a line in geometry, only two points of orientation are necessary to grasp the entirety of the line, thus I have rarely spoken here about God directly. Rather, the divine has been invoked as a natural efflux of plotting the human-animal relation:

in order to say that humans are ascendant above animals, I must explain that, in certain Jewish imaginations, this is so because God ordained it. As Agamben has argued, even the human relation with the divine depends "on that darker one which separates us from the animal."[11] The question that both Singer's Joseph and Derrida raise for us is this: does this tripartite animal-human-divine structure and its instantiation in meat eating play a broader role in religion as such, or at least in Abrahamic religions as such? In sum, is the structure I have theorized in the final chapter of this book as "the humane subject" distinctively Jewish, distinctively Abrahamic, or an even broader phenomena? Can, for example, the humane subject be found in the secular sphere?

THE HUMANE SUBJECT AS A RELIGIOUS STRUCTURE

The humane subject does not require that God or any source of ultimate meaning be explicitly mentioned for that source to be an inherent part of the structure's coherence. A secular person can speak about the distinction of the human (e.g., "human rights") and ethical obligations toward the sentient (e.g., "humane slaughter") to instantiate the humane subject without explicitly invoking the divine. However, plotting these two points (*human, animal*) of the structure of the humane subject always implies a third: some deeper ground of truth that gives ultimate meaning to a distinction between human and animal and sets them in proper relation. This authoritative ground—the *divine* in the Orthodox Jewish case—can also be imagined as the natural order itself without meaningfully changing the structure of the humane subject in terms of its social function. The humane subject has a multiplicity of guises.

All this is to say that the humane subject this book has found in Jewish texts could in theory be found in diverse religious traditions as well as in the secular sphere. It is, one could argue, implicit in U.S. laws like the Humane Methods of Slaughter Act and, as detailed in chapter 3, in the splitting of the natural and human sciences. In diverse contexts humans are propelled into the world through symbolic-and-real vertical relationships of ascendancy over animals and horizontal relationships of similarity in kind with them. There are versions of the humane subject that may first appear to have "no direct bearing on religion" but that nonetheless often represent values, self-imaginations, and life commitments that are best described as fundamentally religious.

When Joseph imagines his dietary choice as "religious," despite the opposition of his coreligionists, he is arguing that the meanings proliferated through meat eating symbolically and in actuality speak to the most fundamental issues of our existence. What Joseph conveys when he imagines that his decision appears to have "no direct bearing on religion" is not that it is without religious charge but rather that it releases, precisely, a religious charge that puts him in conflict with the religious *authorities* of his day and their imagination of the divine. As Joseph tells us, in making the decision to decline meat and fish, he has girded himself to defy even God, or at least a certain vision of God.

Most of the voices that responded to AgriProcessors were explicitly constructed as "religious" in the U.S. and Israeli media. Jews, as Jews, either defended or critiqued AgriProcessors. Scriptures were cited and explicitly religious ethical mandates were invoked. The conflict over AgriProcessors is explicitly a conflict between religious orientations, but what Singer and Derrida give us to think is that even had the chief actors not spoken *explicitly* in the name of religion, even if no scripture had been cited and no historically religious ethical mandates invoked, we perhaps still would have before us a religious conflict. That is, conflicts over the ethics of eating animals, despite their often demeaning popular configuration as lifestyles or personal quirks, are usually best viewed as religious. They are religious conflicts not in the sense of being explicitly tied to historical religious traditions (though this is often the case) but because they are conflicts about the kind of beings we are, about the stories we should tell our children about who they are, about how human society ought to orient itself in the larger drama of the living, about the nature of ultimate concerns, and about how we should encounter, conjure, and dwell within worlds shot-through with meaning.

I hypothesize that Americans who protest the endemic cruelty of modern industrial farming and those who embrace it, no less than the rabbis who defended AgriProcessors and those who were its critics, are acting on a religious stage. This is to say that understanding modern debates around both the treatment of farmed animals and the more basic question of whether we should eat animals are best understood, at least in many cases, not as some recently popular lifestyle or a decades-old "movement," but as persistent and camouflaged conflicts of religion—cross-cultural human conflicts best viewed in the *longue durée* of the history of religions.

This book has situated the views expressed by both Jewish supporters and critics of AgriProcessors within the history of the long-standing tension within Judaism between the human right to rule creation like a king and the consanguinity of the animate (between ascendancy and kindness). This tension and the humane subject it generates are likely as foundational in the secular modern Western imagination as in the Jewish or Christian imagination. Had we more time, it would in fact be easy to show that the kind of hyperdominionist ethos defended in defending AgriProcessors is also a major force in the allegedly secular sphere. Consider, for example, new "ag-gag" laws in the United States that would, through various strategies, restrict current understandings of freedom of press and speech to render it illegal to produce, distribute, or, in some proposals, even possess an undercover video like the one PETA produced of incidents at AgriProcessors.[12] That is, ag-gag laws would in practice (if not in legalistic detail) argue that those who raise animals for food should be exempt from the normal vagaries of media investigations and public critiques; they, as the producers of meat, should be inviolable. These laws, extremely unpopular with the general public, imply that there should be one standard of free speech for (almost) all Americans, and another for those Americans that critique animal agriculture. Now passed in nine states,[13] these laws functionally prioritize the right of those who treat animals as things (often elites empowered through corporate structures) over the rights of those motivated about a concern for sentient life. Ag-gag laws target those humans who would stand with animals and bring animals' absent presences into view, and at the center of the crosshairs are those individuals conducting undercover investigations. These laws also reinforce a broader social impulse to hide slaughter from view. "This is the logic that maps contemporary industrialized slaughterhouses," Pachirat concludes after critically analyzing his six months of undercover work at a nonkosher Midwestern abattoir: "to enable us to eat meat without the killers or the killing, without even—insofar as the smell, the manure, and the other components of organic life are concerned—*the animals themselves*."[14] When one considers the massive impact of the 2004 PETA video of AgriProcessors documented in this book—merely one example of undercover videos functioning to bring animal abuse into view—one can see why agribusiness corporations subscribing to a hyperdominionist ethos would see these videos in general as an existential threat.

My own suspicion is that a more thorough contextualization of AgriProcessors, not in the Jewish context, as this book has done, but rather in the American context, would show that the aberrant extreme of the dominionist

ethos represented by the defense of AgriProcessors flows less from narrowly
Jewish trajectories and more from the ethos of U.S.-style industrialization
with which modern kosher practice has become saturated. Ironically, the
kosher meat system embraced by Orthodox Jews, is, in this sense, highly
assimilationist—it has fully assimilated with the external demands of industrial slaughter. The apparent strangeness of the creation of the most extensive kosher system the world has ever known, usually a marker of Jewish
difference, in the very place—contemporary America—where the forces of
assimilation are strongest can be easily enough explained: the kosher meat
system, now a fully industrial system, represents a variation on assimilation,
not an anomalous exception to it.[15]

If this supposition is correct, the conflict between the Jewish voices that
defended and critiqued AgriProcessors is not ultimately a Jewish conflict—
that is, not *only* a Jewish conflict. Rather, as Derrida suggested, this conflict
pervades the sacrificial logic of Abrahamic religiosity; it is "a war . . . waged
between, on the one hand, those who violate not only animal life but even
and also this sentiment of compassion, and, on the other hand, those who
appeal for an irrefutable testimony to this pity."[16] And the preferred theater
for this war of religion is the practice of eating meat.

"Belief in human dominion does not merely legitimate meat eating,"
writes Nick Fiddes in his masterful study of the symbolic power of meat, "the
reverse is also true: meat reinforces that presumption. Killing, cooking, and
eating others animals' flesh provides perhaps the ultimate authentication of
human superiority over the rest of nature. . . . Meat has long stood for Man's
proverbial 'muscle' over the natural world."[17] Surveying a range of cultural
contexts, but focusing on the contemporary UK, Fiddes's study demonstrates the inadequacy of explanations for the frequency and popularity of
meat eating that point to taste, economics, or health.[18] "Such common-sense
beliefs must be questioned," he argues, "since what seems natural fact to us,
in our particular society, at this particular time, is exposed as mere cultural
orthodoxy when set against the range of beliefs and practices of other societies and in history."[19] As our engagement with Ingold showed, even a brief
attempt to apprehend the world in the manner hunter-gatherers do will il-
luminate the cultural specificity of the border we use to divide human and
animal (for these cultures often have nothing resembling this sacred border). For Fiddes, meat eating generally is more about meaning making than
anything else, and what the present study has found in the particular case

of contemporary American Jews confirms his more general thesis. Meat is meaning become flesh.

Going further, Fiddes argues that "the slaughter of sentient creatures is not just a (perhaps regrettable) necessity in producing a valuable foodstuff. Bloodshed is central to meat's value."[20] As Derrida has it, "The subject does not want just to master and possess nature actively. In our cultures, he accepts sacrifice and eats flesh."[21] Fiddes continues: "Indeed, the visible domination of other creatures is so important that cruelty is widely reputed to be *necessary*."[22] This, too, is a conclusion that our study of AgriProcessors would tend to affirm. Of course, this is rarely spoken as such. We prefer to consciously think of ourselves as humane, as dominant and yet still kind. If we do something cruel, it is "necessary" and thus not really cruel at all. Yet, in moments of crisis like the AgriProcessors scandals, Fiddes's more disquieting thesis can gain credibility: recall that Orthodox Union representatives both acknowledged the cruelty of AgriProcessors and continued to actively promote its products as fully kosher.[23]

The hypothesis I am unfolding is that eating meat today, eating it selectively, and even refusing to eat it are all what scholars of religion might call mythological activities, religious activities. Eating meat is always accompanied with narratives, always embodied in flesh, and always helps tell the story of where we came from and who we are. Myths bridge the microcosm of the everyday realities that constitute our lives, like eating, with the macroscopic issues of meaning that are woven into the human heart, like the macrocosm of human power over so much of the sentient life of this planet. As Doniger expresses it, "Myths form a bridge between the terrifying abyss of cosmological ignorance and our comfortable familiarity with our recurrent, if tormenting, human problems."[24] It is through myths about eating animals and myths uttered silently through eating animals that we negotiate the macro question inherent in being born into the kind of societies we now inhabit: *How should we respond to this inheritance of power over the living that we exercise constantly throughout our lives?* We don't, of course, sit there with our burgers—whether beef or veggie—and say aloud, "I will now instantiate a particular view of the human, the animal, and the divine by (not) eating this animal that has been killed and processed in such-and-such a way." We *can't* do this. We simply aren't the kind of being that can spend its moments consciously confronting these macro issues that are, nonetheless, constantly confronting us.

We can't live our lives if we think only about the galaxies, or the Nazis, or the children who are dying of starvation or disease or gunshot wounds on the streets of our own cities as well as in wars and famines throughout the world. We can't think about those things for long because we are human and we care about *our* lives, about what film we're going to watch tonight. Yet at the same time we know that there are all those galaxies out there and all those children. We never entirely forget. This tension in us, in either direction, haunts us and threatens either to dim the intensity of the pleasure that we rightly take in our lives or to weaken our commitment to causes beyond our lives, causes that we undertake for the sake of those who will inhabit this planet hundreds of years after we have died.[25]

We can't think directly about the terrifying immensity of the worlds we help create through the consumption patterns we adopt. And I do not mean only ideational worlds: livestock occupy a third of the arable land on the planet[26] and are the number one cause of climate change internationally.[27] "Meat is bound up with the story of who we are and who we want to be, from the book of Genesis to the latest farm bill."[28] We can't think constantly about such realities and so we let myths embodied in eating do the work.

When asked to reflect, it is not hard to see the enormous political and social charge of eating or refusing to eat meat, as this study has shown, but we rarely articulate the "stakes of steaks" explicitly. Taking a lead from Derrida,[29] I sometimes ask students the following question: *Can the president of the United States be a vegetarian? Even if a candidate otherwise is charismatic and has views that fit the political climate, do you think Americans would elect a vegetarian? No turkey at the presidential Thanksgiving, no White House Christmas ham, no hot dogs when the president visits a ballpark. Picture the response of your parents and your relatives, of foreign hosts, and of talk show hosts.* My evidence is admittedly quite anecdotal, but my students almost without exception have agreed that they cannot imagine a declared vegetarian becoming president, though few can explain why. My attempt here has been to offer the beginnings of an explanation: meat eating, in the U.S. and many other nations, can be described as a tacit "religious litmus test" for the highest offices of the land.

In the past, when the religious charge of meat eating has been interpreted by scholars, it has always been a charge assigned to meat by a particular religious traditions (halal meat in Islam, Christian ascetic vegetarianism, and so on), and, as far as I know, the religious meaning of meat eating in the contemporary West *as such* is entirely unexplored by the study of religion. This book has largely not been an exception to this rule; I have explored the meaning meat has in a particular and explicitly religious context. What I hypothesize in this epilogue is that the basic structures through which meaning is embedded in meat in explicitly religious contexts—creating various humane subjects—appear to reappear in what we generally consider secular contexts, like nonkosher industrial slaughterhouses.

ANIMALS AS RELIGIOUS SUBJECTS

As I come to a close, let me emphasize an implication of these closing reflections and this work as a whole: the shape of these myths—and thus the shape of the world they propel us to create—is formed not only by human agencies. Just as the myths of one people are shaped by other peoples around them, I submit that part of the lesson of AgriProcessors is that the myths we humans tell are shaped by the animals we live with, by animals. Animals, in a manner parallel to our fellow humans, contribute to the process of narrating us into a meaningful existence. "Animals! The object of insatiable interest, examples of the riddle of life, created, as it were, to reveal the human being to man himself," intones Bruno Schulz, "displaying his richness and complexity in a thousand kaleidoscopic possibilities, each of them brought to some curious end."[30] Why would American agribusiness spend tens of millions of dollars in highly unpopular campaigns for ag-gag legislation simply in the hopes of restricting access to images of animals that they raise and slaughter? What force is being held at bay? The drama of AgriProcessors suggests that, faced with an animal, we cannot narrate any myth we want. The reality of animals, especially when captured on video, constrains our myth and meaning making.

We do not simply have a "view" of animals or a "worldview" in which they appear. We in fact only come to see ourselves as having a view at all after a mythologically fueled removal of ourselves from the world—a division of the world into human and animal, subject and object, male and female, able and disabled, and us and them—and thus the creation of the subject that can have a "view" rather than, for example, an agency taking up directions of movement within fields of relations that crisscross boundaries like human and animal, living and nonliving, subject and object.[31]

Animals—the beings we name animals—are not, strictly speaking, "good to think" (that can be said of all so-called natural kinds),[32] but good to think *with*, good to think *alongside*. Other animals may or may not think in narratives as we do, but it is hard to deny that they mind the world in their way and it is undeniable that the way in which the pleading face of my dog—*take me out, play with me*—affects me is unlike the way in which anything without sentience affects me. Animals may not literally make a case for how we ought to treat them with words and story—with their own narrated myths—the way another human community might, but to say that animals are silent, invested with meaning only from the outside world of purely human myth making, as the study of religion now tends to do, is absurd and ultimately counterintuitive. All communities constantly revise our myths to accommodate the realities that other human communities press upon us. We also revise myths (and there is no pristine myth, only revision and application) when animals confront us and we always have.[33] Judah ha-Nasi was not the first to be confronted by a calf on its way to slaughter and find himself transformed by the encounter, and the viewers of the undercover video of AgriProcessors's abuses are not the last.

Nonhuman animals are by definition not human, and noting the difference is perfectly sensible, but why is it necessary to so constantly affirm this difference as I just did earlier in this sentence? Why do we guard it so jealously? Flattening the entire world of the nonhuman into a blank slate that demands nothing of us, touching neither our hearts nor our myths, is simply not credible. Animals insert themselves, sometimes uncomfortably, into the processes of meaning and mythmaking. Nonhuman animals are not so much part of our religious worldview but, like human animals, agencies that help call forth and shape those views and then, later, appear within their frame.

To engage the question of the animal and religion is in the end to acknowledge the coemergence of *homo sapiens* with the more-than-human world and thus religion's coemergence with both humans and animals. It is to remember that humans cannot disentangle ourselves from the biochemical, somatic, and evolutionary forces that web together all life and that the line between nature and culture is a paradox.[34] To engage this question is to feel the pathos that courses through this ongoing process of coemergence and to surrender what we thought we knew for the sake of a more capacious, transdisciplinary, and less anthropocentric understanding of religion. The stakes are as much practical as philosophical. They have as much to do with the contents of soup as holy books, as much to do with the structure of the food industry as the structure of the academy, and as much to do with our relationship with dogs as gods.

There are acrobatics that can allow us, no doubt, to continue to describe religion as an exclusively human phenomenon with some measure of coherence. I do not hope to have proven this view wrong so much as to have shown that there is nothing necessary about it. I do not see how our understanding of even the human condition benefits from viewing religion as an exclusively human phenomenon. I see how such a view reifies the academy's bifurcation into human and natural sciences and supports a particular instantiation of the humane subject with varying political consequences, but I do not see an intellectually rigorous position requiring that we conceptualize the core phenomena of meaning making that (many) scholars of religion call religion as arising first and only with the human. Some forms of religiosity are surely productively described as unique to *homo sapiens*, but why limit the imaginations of religion to these forms?

Glossary

AGRIPROCESSORS, INC.   Located in Postville, Iowa, AgriProcessors owned and operated one of the largest kosher slaughterhouses in the world until its bankruptcy following a 2008 federal raid. This book examines a series of animal abuse scandals and the response to them that began at this slaughterhouse starting in 2004.

AGUDATH HARABONIM (aka Union of Orthodox Rabbis of the United States and Canada)   The largest contemporary North American rabbinic association for Haredi rabbis.

AGUDATH ISRAEL OF AMERICA   The largest contemporary North American communal association for Haredi Jews.

BAAL TESHUVAH (s. noun)   Literally "one who turns" or "master of turning," a *baal teshuvah* is a person who becomes observant of traditional Jewish law after a period or lifetime of nonobservance; *baal teshuvah* is sometimes translated as "penitent."

BIG FOUR/BIG FIVE   The four largest kosher supervision agencies that have dominated the industry for decades are collectively referred to as the Big Four: (1) the Kashrut Division of the Orthodox Union (aka OU Kosher)—the largest of them all; (2) Kof-K Kosher Supervision; (3) OK Kosher Certification; and (4) Star-K Kosher Certification. In recent years some commentators have begun referring to the Big Five, adding (5) the Chicago Rabbinical Council's kosher certification to the list.

BODEK (s. noun), BODKIM (p. noun)   Kosher examiner or examiners who check both the sharpness of knifes and the slaughtered animals' internal organs. *Bodek* is also used in the phrase "to be *bodek*," referring to the act of "checking" to make certain that Jewish law has been properly followed, whether with kosher or other aspects of the law ("He went to be *bodek* [check] his home for any prohibited bread products during Passover.")

CENTRAL CONFERENCE OF AMERICAN RABBIS (CCAR) The largest contemporary North American rabbinic association for Reform rabbis.

CHABAD-LUBAVITCH (aka Chabad) A major branch of Hasidic Judaism that has built a uniquely large, modern organizational infrastructure. The AgriProcessors slaughterhouse was inspired, owned, and run by members of this movement.

CHUKKIM (p. noun) Sometimes translated as "statutes," *chukkim* is the Hebrew word for Jewish laws that are regarded as having no rational explanation; *chukkim* are understood in contrast to *mishpatim*.

CONSERVATIVE JUDAISM (aka the Conservative movement) See Liberal Judaisms.

THE FORWARD A weekly Jewish paper of historic significance published in both English and Yiddish.

GEMARA See Mishnah.

GLATT (adjective) *Glatt,* often used in the phrase *glatt kosher,* refers to an additional set of stringencies in evaluating the kosher status of certain kosher animals, including the lack of any adhesions in the slaughtered animal's lungs (the lungs must be *glatt,* the Yiddish word for "smooth"). Much of the Orthodox community in the United States insists on the additional glatt stringency for kosher beef.

HALAKHA (s. noun), HALAKHIC (adjective) Etymologically related to a Hebrew verb meaning "to walk," halakha refers to the entire system of Jewish law (*American law, canon law*, and *halakha* would be parallel terms). This legal tradition claims its origin in the ancient texts of the Hebrew Bible and the Rabbinic tradition—especially the Talmud—and is embodied in ongoing rulings by living rabbis. Halakha includes in its purview what contemporary Westerners would see as secular laws (for example, rules regarding theft or accidental damage) and specifically religious laws (for example, the dietary laws of kashrut or holiday observances). It is also crucial to note that the entire conception of law in the Jewish context has different and more positive connotations than the English word *law*. In traditional Judaism, law is above all the primary vehicle through which God communicates God's will and as such law is always infused with life and love.

HAREDI (adjective), HAREDIM (p. noun) See Orthodox Judaisms.

HASID (s. noun), HASIDIM (p. noun) Practitioners of Hasidic Judaism.

HASIDIC JUDAISM (aka Hasidism or the Hasidic movement) A form of Haredi Orthodox Judaism that began in eighteenth-century Eastern Europe. The Chabad-Lubavitch movement is a form of Hasidism that is uniquely concerned with outreach to nonobservant Jews.

HEKHSHER (s. noun), HEKSHERIM (p. noun) A seal indicating that a product has been approved as kosher (common seals include a circle with a *U* in it or a star with a *k* in it). Different kosher supervisions agencies use different *heksherim*.

JEWISH RENEWAL MOVEMENT   A loose-knit movement in American Judaism rooted in the 1960s counterculture that can be found both within Jewish dominations and as an alternative to them. Jewish renewal aims to vivify what it sees as the stultifying state of much of congregational Judaism by drawing on both Jewish and non-Jewish (particularly Buddhist and Sufi) mysticism, contemplative prayer, musical traditions, meditation, and bodily spiritual disciplines like yoga.

KASHRUT (s. noun)   Kashrut refers to the entire set of Jewish dietary laws. Foods that are fit to eat according to kashrut are deemed kosher.

KASHRUT DIVISION OF THE ORTHODOX UNION (aka OU Kosher)   See Orthodox Union.

KOF-K KOSHER SUPERVISION (aka Kof-K)   One of the Big Four (or Five) kosher certification agencies. Kof-K was founded by Rabbi Dr. H. Zecharia Senter who received *semikhah* from the revered *posek* Rabbi Joseph Soloveitchik, who is associated with the development of Modern Orthodox Judaism.

LIBERAL JUDAISMS   The vast majority of affiliated American Jews practice one or another form of Liberal Judaism—that is, types of Judaism in which halakhah is variously understood as either highly flexible, changing, and internally diverse while still authoritative (Conservative Judaism), or in which halakhah is understood to be worthy of study but ultimately is subservient to a commitment to personal autonomy (Reform and Reconstructionist Judaisms). Liberal forms of Judaism can be understood in contrast to Orthodox Judaisms, for which halakhah is binding and more limited in flexibility and internal diversity. While leaders in all forms of liberal Judaism strongly spoke out against the AgriProcessors animal abuse scandals, the Conservative movement has been by far the most outspoken and active on the issue of the ethics of kosher meat production.

LIFNIM MESHURAT HADIN   This traditional rabbinic concept translates as "beyond the letter of the law" (while retaining the law itself). Since this concept points to desirable actions that are not required by halakha, some Jewish thinkers have associated it with a domain of ethical obligation independent from law.

MAGEN TZEDEK   Originally called Hekhsher Tzedek, this Conservative movement initiative hopes to create a seal that will certify that specific ethical standards, including the treatment of animals and workers, have been met by food products that have been certified as kosher by other agencies. Magen Tzedek was created as a response to the scandals at AgriProcessors.

MAIMONIDES   Rabbi Moses ben Maimon or Rambam (1135–1204) is one of the most influential rabbis in Jewish history and arguably the most eminent of the *rishonim.*

MASHGIACH (s. noun, aka *Rav ha-makhsher*), MASHGICHIM (p. noun, aka *Rav ha-makhshirim*)   The title give to rabbis working on kosher certification who are directly charged with making sure the laws of kashrut are properly followed in food production and preparation. This is one of several aspects of kosher supervision in which individuals can specialize professionally.

MELICHA (s. noun)   The salting of meats required by kosher law.

MENAKER (s. noun), MENAKKRIM (p. noun)   Porger or porgers whose role in the process of kosher butchery is to remove residual blood, forbidden fats, and the forbidden sciatic nerve. This is one of several aspects of kosher supervision in which individuals can specialize professionally.

MENSCH (s. noun)   In German *Mensch* means "human being." In Yiddish, a fusion of German and Hebrew that is still the living language of some Haredi communities, mensch continues to mean a human being but includes the connotation of an especially decent, ethical human being. This Yiddish usage of mensch has passed into American English (for example, "what a great guy he is—such a mensch!").

MIDRASH (s. noun), MIDRASHIM (p. noun)   The Midrashim (also referred to collectively as "the Midrash") are one of three central parts of the Jewish scriptural corpus, which also includes the Tanakh and Talmudim. The word midrash literally means interpretation and refers to rabbinic interpretations of the Tanakh; any direct interpretation of the Tanakh that employs the characteristic devices of rabbinic hermeneutics may be referred to as midrashic or a midrash. When used as a proper noun, Midrash refers to the *canonical* compilations of rabbinic midrashim on the Tanakh.

MISHNAH   Next to the Tanakh itself, the Mishnah is the central scripture of rabbinic Judaism. Completed in approximately 200 CE, the Mishnah is a small text that can be bound in a single volume. The rabbinic commentarial tradition on the Mishnah, by contrast, is voluminous and could fill many shelves. The most authoritative commentaries on the Mishnah are known as Gemara and were completed in approximately 400 CE in Israel and 600 CE in Babylonia; when the Mishnah and Gemara are bound together, usually with other commentaries, the resulting compilation is known as Talmud.

MISHPATIM (p. noun)   Sometimes translated as "judgments," *mishpatim* is the Hebrew word for Jewish laws that are understood to be self-evident, such as prohibitions on murder and theft. *Mishpatim* are understood in contrast to *chukkim*.

MITZVAH (s. noun), MITZVOT (p. noun)   Mitzvah literally means a divine command. The laws found in the Decalogue (ten commandments) are the most well known of all the mitzvot, which are traditionally believed to be 613 in number. As it is used in English today, though, mitzvah often has a lighter connotation, meaning something closer to "good deed." The word thus has a broad semantic range denoting both minor acts of kindness and formally commanded behaviors.

MODERN ORTHODOX, MODERN ORTHODOXY   —see Orthodox Judaisms.

NACHMANIDES   Rabbi Moses ben Nachman or Ramban (1194–1270) is one of the greatest of the Rishonim. His insights and conclusions are often contrasted with those of Maimonides.

OK KOSHER CERTIFICATION (aka OK)   One of the Big Four (or Big Five) kosher certification agencies. The listed head of OK, Rabbi Don Yoel Levy, affiliates with the
Haredi Chabad-Lubavitch movement, and received *semikhah* from the highly regarded *posek* Moshe Feinstein, who is associated with Haredi Orthodoxy.

ORTHODOX JUDAISMS   In America, different Judaisms are typically categorized
as either Orthodox or Liberal Judaisms. Orthodox Judaism is highly diverse internally and can be divided into two main forms: Modern Orthodoxy and Haredi
Orthodoxy. All forms of Orthodox Judaism understand Jewish law (halakha) as
binding and less flexible than is the case in liberal Judaisms. In America, Orthodox Jewish practice is marked by the virtually universal observance of Shabbat (the
Jewish day of rest from Friday sundown to Saturday sundown) and kosher (dietary)
laws. Whereas Modern Orthodox Judaism strives for a robust integration with
modern secular institutions, Haredi Orthodoxy is more interested in preservation
and insularity. The sociologist Samuel Heilman describes Modern Orthodoxy as
"acculturative contrapuntalist" or "accomodationist" and Haredi Orthodoxy as
"contra-acculturative" and "enclavist" (2006). The present study found that Modern Orthodox leaders, while far from embracing animal welfare as a serious issue
of institutional attention, were open to advice from secular animal welfare leaders
far more than Haredi Orthodox leaders were. While some very prominent Haredi
leaders have been strong advocates for animals, more often than not Haredi leaders in the Americas have derisively dismissed concerns coming from the national
animal welfare community.

ORTHODOX UNION (aka OU)   The largest contemporary North American communal association for Modern Orthodox Jews. The Kashrut Division of the OU is the
largest of the Big Four (or Big Five) kosher certification agencies. Rabbi Menachem
Genack has headed it for decades; Genack received *semikhah* from the revered
posek Rabbi Joseph Soloveitchik, who is associated with the development of Modern Orthodox Judaism.

POSEK (s. noun) POSKIM (p. noun)   An expert in Jewish law invested with the authority to make Jewish legal decisions (for example, regarding what counts as kosher). It is ultimately the decisions of the most authoritative *poskim* of any given
generation that determine what is licit and illicit under Jewish law.

PSHAT (adjective)   Refers to the most basic level of textual analysis and meaning—
the plain or direct meaning. A *pshat* reading of the text is understood in contrast to
less literal levels of meaning such as allegorical or mystical meanings. In addition
to *pshat*, Jewish tradition refers to *remez*, *derash*, and *sod* levels of textual meaning
and analysis (collectively these four levels of meaning are referred to by the acronym *pardes*, which is also the Hebrew word for "garden").

RABBINICAL ASSEMBLY   The largest contemporary North American rabbinic association for Conservative rabbis.

RACHAMIM (s. noun)   Usually translated as "compassion" or "mercy," *rachamim* is considered on of the most important divine attributes and is a central ethical ideal of Jewish traditions. God's *rachamim* is often contrasted with God's sense of strict justice; in the rabbinic imagination God's justice is balanced by and constrained by God's *rachamim*. Some scholars have argued that *rachamim* is etymologically related to the Hebrew word for womb and have suggested "mother love" as the most literal translation. The ideal of *rachamim* is found with high frequency in Jewish texts that promote regard for animals.

RASHI   An acronym for Rabbi Shlomo Yitzhaki (1040–1105), a highly influential French savant known especially for his comprehensive commentaries on both the Talmud and the Tanakh.

RAV HA-MAKHSHER (s. noun), RAV HA-MAKHSHIRIM (p. noun)   —see *Mashgiach*.

RECONSTRUCTIONIST JUDAISM (aka the Reconstructionist movement)   See liberal Judaisms.

REFORM JUDAISM (aka the Reform movement)   See liberal Judaisms.

RISHONIM (p. noun)   The *rishonim* is the collective designation for Jewish legal authorities that lived between the eleventh and mid-sixteenth century.

SCHECT (verb: to schect, schecting, schected)   To *shecht* means to slaughter an animal in the manner prescribed by Jewish law.

SEMIKHAH   The Hebrew word for rabbinic ordination.

SHACKLING AND DRAGGING   See Shackling and hoisting.

SHACKLING AND HOISTING (similar to shackling and dragging)   A method of slaughter often used on cattle and goats. A significant portion of the U.S. kosher beef market presently comes from animals slaughtered by shackling and hoisting or shackling and dragging in Latin American abattoirs. During the process of shackling and hoisting, a chain is clamped on an animal's leg or legs and the animal is hoisted into the air and will sometimes dangle there for minutes before slaughter. The hoisting often causes bruising, torn flesh, and bone breakage and is thus painful, disorienting, and stressful for the animal. The animals' flailing limbs pose a risk to workers. Slaughter practices that are referred to as "shackling and hoisting" are often closer to shackling and dragging, in which the animals legs are bound, but, instead of being hoisted into the air, the animal is rolled over on its side or back prior to slaughter. This method is also considered inhumane by modern standards and can cause similar distress and injury to both animals and workers.

In the U.S. context, shackling and hoisting was first required by law in 1906 and then became the dominant method for all slaughter, kosher and nonkosher. However, in 1958 U.S. law started to require that animals be stunned before hoisting and deemed shackling and hoisting without stunning inhumane. Because kosher law has been interpreted to mean animals must be conscious at the time of slaughter, the practice of shackling and hoisting in kosher slaughterhouses is

done while animals are conscious and is today almost universally considered inhumane. The Conservative movement has formally condemned both shackle and
hoist and shackle and drag, and the Orthodox Union has refused to certify slaughterhouses in the U.S. that use either method, but has not applied that stricture
abroad.

SHECHITAH (s. noun)   Shechitah is the traditional Jewish method of slaughter, requiring that a specially trained individual called a *shochet* perform a carefully
specified cut to the neck using a perfectly sharp knife (the sharpness of the knife
serves to reduce pain). Blood must be drained from the slaughtered animal. In the
European context, shechitah has historically often been unjustly attacked by an-
ti-Semites as more cruel than other slaughter methods. Contemporary efforts in
Europe to require stunning—which would effectively ban most or all Jewish and
Muslim slaughter—are more complex and appear motivated by a combination of
anti-Semitism, Islamaphobia, and genuine interest in the clear humane advantages of slaughter systems that incorporate stunning. Going back centuries, most
discussions and definitions of shechitah in Jewish sources point to a humane mo-
tive behind the law. Most American Jews, for example, have the notion that kosher
meat is slaughtered in a more humane manner (though there is no evidence that
this is the case). However, the rabbinic leadership that presently dominates kosher
certification argues that kosher law should be dealt with completely apart from
questions of *tza'ar ba'ale chayyim* and have publicly argued that even egregious
animal suffering during shechitah would not jeopardize the kosher status of the
meat. Thus, while for most Jews *shechitah* references (in theory) a humane practice expressive of Jewish ethical values, for other Jews—including virtually all who
hold power in kosher certification—*shechitah* is a nonrational technical procedure
required because and only because it is mandated by Jewish law.

SHOCHET (s. noun), SHOCHTIM (p. noun)   Adult Jews, traditionally male, trained in
the laws and practice of *shechitah*. Jewish textual sources emphasize that *shochtim*
are to be individuals of high moral caliber, but the contemporary role has today become largely technocratic.

STAR-K KOSHER CERTIFICATION (Star-K)   One of the Big Four (or Big Five) kosher
certification agencies. The listed head of Star-K, Rabbi Moshe Heinemann, received *semikhah* from the highly regarded *posek* Moshe Feinstein, who is associated with Haredi Orthodoxy.

TALMUD (s. noun), TALMUDIM (p. noun)   The Talmudim are one of three central
parts of the Jewish scriptural corpus, which also includes the Tanakh and Midrashim. A Talmud is a compilation text including the Mishnah and later rabbinic
commentary on the Mishnah. These commentaries always include Gemara (composed twice) and, in the form that has become standard, include Rashi, Rashi's
grandsons (known as the Tosofot), and sometimes later commentaries.

TANAKH (aka Hebrew Bible)   The Tanakh is one of three central parts of the Jewish scriptural corpus, which also includes the Midrashim and Talmudim. Tanakh is the Jewish term for what Christians call the Old Testament. Tanakh is an acronym standing for *Torah* (Law), *Nevi'im* (Prophets), and *Ketuvim* (Writings).

TANNAIM (p. noun)   Tannaim is the collective name for rabbis of the first two centuries, the earliest generation of rabbis.

TESHUVAH (s. noun), TESHUVOT (p. noun)   Literally "turning" or "turnings," *teshuvot* is the Hebrew word for Rabbinic responsa, that is, for legal decisions made in response to a particular inquiry.

TREYF   A Yiddish term derived from the Hebrew *terefah*, for food that is not fit for consumption according to kosher law.

TZA'AR BA'ALE CHAYYIM   Usually translated as "compassion for animals," *tza'ar ba'ale chayyim* names the broad Jewish legal principle that one should not cause unnecessary pain to living beings. Historically this value has often been associated with the practice of shechitah, but contemporary kosher certification authorities have shown little or no interest in attending to this aspect of Jewish legal tradition (kosher law and laws dealing with *tza'ar ba'ale chayyim* appear in different sections of Jewish legal codes and so can be drawn together or held apart depending upon the particular interpretation).

UNION OF ORTHODOX RABBIS OF THE UNITED STATES AND CANADA   See Agudath HaRabonim.

UNION OF REFORM JUDAISM (aka URJ)   The largest contemporary North American communal association for Reform Jews.

UNITED SYNAGOGUE OF CONSERVATIVE JUDAISM (aka USCJ)   The largest contemporary North American communal association for Conservative Jews.

URI L'TZEDEK   Founded several years after the original AgriProcessors scandals and one year before the 2008 federal raid on AgriProcessors, Uri L'Tzedek is a first-of-its-kind Modern Orthodox social justice organization that has achieved its most prominent victories around food justice. Uri L'Tzedek ran the only organized boycott of AgriProcessors; it lasted six weeks, and the group reported that it achieved certain improvements for workers shortly before AgriProcessors declared bankruptcy. The organization continues to run Tav HaYosher, an ethical certification for restaurants focused on worker justice.

YESHIVA UNIVERSITY   Founded in 1886 in New York City, Yeshiva University is one of the major institutions of Modern Orthodox Judaism. A yeshiva is a type of traditional Jewish school for the study of Jewish sacred texts, particularly the Talmud. Yeshiva University is a major research institution that includes separate men's and women's undergraduate colleges, a law school, a medical school, and a business school.

Notes

INTRODUCTION

1. Despite digitization, VHS was still being used by some activist groups because editing required less expensive equipment and as a security measure.
2. Bloom 2000; Iowa Public Television 2001.
3. Hallmark 2004.
4. As of November 30, 2009 (Bartlett 2009).
5. The phrase is taken from Timothy Pachirat's remarkable ethnographic monograph on the American slaughterhouse, *Every Twelve Seconds: Industrialized Slaughter and the Politics of Sight* (2011).
6. According to the report issued by the USDA inspector general after investigating whether AgriProcessors had violated HMSA (the Humane Methods of Slaughter Act), later obtained through the Freedom of Information Act by People for the Ethical Treatment of Animals, "The investigation determined that employees of AGRI had engaged in acts of inhumane slaughter" (Hayden 2005). Despite this, AgriProcessors was never penalized.
7. Grandin 2004.
8. The Reform Jewish theologian Eugene Borowitz argues that Jewish concern with the "civic behavior" of Jews in general—for example rates of divorce, alcoholism, or violent crime—is an often unnoticed location where Jewish identity, what Borowitz calls "chosenness amid our secularized existence," can flash forth, revealing a subterranean "ongoing folk continuation of Israel's ancient Covenant" (Borowitz 1991:205). Rather than a constant sense of difference that may have reigned in an

earlier European context, these surging, almost revelatory moments play, argues Borowitz, a crucial role in preserving a sense of Jewish distinctiveness.

9. Vonnegut 1990:311.

10. de Waal 2009:138.

11. I interpret "empathy" and "sympathy," to utilize the helpful label proposed by Anne Taves, as basic "building blocks" of religion. By building blocks, I mean "things that strike people as special" and that can be manipulated or "assembled in various ways to create more complex socio-cultural formations, some of which people characterize as 'religions'" (Taves 2009:162). Following primatological studies, I more specifically define empathy as the ability to know or share the emotional state of others and sympathy as the "desire to improve the other's situation" (de Waal 2009:88). The implication of finding a scientific basis for spontaneous mammalian "empathy" will be addressed in chapter 5 in dialogue with Jacques Derrida's thought.

12. Derrida 2008a:28. The full wording in the French: "à la possibilité de partager la possibilité de cet im-pouvoir, la possibilité de cette impossibilité, l'angoisse de cette vulnérabilité et la vulnérabilité de cette angoisse" (Derrida 1999:278–279).

13. Rubashkin 2010; Cooperman 2004.

14. Simon 2004.

15. In her autobiography, *Thinking in Pictures,* Grandin argues that when the cut that is made to the animals' throat during kosher slaughter is done "correctly according to the rules outlined in the Talmud, the animal does not appear to feel it" (Grandin 1995:178). She further describes her experience at a well-run kosher slaughterhouse as follows: "As the life force left the animal, I had deep religious feelings. For the first time in my life logic had been completely overwhelmed with feelings I did not know I had" (Grandin 1995:238). Grandin even received high praise from the Haredi-oriented magazine *Mishpahah* (Wolfson 1998).

16. The full quote reads "an atrocious abomination, nothing like I've seen in 30 kosher plants I've visited here and in England, France, Ireland and Canada" (McNeil 2004a).

17. The idea of "profanation" has been helpfully theorized by both Bruce Lincoln and Michael Taussig (Lincoln 1992; Taussig 1999).

18. Cooperman 2004; USDA Technical Service Center 2004.

19. For a brief description see Postville Resource Center 2012; Argueta 2010.

20. Tony 2008.

21. All these details are discussed further in chapter 2, where extensive source documentation is also provided.

22. Bava Metzia 85a. A variation of the story appears in Bereshit Rabbah 33:3.

23. The phrase "the question of the animal" is most closely associated with the work of Jacques Derrida, especially in regard to his critique of Martin Heidegger's writ-

ings on animals (for example, Derrida 1989). By including this phrase in my title and riffing on it throughout this work (e.g., "the questions of the animal and religion"), I mean to signal my own debt to and sympathy with Derrida's reflections on animals, which will occupy us further in chapter 5.

24. This comparison includes animals we interact with as pets, hunted animals, watched birds, animals dissected for educational purposes, animals in zoos, laboratories, racetracks, and circuses (Wolfson and Sullivan 2005:206).

25. Tillich 1959. Also see the Jewish theologian A. J. Heschel, who conceives of religion as essentially engaged with a certain "ontological category. . . . a dimension of all existence . . . [that] may be experienced everywhere and at all times" (Heschel 1994 [1955]:57).

26. Defining the human in relation to the beings we know as animals appears to be a cross-cultural phenomenon, though a more internally diverse one than we might suspect (for example, some cultures define humans via particular animal species but without ever conceiving a single human/animal border of any significance). Thus the mere fact that in imagining the study of ourselves we would reference animal others is unsurprising. However, the nature of that engagement is infinitely open: animals can be ancestors or root others, fellow creatures or Friday's dinner. For discussion, see my introduction to *Animals and the Human Imagination* (Gross and Vallely 2012).

27. For a comprehensive bibliography of animal studies see Kalof, Bryant, and Fitzgerald 2010.

28. For Levinas, totality designates the realm of the calculable—that which can no longer surprise or challenge because it has been systematized and reduced. In the totality there is no room for "an other refractory to categories." "The void that breaks the totality can be maintained against an inevitably totalizing and synoptic thought only if thought finds itself *faced* with an other refractory to categories" (Levinas 1995 [1969]:40).

29. Calarco 2008:4.

30. See discussion of Derrida in chapter 5.

31. Staal 1990:424.

32. Thomas Berry's phrase is productively engaged in the edited volume of the same title by Waldau and Patton (Waldau and Patton 2006).

33. The question "what is an animal" was posed to a diverse group of scholars from the disciplines of social and cultural anthropology, archaeology, biology, psychology, philosophy, and semiotics in an edited scholarly volume of the same title. In his summary of the divergent positions expressed, anthropologist Tim Ingold, whose work is crucial to chapter 4 of this work, argues that there were two points upon which all the contributors agreed: "first, that there is a strong emotional undercurrent to our ideas about animality; and, secondly, that to subject these ideas to

critical scrutiny is to expose highly sensitive and largely unexplored aspects of the understanding of our own humanity" (Ingold 1988:1).

34. In different ways, the corpus of work by Walter Benjamin and Jacque Derrida (see especially Derrida 1989) on the animal offer a sophisticated analysis of the multiple ways in which animals can be understood as "haunting," shadowy, spectral, and—as Benjamin says of Franz Kafka's animals—"receptacles of forgetting" (Benjamin 2004b:19).

35. From *Concerning the City of God Against the Pagans* as cited in Linzey 1987.

36. Coetzee 1999.

37. Benjamin's reflections on animals are especially rich in his essays "On Language as Such and on the Language of Man" (2004d), "Franz Kafka: *Beim Bau der Chinesischen Mauer*" (2004a), "Franz Kafka: On the Tenth Anniversary of His Death" (2004b), and "Letter to Gershom Scholem on Franz Kafka" (2004c).

38. Lévi-Strauss 1963:89; also see Lévi-Strauss 2001, 2000, 1973, 1983, 1990b, a, 1962.

39. Ingold 2012b:42. Other important works of Ingold that deal with animals are listed in the bibliography.

40. Haraway 2008:19.

41. Ibid.

42. Doniger 2012:351.

43. This understanding is put forth in *The Fundamental Concepts of Metaphysics* (Heidegger 1983b:199, for the German, see 1983a, 93). Heidegger's problematic discussion of animals has been at the heart of a surprising range of inquiries into the meaning of anthropocentrism and the human/animal border. This book will be more interested in those who discuss the animal by way of Heidegger, rather than in Heidegger's own thought.

44. In *Totality and Infinity* and elsewhere Levinas denies that animals have a "face" and thus the ability to call forth the sort of ethical demands he aims to theorize. This is a move for which Derrida bitterly attacks him (Derrida 1978a, 1995). Other scholars, including myself (Gross 2009), however, have found Levinas a resource in constructing new obligations toward and conceptualizations of animals. Parts of his corpus appear "friendly" to animals—for example, his short, haunting piece on a the kindness a dog showed him while confined in Nazi Germany, "The Name of a Dog, or Natural Rights" (Levinas 1990a) and in his Talmudic essays, especially "And God Created Woman" in *Nine Talmudic Readings* (Levinas 1990b).

45. Friedman 1988:329.

46. Agamben 2004:33–38

47. Derrida 2008a:6–7. Important works by Derrida on the animal available in English include Derrida 1978a, 1986, 1989, 1995, 2002a, 2004a, 2008a, 2008b, 2009.

48. For discussion of Derrida as engaging in midrash, see Handelman 1982; Hartman and Budick 1986.

49. For an insightful exploration of the correlation of animal and Jew, see Benjamin 2011.

50. Lévi-Strauss reflects, "What is significant is not so much the presence—or absence—of this or that level of classification as the existence of a classification with, as it were, an adjustable thread which gives the group adopting it the means of 'focusing' on all planes, from the most abstract to the most concrete . . . without changing its intellectual instrument" (Lévi-Strauss 1973:136). Lévi-Strauss considers animals well suited to function as just such an "adjustable thread."

51. Derrida 1995:281

52. For further discussion see my introduction in Gross and Vallely 2012.

53. The term *hunter-gatherer* has been justly problematized because of its connection with colonialist and racist discourses and because of the privilege given to hunting by naming it before gathering despite the fact that gathering is generally more significant in providing sustenance. Following Tim Ingold (1996a) I continue to use *hunter-gatherer* as the least problematic among the available options.

54. The monstrous, as in the *OED* definition, is often defined by the blending of features from animals and humans. It is perhaps this vertigo-introducing boundary blurring that threatens to expel those who gaze upon it out of the world of the animate, turning them, as the myth relates, into stone.

55. Derrida 1989:9.

1. ETHICAL TROPES IN AMERICAN KOSHER CERTIFICATION

1. In utilizing this articulation of the scholarly bifurcation of ethics and emphasizing the interrelation of and fuzzy boundaries between these two forms of ethics, I follow Jonathan Schofer, whose work on rabbinic and comparative ethics draws on such diverse thinkers as Max Kadushin, Charles Taylor, and Paul Ricoeur. Schofer argues that while "there are significant conceptual differences between character and procedural ethics. . . . I believe (for both theoretical and descriptive projects) that we need to address their interrelations along with their conflicts" (Schofer 2005:10). Also see Schofer's endnotes 18, 23, and 24 (2005:180–181).

2. A famous Midrash (Bereshit Rabbah 44:1) asks the rhetorical question of whether God cares about such details as whether humans slaughter animals "by the throat or the nape of the neck." This Midrash is often a point of departure for Jewish discussions of the role of ethics in Jewish life.

3. For a thorough review of the questions about the relationship of Jewish law and Jewish ethics, I recommend the first three chapters of Louis Newman's *Past Imperatives*; see especially pages 49–51, which describe the parameters of the debate, and note 1 on page 238, which offers a list of diverse scholarly sources that have engaged the issue (Newman 1998).

4. Halivni 1978:165 as cited in Newman 1998:50. Note that Halivni leaves open the question of *unconscious* influence in what we might call ethics.

5. One of the most lucid defenders of this position has been Elliot Dorff; see, for example: Dorff 1977. For a discussion of Dorff's and other positions and a productive reframing of these issues, see Newman 1998:45–62. Newman ultimately concludes, with great insight, that "there is a certain paradox at the heart of traditional Judaism, inherent in its dual character as a functioning legal system and as a system of religious instruction, which necessitates that the boundary between law and ethics always be ambiguous" (Newman 1998:11). Joseph Dan, who is particularly attentive to the relationship between Jewish ethics and Jewish mysticism, readily acknowledges, like Dorff and Newman, that *halakhah* (Jewish law) and ethics are difficult to distinguish, but does so by arguing that "*halakhah* defines the obligatory minimum; ethics, and the aggadah, describe the unending road toward perfection" (Dan 1996 [1986]:5). He thus links ethics with a messianic trajectory. Another unique characteristic of Jewish ethics that distinguishes it from law, argues Dan, "is the emphasis on explanation and inducement, rather than simple statement of the actions that should be performed" (ibid., 5).

6. Bava Metzia 30b.

7. Of course, explanation is used not only to justify extant practices but also to propel Jewish ethics into new arenas. For example, see Crane 2007 on how modern Jews used rationales to align Judaic thought with modern Western "human rights" discourse.

8. Lipschutz 1988:16.

9. Orthodox Union, Kashrut Division 2004a.

10. A full list of the hundreds of extant kosher certification agencies is maintained on the kashrut.com Web site. For further details on the Big Four, see the glossary.

11. OK Kosher Certification 2004.

12. United Jewish Community in Cooperation with the Mandell L. Berman Institute–North American Jewish Data Bank 2003.

13. For discussion see Newman 1998:4–5.

14. Union of American Hebrew Congregations 1995 [1885].

15. For discussion of the Reform rejection of kashrut and the contemporary resurgence of interest in kashrut, see Gross 2004.

16. For example, Rabbi Yacov Lipschutz, writes "even a commonplace function such as physical nourishment . . . sanctifies the human body. Conversely the consumption of forbidden foods defiles the holy spirit and its sanctity is injured" (Lipschutz 1988:15).

17. For example, on the Orthodox Union's Web site it is explained that "none [of the kosher animals] are aggressive; none are violent carnivores. . . . In other words, we start out with species with good 'interpersonal' qualities" (Meir 2004). Or consider these citations from two of the other big four certifiers, OK Kosher Certifica-

tion and Star-K Kosher Certification respectively: "Birds of prey and carnivorous animals, having the power to influence the eater with aggressive attributes, are among the foods that are forbidden" (OK Kosher Certification 2004) and "qualities from specific species can enter our spiritual bloodstream. . . . [A kosher animal] is not a predator that tears its victims limb from limb" (Feldman 1994).

18. A frequently heard refrain is "the *Torah* is not a mere health manual" (Feldman 1994).

19. For example, on the OU Web site *shechitah* is described as follows: "The trachea and esophagus of the animal are severed with a special razor-sharp, perfectly smooth blade, causing instantaneous death with no pain to the animal" (Othodox Union, Kashrut Division 2004a). The Star-K Web site also invokes the theme of humaneness: "Poultry and meat are permissible from animals that are slaughtered by humane methods dictated by Jewish Law" (Star-K Kosher Certification 2004).

20. Rosenberg 2004f.

21. Othodox Union, Kashrut Division 2004b (emphasis added).

22. Feldman 1994.

23. Rosenberg 2004.

24. OK Kosher Certification 2004.

25. Othodox Union, Kashrut Division 2004b.

26. Ibid.

27. Douglas 1966.

28. Derrida 2008a:28.

2. THE EVENT AND RESPONSE

1. Chidester 2005:34. Chidester is defining the iconic, not referencing Agri-Processors.

2. Helpful but incomplete narratives have been offered by Fishkoff 2010a:278–295 and Pava 2011:125–134.

3. Jane 2008; Rosenberg 2008b.

4. Pava 2011:126.

5. At this time I had completed a MTS at Harvard Divinity School and was enrolled as a PhD student at University of California, Santa Barbara, where Jewish traditions were my primary field of study. For those interested in my personal views on contemporary farming, see the Web site of the nonprofit animal protection organization I founded in 2007, www.FarmForward.com.

6. PETA 2009.

7. Friedrich was well known at PETA because he was among the only members of their leadership who believes strongly in the positive role religions have and can play in advancing animal protection. Friedrich views the Jewish tradition as hav-

ing the strongest tradition of animal protection among the Abrahamic traditions and admires the Jewish community for this reason. Friedrich is himself a committed Catholic and formerly lived for several years in a Catholic Worker community.

8. Dr. Steve Gross, a former business consultant who assisted PETA with several negotiations with industry—and who is also my father—signed the letter. PETA staffers penned the letter and asked Steve to review and sign it, as they felt it might be better received if signed by a Jew and because he had volunteered to donate his time in negotiating with AgriProcessors should they have responded favorably.

9. Lewin, while loved by many in the Orthodox world, is also a source of immense frustration to other Orthodox. In my conversations with Modern Orthodox leadership who were actively defending AgriProcessors and therefore in alliance with Lewin, I more than once encountered a sigh after I shared one of Lewin's accusatory statements (for example his comparison of PETA to the Nazis) and was told that Lewin needs to be taken with a grain of salt. A telling example of Lewin's failure to remain fully credible in his own community occurred when he agreed to a debate with PETA's Friedrich at an Orthodox synagogue to an Orthodox audience. According to all reports, in defiance of all expectations, and based on my own observation after listening to the audio recording of the talks made by PETA, the audience was more sympathetic to Friedrich, who explained that if the plant took modest steps forward to address the abuse problems, PETA would pull the entire campaign against AgriProcessors from its Web site. This surprising result suggests to me that Orthodox leadership's response to PETA was more hostile than what would have been the response of most of the community's membership.

10. PETA (Steven Jay Gross) 2003.

11. Lewin and Lewin (Nathan Lewin) 2003.

12. The absence of sadists cannot be taken for granted in this context. Grandin, citing other studies and her own observations, reports that this is a regular problem in slaughterhouses (Grandin 1988).

13. Though "abuses" has frequently been used to describe the incidents at AgriProcessors, it is potentially misleading. The word abuse *implies* moments of nonabuse—a violence that occurs only occasionally or periodically (thus the frequent attachment of the adjective *systematic* to *abuse*).

14. PETA's internal analysis, calculated by Friedrich, suggested that at least 25 percent of the animals were conscious after release from restraints. My estimate of 20 percent is slightly more conservative than the 25 percent estimate that Friedrich arrived at for use by PETA because I have not included in my count of incidents of sensibility any of the scenes where the animal was obscured and therefore sensibility was impossible to judge with certainty. Otherwise my count matches that arrived at by PETA. Ideally these numbers would be verified by a scholar specializing in animal behavior.

15. The Rubashkins have sometimes explained that the second cut was meant to increase blood flow and that this would ultimately speed unconsciousness. Grandin does not believe this explanation to be credible. Other statements by supporters of AgriProcessors indicate that the methods of slaughter used at AgriProcessors were causing them problems with poor bleed out, "blood splash," and "blood spots," ultimately affecting either the kosher status of the animals or discoloring the meat. Rabbi Kohn of KAJ, one of the agencies certifying AgriProcessors, explained that the purpose of the procedure "is not to make the animal unconscious faster. . . . I would never say that," but rather to make the animal bleed out faster and to prevent blood spots and bruises on the meat (Rosenberg 2004c). The head of OU Kosher, Rabbi Menachem Genack, explained, "This [second cut] is not done for kashrut reasons, for after the trachea and esophagus have been severed the *shechita* is complete, but rather for commercial reasons, to avoid blood splash, which turns the meat a darker color" (Genack 2004).

16. See, for example, Rosenberg 2004d.

17. Grandin 1994.

18. Food Marketing Institute and National Council of Chain Restaurants 2003.

19. Rosenberg 2005.

20. Bloom 2005.

21. PETA (Lori Kettler) 2004.

22. Orbach 2008.

23. Rosenberg 2004e.

24. Several popular press sources inaccurately reported this incident, saying or suggesting that Rabbi Cohen had been deceived by PETA, a deception that appears to be connected to remarks by AgriProcessors attorney Nathan Lewin. This suggestion is a complete fabrication. Rabbi Cohen did distance himself from PETA, but adamantly denied that PETA had deceived him.

25. Rabbi Kohn appears to have had little interest in what scientific experts suggested about the pain involved in the procedures at AgriProcessors. According to the Orthodox muckraking blogger Shmarya Rosenberg, whose reporting on the AgriProcessors events on FailedMessiah.com has been rigorous and reliable, Rabbi Kohn

> claimed that the animal felt no pain when the hook was inserted and the second cut made, even though the animal had not yet bled-out. I told him the experts like Dr. Grandin differ with him. He said, "We know the animal feels no pain. We rely on Halakha that says so." He also called Dr. Grandin— arguably the world's expert on animal slaughter and who is widely regarded as a friend of shechita (please see the article about her from Mishpacha Magazine, posted below)—a "self-appointed expert. We have other experts who disagree with her," he said. Rabbi Kohn did not name those "other experts." (Rosenberg 2004c)

The article Rosenberg refers to in *Mishpacha* is of interest as a positive Haredi view of Grandin's work on religious slaughter issues and deserves an extended quotation. "You may wonder why the Rabbayin [the Rabbis] listen to a gentile, autistic woman?" the article asks (itself an interesting commentary). The fact that Grandin has a PhD, the recognition of both the meat industry and animal protection groups, and functions as the nation's de facto most influential scientist on questions of humane slaughter would not impress rabbis like Kohn or likely most readers of *Mishpacha,* a leading Israeli-based Haredi periodical. The article continues,

> One reason may be because she knows the laws of shechita very well. She was told about the Talmud and went to the library and found Mesechet Chulin, in English and read it. Then, she applied science to what she learned in the Gemorrah and published an article called, "Slaughter," for a scientific journal in the meat industry. In that journal article she relates some important facts. She studied the reaction time of death from the initial incision of the knife until the death of the animal. She wanted to know if it was painful to cut the animal's throat. She did this by observation of the animal. What she saw was that when animals were led quietly into a restraining device where they stood upright, into a frame that supplied chin and head support, the animals had "little or no reaction to the cut." She said that her observations in kosher slaughter houses where there was a poorly designed holder was that the cut allowed the neck to close back over the knife and it resulted in vigorous reactions from the cattle during the cut. She also states that when the moving and holding devices are not well designed, the animal will kick and twist and occasionally go into spasms. She says that when a shochet uses a rapid cutting stroke, on a calm, upright animal, 95% of the calves she observed collapsed almost immediately. She says in her paper: Some rabbinical authorities prefer inverted restraint and cutting downward because they are concerned that an upward cut may violate the Jewish rule which forbids excessive pressure on the knife. There is concern that the animal may tend to push downward on the knife during an upward cut. Observations indicate that just the opposite happens. When large 800 to 950 kilogram bulls are held in a pneumatically powered head restraint which they can easily move, the animals pull their heads upwards away from the knife during a mis-cut. This would reduce pressure on the blade. When the cut is done correctly, the bulls stood still and did not move the head restraint. Equal amounts of pressure were applied by the forehead bracket and the chin lift. (Wolfson 1998)

26. Wagner 2004a.
27. Wagner 2004b.
28. Eby 2004.

29. Ibid.

30. Waddington 2008a; FailedMessiah.com provided the most comprehensive reporting on the behavior of Judge. For further discussion, see Rosenberg 2004b.

31. Simon 2004; Cooperman 2004; Frank 2005; *Jerusalem Post* 2004; Wagner 2004a, 2004b, 2006; Allen 2004.

32. Rubashkin 2010.

33. All citations in this paragraph are from Lewin 2004.

34. Ibid.

35. Zirkind 2009.

36. Ibid.

37. Rosenberg 2009.

38. Elchonon 2004.

39. Lewin 2004; Rosenberg 2004a, 2008a.

40. McNeil 2004a.

41. Ibid.

42. By contrast, the Rubashkins, while beloved by many in the Haredi community, were regularly referred to as arrogant and corrupt. Nathan Lewin, despite his fame, is also an ambivalent figure in the Orthodox world, and I was frequently given the impression that his allies also saw him as a headache.

43. This is the general picture painted from multiple conversations with people close to the events, but especially by details shared with me by food science professor Joe Regenstein (Cornell University), an expert on animal welfare in kosher slaughter.

44. McNeil 2004b.

45. Ibid.

46. Hersh 2004.

47. Ibid.

48. Rubashkin's remarks are not dated, but he refers to the video being released only days before. Another example: "'This is the way we did it in the Holy Temple all those years. This is basically the exact way that God asked us to do it,' said Rabbi Sholem Fishbane, who administrates kosher slaughterhouses for the Chicago Rabbinical Council" (Simon 2004).

49. Hersh 2004.

50. Rosenberg 2004e.

51. Popper 2006b.

52. Ibid.

53. PETA 2010a.

54. Iowa Attorney General's Office 2008.

55. Preston 2008a.

56. Ibid.

57. Ibid.

58. Black 2010.
59. Tony 2008.
60. Associated Press 2009.
61. Legal Info 2009.
62. Preston 2010.
63. Ibid.
64. Significantly, the assumption that these abuses can be easily delineated is not inherently a more obvious starting point than the assumption that they are connected.
65. Waddington 2008b.
66. Grandin commented in an interview that AgriProcessors was in the bottom 10 percent of the bottom 20 percent of American slaughterhouses (Waddington 2008c).
67. Rosen originally issued his comment, later circulated in the press, at my request. Milikowsky spontaneously contacted PETA with his comment, which they helped to distribute (I personally confirmed this with Milikowsky and PETA). Greenberg was prompted to comment by novelist Jonathan Safran Foer, who featured him in an activist-style video he released in 2006 (I heard this from Foer).
68. Rosen 2004. Well before starting on this book, I solicited this statement from him and passed it to PETA for distribution to the media. Rosen's statement is widely cited in media in parts. I have cited the original statement from my correspondence in its entirety.
69. PETA has its own list of response statements at www.peta.org/features/Agriprocessors-experts.aspx.
70. Foer 2006. I assisted Foer in his work on this video, which was distributed with the help of PETA.
71. Freedman 2010.
72. Rosenberg 2013.
73. Freedman 2010.
74. Only six out of twenty-five votes are required to "pass" Conservative movement *teshuvot,* which are not binding upon all members of the movement.
75. Dorff and Roth 2002.
76. Rank 2004.
77. In June 2010 Joe Regenstein—one of probably *the* most trusted consultants on humane kosher slaughter—shared with me that he assisted Rank in editing this letter and encouraged him to "tone it down," which makes the strength of this letter all the more interesting.
78. For example, in 2008 *Newsweek* magazine declared Wolpe the number 1 pulpit rabbi in the nation (Lynton, Ginsberg, and Sanderson 2008). In 2012 he was number 1 on *Newsweek*'s list of "50 Influential US Rabbis" (*Newsweek* 2012).

79. See Nachmanides' comments on Deuteronomy 22:6–7 in his *Commentary on the Torah*. Available translations include the 1976 translation of Charles Chavel published by Shilo and a 2008 annotated translation published in Mesorah Publication's ArtScroll series.
80. For example, Schwartz 2004.
81. I took a lead role in writing and distributing this statement to American rabbis. Others include Joe Regenstein, who helped edit it, and Richard Schwartz, who helped invite many of the signatories.
82. Shapiro 2008.
83. Koenig 2010.
84. Sue Fishkoff recalls a slightly different version of Hazon's founding in 2000, seeing the organization as formed primarily to promote the ecological benefits of bike riding and turning its focus to food sustainability and Jewish agricultural education only in 2004 (Fishkoff 2008).
85. Savage 2010.
86. Union for Reform Judaism 2011.
87. In my direct conversations with Magen Tzedek leadership, their self-understanding is that, in regards to animal welfare, the program aims only to eliminate the bottom-of-the-barrel animal abuse at the slaughterhouse (what Grandin describes as the bottom 10 percent of slaughterhouses), not to set forth an ideal. Indeed, the standards even allow inversion before slaughter, despite the movement's own *teshuvah* declaring it a violation of Jewish law, and the standards make no attempt to address the plight of animals on the farm.
88. 54 percent of American Jews do not affiliate with a synagogue and thus have no formal connection with any particular form of Judaism. Liberal forms of Judaism include, in order of size, Reform (39 percent of the affiliated American Jewish population), Conservative (33 percent), and Reconstructionist (3 percent; United Jewish Community in Cooperation with the Mandell L. Berman Institute–North American Jewish Data Bank 2003).
89. Ibid.
90. Shapiro 2008.
91. Ibid.
92. *Igerot Moshe* (*Even ha-Ezer* 4:92) as cited in Sears 2003:80; Shapiro 2008.
93. For a definition and discussion of factory farming, see Gross forthcoming.
94. de Waal 2009.

3. THE ABSENT PRESENCE

1. Tillich 1959.
2. Heschel 1994 [1955]:56.

3. My use of "absent presence" is indebted to Carol Adams's theorization of animals and women as "absent referents" (Adams 2010 [1990]).

4. Many of the deconstructive gestures of this analysis are indebted to feminist theory. The multiplicity of revolutions in our thinking about sex and gender that mark recent decades is a crucial part of what has made this present inquiry into animals legible to a large audience. Similarly, the critique of racism, race theory more broadly, and the revaluation of earlier attitudes toward native peoples play—as will be quite evident as we proceed—an important role in increasing the intelligibility of critical thinking about animals. It is not that there is some natural order of progression, as is often imagined, in which human liberation must precede animal liberation. Rather there is a common critical gesture at work in feminism, race theory, postcolonial theory, and queer theory and in most of what we call cultural studies that is also at work in critically thinking about animals. Every time this critical gesture is made—the essence of which we might imagine as a challenge to a certain vision of the subject as a male, virile, white, heterosexual, and, we should not forget, human and carnivorous—it weakens the grip of this dominant schema of the subject.

5. David Biale, in his book *Not in the Heavens,* pursues the ambitious project of rigorously defining Jewish secularism and ultimately conveying an understanding of it as a lineage and countertradition that works "to fashion a new identity out of the shards of the past. This lineage consists of a chain of ideas that arose in rejection of the religious tradition yet were still tied to that which they overturned" (Biale 2011:14).

6. Chief among those problematically Jewish Jews is Derrida, Reb Derissa; Derrida "signs" his name at the end of *Writing and Difference* as "Reb Derrisa" (Derrida 1978b:300). For discussion, see Caputo 1997:232; Handelman 1982:163–178.

7. Carlson 2008:187.

8. For discussion, see the introduction to Alexander 1988:5–6.

9. Durkheim and Mauss 1963:7.

10. Durkheim 1995:14.

11. Ibid., 446.

12. Ibid., 440.

13. Berger 1990:4.

14. See, for example, Durkheim 1995:220, 228.

15. Ibid., 220.

16. Ibid., 229.

17. Ibid., 229.

18. Cassirer 1972 [1944]:24.

19. *Speciation* as defined by the *OED* means "the formation of new and distinct species in the course of evolution."

20. Cassirer 1972 [1944]:27, 32.

21. Ibid., 36.

22. For a more recent proposal to separate the animal from the human because of the manner in which humans are "thrown" into a past that is itself the product of humanity, see both Tom Carlson (2008:185–205) and Robert Harrison (2003). Harrison argues, "We share with the animals our throwness into gender and into our species-being, but in addition to the determinations we are also thrown into the authority of the past" (ibid., 86; for discussion, see Carlson 2008:204).

23. Cassirer 1972 [1944]:36.

24. Ibid., 34, 36, 41.

25. Durkheim 1995:118.

26. Ibid., 148.

27. Ibid., 149.

28. Ibid., 63.

29. Cassirer 1972 [1944]:100.

30. Ibid., 82.

31. Durkheim 1995:83 (emphasis added).

32. In *Myth and Reality* Eliade offers perhaps his most lucid definition of myth, arguing that myth always "describe[s] . . . dramatic breakthroughs of the sacred" (1998:6).

33. Eliade 1984 [1969].

34. Eliade 1981:xiii.

35. Boesch 2003. Boesch provides citations to a range of studies of primate tool use.

36. Some fish will fire darts of air to dislodge insects and others will use rocks to crack open mollusks. More impressively, observations as early as the 1950s (and repeatedly confirmed since) have shown that several species of fish will use floating leaves as baby carriages to ferry their eggs more quickly to safety. Some "grazing" fish even do a bit of gardening, removing unwanted algae to promote the growth of tasty species on a favored plot. Two excellent summaries of studies of fish tool use are Bshary, Wickler, and Fricke 2002 and Brown 2004.

37. Eliade 1981:4.

38. Ibid., 5.

39. Derrida 1995:278.

40. Eliade 1981:5.

41. Cassirer 1972 [1944]:82.

42. As we will see in chapter 5, Jacques Derrida will argue that a deployment of the human/animal binary may be what brings all philosophers as such together.

43. Eliade 1981:xiii.

44. Ibid., 3.

45. Strictly speaking, Staal does not suggest a continuity between animal and human religious practices, but between animal and human "rituals." Staal associates the former with meaning making and considers the latter meaningless, defining rit-

ual as "a system of acts and sounds, related to each other in accordance with rules without reference to meaning" (1990:433). Therefore his thinking is consistent with the exclusion of the animal from religion that we have seen in Durkheim and Eliade, but not ritual. However, Stall combines this intellectual move with an elevation of the status of ritual in general, making it a fundamental feature of the human. And, in any case, the ritual practices that Staal argues have continuities with animal behavior are usually considered "religious" rituals (for example, the *agnicayana*); thus, from a certain perspective, Staal does seem to be connecting what might be called religious behavior with animal behavior and therefore is presenting a new approach to "religious" practice. As Staal himself articulates it, though, he is only linking human ritual activity—which is distinct from religious activity—with animal behavior.

Unlike Staal, Burkert explicitly argues that religion is a blend of nature and culture, thus allowing data from ethology to bear directly on the phenomena of religion, particularly rituals. "Religion's hybrid character—between biology and culture—calls for an interdisciplinary meeting of methods" (Burkert 1996:23).

46. Smith 1988b:xi.
47. Ibid., 102.
48. Ibid.
49. Ibid., 104.
50. "Reason," we can note, is the classic capacity used to draw the human/animal binary in a long arc of philosophical thought that we could trace back to Aristotle.
51. Waldau and Patton 2006:12
52. Smith 1993:294.
53. Cassirer 1972 [1944]:100, 101.
54. Patton 2006:37.
55. Cassirer 1972 [1944]:100–101.
56. Ibid., 100–101.
57. Smith 1993:274.
58. Cassirer 1972 [1944]:100.
59. Note Cassirer's relativization of "our own point of view."
60. Note how here Cassirer, whatever the accuracy of his view, works to bridge what remains a significant difference, balancing a sense of strangeness and similarity in a careful manner.
61. Cassirer 1972 [1944]:83.
62. Ibid., 84.
63. Ibid., 100.
64. Smith 1988a:57.
65. Ibid., 59.
66. Ibid. (brackets are in the original).

67. Agamben 2004:29.

68. Smith 1993:294.

69. Ibid., 294.

70. Agamben 2004:25.

71. Ibid.

72. Ibid., 30.

73. Ibid., 34.

74. Kubrick 1968.

75. See discussion on page 76 in this book.

76. Agamben 2004:37–38.

77. Ibid., 37.

78. Smith 1993:294.

79. Agamben 2004:15.

80. Ibid., 16.

81. Ibid., 21.

82. Ibid., 12.

83. Waldau and Patton 2006:12

84. See the bibliography for select important works by Coetzee, Doniger, and Haraway.

4. AFTER THE SUBJECT

1. Ingold 1996a:150, 2012b:49.

2. The study of religion as an academic institution is justifiably most interested in religion as it appears in our own human communities—for example, its role in creating social solidarity and founding ethical norms (two areas of concern to the present study)—but the phenomena itself are larger. An engineer may focus on building bridges that facilitate human transportation, but she operates—and this is of decisive pragmatic and theoretical importance—in a world in which the gravitational forces she considers are understood to apply equally to matter anywhere in the universe.

3. Although the word *agent* can be read as another name for a *subject*, I use the word *agent*, following Ingold, as an alternative to thinking about living beings as subjectivities. In an essay entitled "No More Ancient; No More Human: The Future Past of Archaeology and Anthropology," Ingold, who is keen to move beyond talk of subjects and objects, imagines a future scholarly utopia when the subject/object binary has been overcome. At some point in the near future, Ingold imagines the concept of agency displaces that of subjectivity: "The word [*agency*] was introduced to fix an insoluble conundrum: how could anything happen in the world of solid and immutable forms? The answer was to endow them with an intrinsic, but ultimately mysterious, capacity to act. Huge efforts and millions of words were

expended in the futile search for this capacity. Fortunately, we can now [in 2053] put all that behind us" (Ingold 2010b:163).

4. Haraway 2008:19.

5. Ingold 2010a:361 (emphasis added).

6. I do believe that a "science," a *Wissenschaft*, of religion is possible, but this science is not that articulated by philosophers of science like Thomas Kuhn or Karl Popper, but closer to the "anything goes" understanding of science advanced by Paul Feyerabend in his classic text *Against Method* when he asserts that "science is an essentially anarchic enterprise: theoretical anarchism is more humanitarian and more likely to encourage progress than its law-and-order alternatives" (1993 [1975]:9).

7. Agamben 2004:21.

8. Ingold 2001b:255.

9. Agamben writes, "Several of Benjamin's texts propose an entirely different image of the relationship between man and nature and between nature and history: an image in which the anthropological machine seems to be completely out of play" (Agamben 2004:81). In turning to Derrida in the next chapter, we will also draw on related Western intellectual traditions. Both Benjamin and Derrida are, for example, heirs to a common intellectual heritage on the question of the animal: heirs to Nietzsche, Freud, Marx, and to certain aspects of rabbinic tradition.

10. *Enskillment* is a neologism of Ingold's that attempts, like his reference to the human condition as one of being immersed in an "active, practical and perceptual engagement with constituents of the dwelt-in world" (Ingold 1996a:120–121), to avoid a classic analysis in which an autonomous subject gains knowledge about an external world of objects. As we will see, in place of this classic analysis, Ingold proposes we utilize hunter-gatherers' own "ontologies." Writing on the Koyukon, he explains that, for them,

> Learning to see, then, is a matter not of acquiring schemata for mentally constructing the environment but of acquiring the skills for direct perceptual engagement with its constituents, human and nonhuman, animate and inanimate. To adopt a felicitous phrase from the founder of ecological psychology, J. J. Gibson, learning is an "education of attention," a process not of enculturation but of enskillment. If the Koyukon hunter notices significant features of the landscape of which the Western observer remains unaware, it is not because their source lies in "the Koyukon mind," which imposes its own unique construction on a common body of sensory data, but because the perceptual system of the hunter is attuned to picking up information, critical to the practical conduct of his hunting, to which the unskilled observer simply fails to attend.   (Ibid., 141–142)

11. Since writing this paragraph, in which I argue for a resonance between Ingold and Agamben's efforts (an early version is found in my dissertation, Gross 2010), Ingold has himself embraced Agamben and utilized Agamben's metaphor of the anthropological machine. See Ingold 2010b:167–168, 2010a:363.

12. Ingold 2008a [2000]:75.

13. This is to say that the hunter-gatherer rejection of a division of the world in to human and animal does not mean that these communities would have any difficulty understanding this binary as an analytic distinction; this is not in question. They can make the analytic distinction, but simply do not view it as important, any more than other people would view a division of the world into Aaron/not-Aaron as an important binary.

14. Ingold 1996a:121–122, 2012b:35.

15. Ingold 2010b:160.

16. Ibid., 354.

17. Durkheim and Mauss 1963.

18. For discussion, see Ingold 2013.

19. Steven Lukes as cited in Smith 1993:285.

20. Ingold 2010a:355.

21. Ibid., 356.

22. Ibid.

23. Ibid., citing Nuttall 2009:299.

24. Ibid.

25. Ingold 1996a:117; 2012b:31.

26. This doubling of *nature* can be connected to the doubling of another, related, and equally foundational term of Western ontology, *spirit,* as it appears in the work of Martin Heidegger and as it is critiqued by Derrida in *Of Spirit* (1989). While space constrains me from elaborating Heidegger's use or Derrida's critique here, I nonetheless mention it as we will be considering *Of Spirit* in the next chapter. Briefly, the doubling of *nature* Ingold considers here and the doubling of *spirit* (really of *Geist*) Derrida considers are both products of an attempt to think one's way out of the knot of binaries that constrain Western thought (nature/culture, object/subject, and, by extension, animal/human) or, to put it another way, to reach a place more primary—the very opening of questioning: a place, we might say, where binaries paradoxically cease to be oppositional. The doubling is also a haunting, the ghostly return of a primacy that can never cease to be spectral. The question I will consider in the next chapter, in a more careful consideration of Derrida, is whether these doublings, which are also sincere attempts at originary thinking, are symptomatic of a disavowal of animals. To the extent that the primary questions we are considering do not allow us to avoid some of this spectral doubling, is there a more adequate structure of doubling? If the doubling of *nature* that Ingold

considers in "conventional" anthropology and the doubling of *spirit,* or *Geist*, Derrida considers in Heidegger merely "pretend" to take us past this knot of binaries, while ultimately reinscribing the animal/human binary, what articulation—if any—might be more sufficient?

27. "It is recognized that the concept of nature, in so far as it denotes an external world of matter and substance 'waiting to be given meaningful shape and content by the mind of man,' is part of that very intentional world within which is situated the project of Western science as the 'objective' study of natural phenomena" (Ingold 1996a:119, 2012b:33).

28. Ibid.

29. For discussion, see the section "The Alliance Between Philosophy and Common Sense" in the next chapter.

30. Ingold 1996a:120, 2012b:34.

31. Ibid.,118, ibid., 32.

32. Ingold 2008a [2000]:76.

33. Ibid.

34. I would want to say the "human religious condition."

35. Note Ingold's use of this religiously laden term *creature.*

36. Ingold 1996a:120–121, 2012b:134.

37. Ibid.

38. Ibid., 120, ibid.

39. See, for example, Serpell 1996. For further discussion also see Burkert 1983:12–22, Burkert 1996:150; Frazer and Gaster 1959:471–479; Ingold 2008a [2000]:69; and Milgrom 1991:712–713.

40. As cited in Ingold 1996a:8 (my emphasis).

41. Smith 1993:267.

42. This alignment and interrelations of series of binary oppositions is a key insight of Lévi-Strauss, and we will return to it and to Derrida's reconsideration of it in the section "Structural Links" in the next chapter.

43. Ingold 1996a:130–131, 2012b:42.

44. Steven Lukes as cited in Smith 1993.

45. Ingold 2012a.

46. Freud writes,

> In the course of centuries the naive self-love of men has had to submit to two major blows at the hands of science. The first was when they learnt that our earth was not the center of the universe but only a tiny fragment of a cosmic system of scarcely imaginable vastness. This is associated in our minds with the name of Copernicus, though something similar had already been asserted by Alexandrian science. The second blow fell when biological re-

search destroyed man's supposedly privileged place in creation and proved his descent from the animal kingdom and his ineradicable animal nature. This revaluation has been accomplished in our own days by Darwin, Wallace and their predecessors, though not without the most violent contemporary opposition. But human megalomania will have suffered its third and most wounding blow from the psychological research of the present time which seeks to prove to the ego that it is not even master in its own house, but must content itself with scanty information of what is going on unconsciously in the mind. (Freud 1963:284–285)

47. Nietzsche 1989:155. The full German reads, "Er ist Tier geworden, Tier, ohne Gleichnis, Abzug und Vorbehalt, er, der in seinem früheren Glauben beinahe ('Kind Gottes,' 'Gottmensch') war" (Nietzsche 2005:1042).

48. Ingold 2008b:49.

49. Ingold 2010b:163.

50. Ingold 2008b:51.

51. Wemelsfelder as cited in Bekoff 2007:46.

52. Thomas 1983:119.

53. Ingold 1996:135, 2012b:46.

54. Buber's views toward animals could benefit from greater attention not only because of the insights they carry about human-animal relationships but also because of the new light they might cast on how Buber understood religion and especially religious experience. The key passage from *I and You* is worth quoting at length:

The eyes of an animal have the capacity of a great language. . . . I sometimes look into the eyes of a house cat. The domesticated animal has not by any means received the gift of the truly "eloquent" glance from us, as a human conceit suggests sometimes; what it has from us is only the ability—purchased with the loss of its elementary naturalness—to turn this glance upon us brutes [uns Untieren]. . . . Undeniably, this cat began its glance by asking me with a glance that was ignited by the breath of my glance: "Can it be that you mean me? Do you actually want that I should not merely do tricks for you? Do I concern you? Am I there for you? Am I there? What is that coming from you? What is that around me? What is it about me? What is that?!" ("I" here is a paraphrase of a word of I-less self-reference that we lack. "That" represents the flood of man's glance in the entire actuality of its power to relate.) There the glance of the animal, the language of anxiety, had risen hugely—and set almost at once. My glance, to be sure, endured longer; but it no longer retained the flood of man's glance. . . . No other event has made me so deeply aware of the evanescent actuality in all relationships to other beings, the sublime melancholy of our lot, the fated lapse into It of every single You.   (Buber 1996 [1970]:144-145)

In the afterward, Buber clarifies the human

obtains from them an often astonishing active response to his approach, to his address—and on the whole this response is the stronger and more direct, the more his relation amounts to a genuine You-saying. Not infrequently animals, like children, see through feigned tenderness. But outside the tamed circle, too, we occasionally encounter a similar contact between men and animals: some men have deep down in their being a potential partnership with animals—most often persons who are by no means "animalic" by nature but rather spiritual. . . . In the perspective of our You-saying to animals, we may call this sphere the threshold of mutuality.   (172–173)

Buber's argument that there are spiritually inclined persons who have especially strong I-You encounters with animals can be understood in the context of his study of Hasidism. Buber notes that a number of Hasidic masters were reported to have unique relationships with animals. For example, in the one brief paragraph he devotes to Rabbi Zev Wolf of Zbarah (died about 1802), he describes him as known for refusing "to treat the wicked differently from the good. Wolf lavished his love on all human beings who came his way and even on animals. He held that man should love all that lives" (Buber 1975 [1947]:22).

55. Note that Ingold again invokes the religious term *creature*.

56. Ingold 1996a: 136, 2012b:46–47.

57. Derrida, too, explicitly wants to challenge the notion that animals lack society. He speaks of "the hardly contestable fact that there are animal societies, animal organizations that are refined and complicated in the organization of family relations and social relations in general, in the distribution of work and wealth, in architecture, in the inheritance of things acquired, of good or non-innate abilities, in the conduct of war and peace, in the hierarchy of powers, in the institution of absolute chief" (Derrida 2009:16).

58. Ingold 1996a:136, 2012b:47.

59. Ingold 2008a:69.

60. Ibid., 69.

61. Ibid., 72.

62. Ibid., 71.

63. Ingold 1996a:121, 2012b:34.

64. Derrida 2002a:26, 1999:276. When two citations are given for a single quotation, the first will be an English translation and the second will cite the original language. Where it is helpful, I will follow these citations with the original language text.

65. Ingold 2001b:255.

66. Derrida 2002a:26, 1999:277. "l'immense question du pathos et du pathologique, justement, de la souffrance, de la pitié et de la compassion. Et de la place qu'il faut accorder à l'interprétation de cette compassion, au partage de la souffrance entre des vivants."

67. Ingold himself makes an argument that medieval and modern approaches to animals in the West differ in a manner parallel to the differences he earlier argued (as detailed in this chapter) are present when contrasting civilizational and hunter-gatherer apprehensions (Ingold 2013).

68. Acampora 2006:4.

69. Ibid., 5.

70. Ibid.

71. Ibid., 5.

72. See note 6 in this chapter on science.

73. Ingold 2010b:160.

74. Derrida 2002a:26, 1999:276.

75. It may at first seem odd, perhaps even inappropriate, to bring up agriculture at the conclusion of a theoretical essay, but livestock occupy a third of the surface area of the earth and most of us are actively involved in supporting factory farming on a daily basis. Nothing so pervasive should be easily put out of discussion. My bringing up contemporary animal agriculture in relation to the question of the animal in the study of religion, I argue, could not be more necessary (not a radical scholarly move, but something dictated by the most basic requirements of critical thought and scholars' duty to contextualize). Not to do so would be like attempting to understand the study of Judaism without considering the presence of anti-Semitism in the history of the West; any such study would be manifestly incomplete.

76. This is so because the one federal law that could protect animals at the point of slaughter, the Humane Methods of Slaughter Act, has been interpreted to exclude chickens, which constitute more than 99 percent of land animals slaughtered in the United States (Farm Forward 2010, 2013).

77. Derrida 1995.

78. For discussion of the complementarity and obviation approaches, see Ingold 2001b.

5. DISAVOWAL, WAR, SACRIFICE

1. Derrida 2009:15, for the French, see Derrida 2008b:36.

2. Ibid., ibid.

3. The notion of "following" is an important one in Derrida's texts. For a helpful discussion of Derrida's and other French thinkers' use of the French verb *suivre*, "to follow," see Lawlor 2007:86–96.

4. Mark Payne productively puts Derrida's encounter with his cat, which I will shortly discuss here, in dialogue with hunting narratives in which the hunter feels accused by the hunted animals gaze (Payne 2010:introduction).

5. Derrida 2008a:277. *The Animal That Therefore I Am* was originally written and delivered as a ten-hour lecture in a 1997 conference entitled "L'Animal Auto-biographique," or "The Autobiographical Animal." The first part of the lecture, "L'Animal Que Donc Je Sui (á Suivre)," later translated as "The Animal That Therefore I Am (More to Follow)," was originally published in French in the edited volume produced from this conference, *L'Animal autobiographique* (Derrida 1999) and later in English in the journal *Critical Inquiry* (Derrida 2002a). It was always Derrida's intention to publish the full lecture—this is one reason for the "(*á Suivre*)," which could also be translated as "to be continued," that Derrida added to the first publication. The full work would not be published until after his death, the French in 2006 and English in 2008.

6. Derrida 2008a:41, for the French, see 1999:291.

7. In French there is a wordplay here: *bête* can mean both "beast" and "stupid" in French. In a seminar that ran between 2001 and 2002, which Derrida entitled *La bête et le souverain* (2008b), *The Beast and the Sovereign* (2009), he spends considerable time exploring the resonances of *bête* and etymologically related words (in the English edition, see especially pages 68, 98, and the fifth and sixth sessions). Also see Ronell 2002.

8. The allusion to Lewis Carroll is Derrida's own (2008a:7), for the French, see 1999:257–258.

9. Derrida's use of the theme of nudity is indebted to and in dialogue with Emmanuel Levinas. In *Totality and Infinity* Levinas makes a distinction between nudity of things, which is absurd, and the nudity of the other person that he theorizes as the "face," arguably his most influential idea. For Levinas, humans, through language—which is not incidentally denied animals—enter relationships with "a nudity disengaged from every form, but having meaning by itself . . . *always a positive value. Such a nudity is the face*" (Levinas 1995 [1969]:74). Nudity is an exposédness that is also a sign and trace of the radical vulnerability of the other that initiates the ethical relation. Nudity "signifies for me an unexceptionable responsibility. . . . The disclosing of the face is nudity, nonform, abandon of self, ageing, dying, more naked than nudity. It is poverty, skin with wrinkles, which are a trace of itself" (Levinas 2004 [1981]:88). As these lines suggest, neither Levinas nor Derrida attempt to use naked in a way totally divorced from its common sense meaning. The nakedness of the other's face, Levinas explains, "extends into the nakedness of the body" (1995 [1969]:75). For Levinas, the concept of nudity is never far from the possibility of violation and pain, and, especially interesting for our purposes, is sometimes associated with sacrifice. Levinas writes, nudity "is

sacrificed rather than sacrificing itself, for it is precisely bound to the adversity or suffering of pain. This existence, with sacrifice imposed on it, is without conditions" (2004 [1981]:49–50).

10. Derrida 2008a:13, for the French, see 1999:264–265.

11. Ibid., 2008a:4, ibid., 253–254. Derrida uses the phrase *face to face* with its biblical (Exodus 33:11) and Levinasian implications in mind. Levinas argues that the face to face "involves a calling into question of oneself, a critical attitude which is itself produced in face of the other and under his authority. . . . The face to face remains an ultimate situation" (1995 [1969]:81). See also Levinas 1995 [1969]:39.

12. Derrida 2008a:9, for the French, see 1999:259.

13. Ibid., 4, ibid., 254.

14. Ibid., ibid.

15. "Seen seen," as I read Derrida, points toward those individuals who have never allowed themselves to be seen in a moment when they avow having been seen by the animal.

16. Derrida 2008a:13. The French reads, "Il y aurait d'abord les texts signés par des gens qui ont sans doute vu, observé, analysé, réfléchi l'animal mais ne se sont jamais vus vus par l'animal; ils n'ont jamais croisé le regard d'un animal posé sur eux. . . . Cette catégorie de discours, de textes, de signataires . . . est de très loin la plus abondamment fournie" (Derrida 1999:264).

17. Derrida 2008a:13; for the French, see Derrida 1999:264.

18. Ibid., 41, ibid., 291.

19. Calarco 2008:4.

20. Derrida 2008a:13. The French reads, "elle est sans doute celle qui rassemble tous les philosophes et tous les théoriciens en tant que tells" (Derrida 1999:264).

21. See, for example, Derrida's discussion of the unthought in chapter 2 of *Of Spirit* (Derrida 1989, for the French, see Derrida 1987).

22. Derrida 2009:108, for the French, see 2008b:155.

23. Derrida 2008a:28–29, for French, see Derrida 1999:279.

24. Derrida 2008a:29. The French reads, "L'animal nous regarde, et nous sommes nus devant lui. Et penser commence peut-être là" (Derrida 1999:279).

25. Elsewhere, Derrida accepts that one may also move beyond the concept of "the fellow" by a radical expansion of the concept rather than eliminating it. For Derrida, these two strategies—on the one hand, the path of the unthought and, on the other hand, the radicalization of what is thought—if pursued with sufficient rigor, point in the same salutary direction. Derrida imagines someone objecting that what he is doing

> is simply an almost limitless broadening of the notion of "fellow" and that in talking about the dissilmilar, the non-fellow I am surreptitiously extend-

ing the similar, the fellow, to all forms of life, to all species. All animals qua living beings are my fellows. I accept this counter proposition, but not without twice further upping the ante by pointing out: 1. In the first place, the first upping of the ante: that this broadening would already, of itself, be markedly, significantly, and obviously in breach with everything that everyone has in mind . . . when the talk about the fellow. . . . 2. In the second place, the second upping of the ante: it is not enough to say that this unconditional ethical obligation, if there is one, binds me to the life of any living being in general. It also binds me twice over to something nonliving, namely to the present nonlife or the nonpresent life of those who are not living . . . —i.e. dead living beings and living beings not yet born.

(Derrida 2009:109–110, for the French, see Derrida 2008b:156–157)

26. Derrida 2008a:28; for the French, see 1999:278–279.

27. Ibid., ibid.

28. Derrida 2009:120, for the French, see Derrida 2008b:169.

29. Derrida 2008a:1. The French reads, "Je voudrais élire des mots qui soient, pour commencer, nus, tout simplement, des mots du Coeur" (Derrida 1999:251).

30. Derrida 2008a:17, for the French, see 1999:267.

31. Derrida 2008a:25. The French reads, "violence, fût-ce au sens moralement le plus neutre de ce terme" (Derrida 1999:276).

32. Freud 1950:157.

33. Payne 2010:189.

34. Derrida 2008a:28. The French reads, "Personne ne peut nier la souffrance, la peur ou la panique, la terreur ou l'effroi qui peut s'emparer de certains animaux, et dont nous, les hommes, nous pouvons témoigner. (Descartes lui-même, nous le verrons, n'a pu alléguer l'insensibilité des animaux à la souffrance)" (Derrida 1999:279).

35. Levinas 2004 [1981]:49–50.

36. Derrida 2008a:28. Derrida here targets the Heideggerian privileging of questioning and, in a way often associated with Levinas, argues that an ethical relation is more fundamental. The French reads, "à la question « Can they suffer ? » la réponse ne fait aucun doute. Elle n'a d'ailleurs jamais laissé place au doute; c'est pourquoi l'expérience que nous en avons n'est pas même indubitable: elle précède l'indubitable, elle est plus vieille que lui" (Derrida 1999:279).

37. As noted in the introduction, by "building blocks" I mean, following Anne Taves, "things that strike people as special" and that can be manipulated or "assembled in various ways to create more complex socio-cultural formations, some of which people characterize as 'religions'" (Taves 2009:162).

38. de Wall 2009.

39. More specifically, Hrdy describes her book *Mothers and Others* as

about the emergence of a particular mode of childrearing known as "cooperative breeding" and its psychological implications for apes in the line leading to Homo sapiens. . . . "Cooperative breeding" refers to any species with alloparental assistance in both the care and provisioning of young. I will propose that a long, long time ago . . . before such distinctively human traits as language (the hallmark of behaviorally modern humans), there emerged in Africa a line of apes that began to be interested in the mental and subjective lives—the thoughts and feelings—of others, interested in understanding them. These apes were . . . emotionally modern.

(Hrdy 2009:30)

40. de Waal 2009:79.

41. Ibid.

42. Ibid.

43. Coetzee 2004:80. Undine Sellbach (2012) offers a compelling discussion of Coetzee's conception of the sympathetic imagination. Coetzee is explicitly critiquing Thomas Nagel's famous essay "What Is It Like to Be a Bat." For a productive reading of Coetzee's engagement with Nagel, see Payne 2010:187–234.

44. Derrida 2008a:28; for the French, see Derrida 1999:279.

45. Ibid.

46. Derrida 1992a:95.

47. Derrida 2008a:26; for the French, see the following note.

48. Ibid. The French reads,

Je n'abuserai pas de la facilité avec laquelle on pourrait donner toute sa charge pathétique aux évidences que je rappelle ainsi. Tout le monde sait quels terrifiants et insoutenables tableaux une peinture réaliste pourrait faire de la violence industrielle, mécanique, chimique, hormonale, génétique, à laquelle l'homme soumet depuis deux siècles la vie animale. Et ce que sont devenus la production, l'élevage, le transport, la mise à mort de ces animaux. (Derrida 1999:277)

49. Derrida 2008a:51. The French reads, "L'animal en général, qu'est-ce que c'est ? Qu'est-ce que ça veut dire ? Qui est-ce ? « Ça » correspond à quoi ? A qui ? Qui répond à qui ? Qui répond au nom commun, général et singulier de ce qu'ils appellent ainsi tranquillement l'« animal » ? Qui est-ce qui répond ?" (Derrida 1999:301).

50. Derrida 1995:286, for the French, see Derrida 1992b:300.

51. Derrida 2008a:28–29, for the French, see Derrida 1999:279.

52. Derrida 2009:30, for the French, see Derrida 2008b:55.

53. Derrida 2008a:24, for the French, see Derrida 1999:275.

54. Derrida 2008a:25. The French reads, "Eh bien pour rappeler, par commodité initiale et sans prétendre ici à aucune exactitude, quelques indices préalables qui nous permettent de nous entendre et de dire « nous » aujourd'hui" (Derrida 1999:275).

55. Wolfson and Sullivan 2005.

56. Derrida 2008a:25, for the French, see Derrida 1999:275–276.

57. Ibid., ibid., 276.

58. Derrida 2008a:25. The French reads,

> par l'élevage et le dressage à une échelle démographique sans commune mesure avec le passé, par l'expérimentation génétique, par l'industrialisation de ce qu'on peut appeler la production alimentaire de la viande. animale, par l'insémination artificielle massive, par les manipulations de plus en plus audacieuses du génome, par la réduction de l'animal non seulement à la production et à la reproduction suractivée (hormones, croisements génétiques, clonage, etc.) de viande alimentaire mais à toutes sortes d'autres finalisations.   (Derrida 1999:276)

59. Derrida 2008a:25, for the French, see Derrida 1999:276.

60. Pauly, Watson, and Adler 2005.

61. Koslow 2007.

62. Ibid.

63. Worm et al. 2006.

64. I make reference here to the UN's Livestock's Long Shadow report (Steinfeld et al. 2006).

65. Derrida 2008a:25. The French reads, "De quelque façon qu'on l'interprète, quelque conséquence pratique, technique, scientifique, juridique, éthique ou politique qu'on en tire, personne aujourd'hui ne peut nier cet événement, à savoir les proportions sans précédent de cet assujettissement de l'animal" (Derrida 1999:276).

66. Derrida 2008a:25–26. The French reads, "Personne ne peut davantage dénier sérieusement la dénégation. Personne ne peut plus nier sérieusement et longtemps que les hommes font tout ce qu'ils peuvent pour dissimuler ou pour se dissimuler cette cruauté, pour organiser à l'échelle mondiale l'oubli ou la méconnaissance de cette violence que certains pourraient comparer aux pires génocides (il y a aussi des génocides animaux)" (Derrida 1999:276).

67. In asking what Derrida might mean in his association of the factory farm with genocide, we should keep in mind his own proximity to the Shoah; Derrida was fifteen years old when the concentration camps were liberated, and he himself had been expelled by his own French government from his school in Algeria a few years before under the power of anti-Semetic Vichy legislation. His voice, his provocation in making this dreaded and despised comparison comes to us with the authority of a biography enmeshed in these historic events.

68. Derrida 1995:278, for the French, see Derrida 1992b:292.
69. Derrida 2008a:26. The French reads, "De la figure du génocide il ne faudrait ni abuser ni s'acquitter trop vite. Car elle se complique ici: l'anéantissement des espèces, certes, serait à l'oeuvre, mais il passerait par l'organisation et l'exploitation d'une survie artificielle, infernale, virtuellement interminable, dans des conditions que des hommes du passé auraient jugé monstrueuses, hors de toutes les normes supposées de la vie proper aux animaux ainsi exterminés dans leur survivance ou dans leur surpeuplement même" (Derrida 1999:276–277).
70. Wolfson and Sullivan 2005:213. Princeton bioethicist and utilitarian philosopher Peter Singer and lawyer Jim Mason went undercover to work as turkey inseminators to document the violence of this artificial insemination in their book *The Way We Eat* (2006:28–29).
71. If left to their own devices these breeder birds will literally eat themselves to death in a frustrated effort to fill their stomachs, for their desire has not been bred out, only the possibility of its satisfaction. Thus the industry must "feed restrict" these birds to keep them alive sufficiently long to be profitable. The following extended citation is from an informative essay distributed to poultry farmers being solicited to buy computer systems for their barns; written by an industry CIO with a doctorate in animal genetics, the essay provides not only a genuinely helpful historical overview, but is illustrative of how the industry understands itself:

> As a result of breeding for large and fast growing broilers [i.e., modern chickens raised for meat as opposed to those raised for egg production] the modern broilers and their parents were genetically inclined towards uncontrolled eating, unchecked by the natural "feeling" of satiation [note the disavowal of the quotation marks used around *feeling*]. The destruction of satiation and feeding control mechanisms seriously affected laying ability, fertility and even the hatching percentage of fertile eggs [after all, these are distressed animals]. . . . From the early 1970s it became clear to growers that in order to maintain an acceptable level of laying ability the feed intake of pullets designated for broiler breeding flocks has to be controlled from an early age throughout their productive cycle. Consequently feed restriction was derived from comparison of an optimal weight chart and feeding schedules. . . . With the continuing success [!] of the selection programs the difference between the recommended restricted feed allotment and every new generation's growing appetite increased. To maintain the balance between growing appetites and the optimal feed ration the time allotted daily to consume the feed ration was shortened. For this purpose specialized feeders were developed to ensure a uniform and rapid feed rationing. . . . Since the 1980's breeder males were diagnosed as suffering the same feed related afflictions as the females and in addition from too heavy breasts.

> It became clear that in order to attain proper flock fertility performance males needed separately monitored feeders and different quantities of food. Later, the continuing genetic changes caused a more dramatic drop in fertility and forced the "spiking" of broiler breeder flocks with young males in the middle of the production cycle. The timing decisions connected with this "spiking" . . . became ICT [Information and Communication Technology] dependent. (Yoav 2008)

72. Derrida 2008a:26, for the French, see 1999:276–277.

73. Derrida emphasizes, even "the most original forms that this discourse might assume today, for example, in Heidegger or Levinas" (Derrida 2008a, for the French, see 1999:277.

74. Foer 2009:37.

75. Derrida 2008a: for the French, see 17, 1999:268.

76. Ibid., 14, ibid., 265.

77. Derrida 1995:278, for the French, see Derrida 1992b:292.

78. Ibid, ibid.

79. Ibid., ibid.

80. Note: "the question" rather than "this question."

81. Derrida 1995:278 (emphasis added), for the French, see Derrida 1992b:292.

82. Ibid., 286, ibid., 300.

83. Ibid., 278, ibid., 292.

84. *Corpus deliciti* (literally Latin for "body of crime") is a legal technical term referring to the requirement that the fact of a crime having occurred must be established before anyone can be tried for it.

85. Derrida 2008a:91, for the French, see 2006:128.

86. Derrida 1995:278, for the French, see 1992b:293.

87. Derrida 2002b:86.

88. Ibid., 85–86.

89. Ibid., 86.

90. Derrida 1995:279, for the French, see Derrida 1992b:293.

91. For discussion of Levinas's view, see Gross 2009.

92. Derrida 1995:279, for the French, see Derrida 1992b:293.

93. Ibid., 281, ibid., 295.

94. Ibid., ibid., 295–296.

95. Ibid., 280, ibid., 294. Derrida revisits, as he says, "everything I nicknamed carnophallogocentrism" in his lecture courses; see Derrida 2009:15, for the French, see Derrida 2008b:35.

96. Derrida 1995:280 (emphasis added), for the French, see Derrida 1992b:294.

97. Ibid., 284, ibid., 298.

98. Derrida 2008a:90, for the French, see Derrida 2006:126.

99. Ibid., 90–91, ibid., 127.

100. Ibid., 103–104, ibid., 143–144.

101. Benjamin 2011:110. In *Of Jews and Animals* (2011) the exempla include figurations of animals in the art of Piero della Francesca and Bartolomé Bermejo (chapter 6); Pascal's Pensées 102 and 103 (chapter 7); the art of Jan van Eyck and his school, Albrecht Dürer, and Velásquez (chapter 8); and what Benjamin calls "the logic of the synagogue," for example, in the image of the defeated *synagogia* in contrast to the triumphant church in European painting (chapters 7–8).

102. Benjamin 2011:4.

103. Derrida 2008a:104, for the French, see Derrida 2006:144.

104. Derrida 1995:278, for the French, see Derrida 1992:293.

105. Ibid., 281, ibid., 293.

106. Ibid., 282, ibid., 296.

107. See the epilogue for further discussion.

6. SACRIFICING ANIMALS AND BEING A MENSCH

1. See entry for mensch in the glossary.

2. For a remarkable examination of ethics as responsibility and responsiveness, see Gibbs 2000.

3. Foer 2009:11.

4. The German reads "Der Mensch ist, was er isst." I quote Feuerbach from the brief but helpful discussion of him in Fox 1999:24. Fox's book also provides variations on this quip in French and English texts as early as 1642 (291).

5. Ingold 2010a:361.

6. Ibid.

7. In addition to examples cited later in this discussion, a survey of "Jewish eating" has been provided by Kraemer 2007.

8. Feely-Harnik 1981:xiii–xvi.

9. Rosenblum forthcoming.

10. Rosenblum 2010:79–80

11. Brumberg-Kraus 2004:310.

12. Wolfson 2006:40.

13. My translation based on text in Bar Ilan's Judaic Library Plus Responsa Version 12 CD rom.

14. In forthcoming publications I discuss the way in which dietary rules interact with processes of "racial formation" (Omi and Winant 1986) and I consider how, in the

case of the Chabad-Lubavitch community that owned, ran, and bought meat from AgriProcessors, particular kinds of racial thinking promoted the mistreatment of non-Jewish workers in the slaughter plant.

15. Bourdieu 1990:68. For a brief discussion of how Bourdieu's idea of habitus can apply to meat eating, see Fiddes 1991:4–5.

16. Bourdieu 1990:69.

17. See earlier the discussion of Derrida in chapter 5 under the heading "Sacrifice of Sacrifice."

18. For Agamben's analysis of the "anthropological machine" see Agamben 2004:34, ch 9. See my discussion of Agamben on pages 91–93.

19. Smith 1993:299.

20. Doniger 2011:xii.

21. Biblical citations follow the 1999 JPS Tanakh.

22. Cohen 1989:66.

23. Gunkel 1997 [1922]:114; Cohen 1989:16.

24. Skinner 1930:35.

25. Gunkel 1997 [1922]:115.

26. Westermann 1994:165.

27. Delitzsch and Dillmann, like the analysis I have given, argue for the relative lack of emphasis on the difference between the diet mandated for humans and animals. Delitzsch describes the difference as "unimportant . . . herbs only being allotted to beasts, but to man fruit trees as well" (1978 [1888]:102). Dillmann calls it "a distinction in the lump" (Dillmann 1897:86). Both likewise concur with my emphasis on the implied vegetarianism. Delitzsch opines, "The main point is not what is expressed, but its reverse; for the direction to vegetable diet means the restriction to this, to the exclusion of the flesh of animals" (Delitzsch 1978 [1888]:102) and Dillmann observes, "But the distinction of the world of plants among living creatures is not the only point of view under which the passage has to be considered. The omission to mention flesh as a food of man . . . leads . . . to a deeper thought. . . . The use of flesh for food costs an animal its life" (87). Later commentators have generally followed this reading by noting (with small variations) the distinction in the assigned food, but emphasizing the significance of the implied vegetarianism and concomitant lack of violence. Driver assigns humans "seed and fruit" and animals "leaves" (Driver 1954 [1904]:16). Skinner makes essentially the same distinction: humans are given "seeding plants . . . and fruit-bearing trees" and animals "the succulent leafy parts [of plants]," adding the helpful comment that the significance of the seeding plants may be connected with their role in cultivation (1930:34). This same distinction is perceived by Gunkel and Westermann (Gunkel 1997 [1922]:114; Westermann 1994:162). Wenham assigns "plants and fruit" to humans and "plants" to animals (Wenham 1987:34).

28. Brueggemann 1982:30. Sarna makes the same point (Sarna 1989:11).

29. This observation is a long-held interpretive consensus, and several commentators strengthen it by noting extrabiblical parallels for the tradition of a primordial human-animal peace. Delitzsch concludes from 1:29–30 that "at the beginning peace prevailed between man and the beasts, and among the beasts towards each-other" (Delitzsch 1978 [1888]:102). Dillmann similarly argues that "the Creator did not desire war and the thirst for blood, but peace among His creatures" (Dillmann 1897:87) and provides a list of ancient Greek and Roman sources that show similar attitudes. Driver, citing Perowne, describes 29–30 as portraying "an *ideal*. 'Animal food can only be had at the cost of animal life, and the taking of animal life seemed to him to be a breach of the Divine order, which from the beginning provides only for the continuance and maintenance of life'" (1954 [1904]:17). Skinner describes "a state of peace and harmony in the animal world" (1930:34) that is motivated by "horror of bloodshed, sympathy with the lower animals, and longing for harmony" (35). Gunkel emphasizes his conclusion that 29–30 represents a separate intellectual tradition that, he argues citing Usener, portrays "the image of the land of the gods where 'the blessed gods lead their lives of joy every day,' where eternal peace reigns, where even the animals abandon their enmity" (1997 [1922]:115). Cassuto likewise calls the portrait "idealized. . . . Not only man but even the animals were expected to show reverence for the principle of life" (1998 [1961]:59). Von Rad speaks of a "paradisiacal peace in the creation as it came God-willed from God's hand" (Rad 1974:61). Westermann, following Dillmann, sees in these verses "the awareness that the killing of living beings for food by other living beings is not right, and so not in accordance with the will of the creator at the beginning" and emphasizes that this sentiment is "a question of what we could call human traditions, because it is restricted neither to place nor to a culture . . . [it is] common to humanity" (Westermann 1994:164). Wenham's discussion of this issue is peculiar; he neither denies nor affirms the tradition of a peaceable beginning, although he cites (approvingly?) Westermann's discussion of this tradition as common to multiple peoples. Sarna follows the main line, emphasizing that human ascendancy must be understood "within the context of a 'very good' world in which the interrelationships of organisms with their environment and with each other are entirely harmonious and mutually beneficial, an idyllic situation" (1989:13). Milgrom, commenting on Genesis 9:4 as part of his commentary on Leviticus follows Dillmann and Westermann in noting that the concern for human-animal harmony demonstrated here is widespread, "The ethical sensitivity displayed by this rationale need not surprise us when we consider the background. Anthropological and comparative evidence indicates that the reluctance to kill an animal harks back to a much earlier period" (Milgrom 1991:712; for a related discussion, see ibid., 442).

30. See Cassuto 1998 [1961]:59; Delitzsch 1978 [1888]:104; Dillmann 1897:89; Driver 1954:13; Gunkel 1997 [1922]:115; Jacob 1974; Sarna 1989:114; Skinner 1930:34–35; Rad 1974:61; Wenham 1987:34; Westermann 1994:165.

31. Skinner 1930:34.

32. Rad 1974:61. Brueggemann, by contrast to this paper's analysis, argues that "the 'good' used here does not refer primarily to a moral quality, but to an aesthetic quality" (Brueggemann 1982:37).

33. Fishbane 1989:318–321.

34. See Gunkel 1997 [1922]:154; Skinner 1930:169.

35. In this connection, Cassuto suggests two points that emphasize the work animals do in establishing the unique ascendancy of man: (a) "This attitude of fear and dread may be due to the fact that the creatures were saved from the Flood on account of man and through his action; from now on they would realize more clearly the superiority of the human species" (Cassuto 1998 [1961]:125) and further (b), the particular order of animals who will experience this fear is arranged so that the animals normally least afraid of man are first "in order to show how far it [fear and dread] reached" (ibid). Humans are not only marked as unique by virtue of their mastery over animals, but their uniqueness is now marked by animals' own subjective states, namely their fearful response to humans. Significantly, this text transforms the frightened response of animals to humans that was undoubtedly frequently observed by the Bible's authors and audience in their own lives into a teaching about human ascendancy. Moreover, Cassuto's hypothesis also suggests how the particular qualities of specific categories of animals—like their relative fearfulness—are marshaled to highlight human qualities.

36. Delitzsch notes, "The אך which follows . . . introduces a limitation of that participation of flesh which is now permitted" (Delitzsch 1978 [1888]:283). Dillmann similarly observes, "These rights of dominion on the part of man are restricted by two prohibitions, both introduced by אך, only, nevertheless" (Dillmann 1897:292). Driver introduces 9:46 as "two limitations upon man's too absolute authority" (Driver 1954:96). Skinner calls verses 4 and 5 the "first [and] second restriction" (Skinner 1930:170). Cassuto, in almost identical terms, calls verses 5–6 "one restriction followed by another" (Cassuto 1998 [1961]:126). Westermann similarly concludes that 9:4–6 is "intended as a restriction of the concession in v. 3" in part on the basis of "the twice repeated אך" (Westermann 1994:464).

37. For discussion, see Cassuto 1998 [1961]:127; Delitzsch 1978 [1888]:186–187; Dillmann 1897:295; Driver 1954:97; Rad 1974:32–133; Sarna 1989:61–62; Skinner 1930:170–171; Wenham 1987:193–194; Westermann 1994:468.

38. Westermann 1994:462.

39. Ibid., 463.

40. Ibid.

41. In this connection we can note that Westermann distinguishes between what he calls the "original" meaning of verse 4 and "the meaning of the sentence in P" (Westermann 1994:465). Westermann argues that "[v]. 4, as such, reflects . . . a specifically primitive notion that the life *of every living being* is identical with the pulsation of the blood" (ibid., emphasis added). He further argues that the prohibition is not on consuming blood, but on consuming flesh from a still living animal (i.e., one with the blood pulsating through it). Westermann's reconstructed original meaning of the prohibition appears similar to the rabbinic tradition of the Noahide law prohibiting cutting a limb off of a living animal, אבר מן־החי, which is based on this verse (for discussion, see Delitzsch 1978 [1888]:283; Gunkel 1997:150; and especially Sarna 1989:60–61, 376–377). In regard to the verse's meaning in P, Westermann writes, "It is a recognition of the connection between murder and brutality that has brought these two restrictions [vs. 4 and 5] together. P shows great wisdom in illustrating the phenomenon of brutality by resuming the old [i.e., original] prohibition and relating it to human conduct towards animals" (Westermann 1994:465). Milgrom brings 9:4–6 together in a similar manner in his work on Leviticus (Milgrom 1991:713).

42. Milgrom's analysis of the ethical basis of the Jewish dietary laws and thus the blood prohibition in 9:4 are first given in his 1963 essay "The Biblical Diet Laws as an Ethical System."

43. Milgrom 1991:718, 733, 735–736, 741; Douglas 1999:137.

44. Delitzsch 1978 [1888]:284; Dillmann 1897:293. The relevant passages are worth quoting at length; Delitzsch writes, "Blood and life are one, inasmuch as they are in one another in a relation of intercausation. . . . This relation of the life to the blood . . . is indicated by the juxtaposition of נפש and דמו, which at the same time suggests the reason for this prohibition of the blood, viz. a sacred reverence for that principle of life flowing in the blood" (Delitzsch 1978:284). Similarly, but with more emphasis on the benefits to human morality rather than for animal life, Dillmann asserts, "The blood is a sensible and palpable manifestation of the soul. But the life belongs to God, the Lord of all life. Men are forbidden to use it for the gratification of their palate, are required, on the contrary, by abstinence from it to preserve their respect for the divineness of life and to find protection from savagery and coarseness of feeling" (Dillmann 1897:293).

45. Westermann 1994:465.

46. Milgrom 2000:1295.

47. Ibid.

48. Milgrom 1991:713.

49. It is also worth emphasizing that the particular commandments of Gen. 9:1–7—a prohibition pertaining to consuming animal blood and a prohibition on murder of humans—are not merely particular commands among others, but explicitly foun-

dational for the new order established after the flood. Thus early biblical critics like Dillmann and Budde call the permission to eat animal flesh given in 9:3 "a chief distinction of the present in contrast to the first age of the world" (Dillmann 1897:292). Gunkel, going farther, argues that for P the blood prohibition (9:4) is "the basis of all order and morality" (Gunkel 1997 [1922]:149). Surely reading the text in a similar direction, some of the earliest extant Jewish interpretations of the text, Targum Onkelos and Pseudo-Jonathan, seize upon these verses as foundational for the court system and add the details that witnesses and a sentence of a judge are required for the death penalty.

50. Cohen 1989:99–105.

51. Ibid., 187.

52. As translated ibid., 184.

53. As a brief excursus, consider that the same basic idea of the human as uniquely neotenic we encountered in Durkheim plays a role in another imagination of the human as uniquely technological, found, as Tom Carlson has shown, in both "mystical theological traditions, on the one hand, and the religious or mystical character of today's technological culture, on the other" (Carlson 2008:207). Carlson has theorized this imagination of the human as "indiscrete image," always inevitably nondiscrete because always and inevitably changing in its co-constitution with technology. "The hypothesis I've been working out here, through the twofold path of mystical theological tradition and more recent post-human discourse, is that the human, precisely as creature of inheritance, or of tradition is inevitably technological—and that the founding condition both of inheritance and of technological existence should be understood not in terms of human property and possession, definition or measure, placement and belonging, but rather, indeed, in terms of an indetermination, a lack of measure or of property . . . that enable and demand the creative—or the genetic—capacity of the human" (ibid., 188). Carlson is not merely documenting intellectual history but proposing this thinking of the human as indiscrete image as a model for religious studies (ibid., 210).

54. Accordingly we can say that the religious and the technological are inevitably thought together; see the discussion of Tom Carlson in the previous note.

55. Cohen 1989:186.

56. This and subsequent translations of Rashi's commentary on Genesis are my own based on the text in Bar Ilan's Judaic Library Plus Responsa Version 12 CD rom.

57. Curiously, Rashi says החיה, switching from the plural to the singular in his reference to animals.

58. Bleich 2001b.

59. Albo 1946:130.

וזה להעיר על היתרון שיש בין מין האדם לזולתו מבעלי חיים.

60. Ibid., 131.

אבל עיקר החטא היה לפי שלא חשב היתרון שיש לאדם על הבעלי חיים לכלום, וחשב גם כן היותו אסור בהריגת הבעלי

חיים אחר היותו שוה אליהם לפי דעתו כי כמות זה כן מות זה.

61. Ibid., 132.

אבל לא שיהיה מותר בהריגתן, כי לא חשב שיהיה לאדם יתרון על הבעלי חיים בזה. . . . ולזה נהרג הבל להיות זה הדעת

קרוב מאד מדעת קין ויותר מוכן לטעות בו האנשים ולהמשך אחריו.

62. Ibid., 133.

כלומר אמת הוא כדברך כי עיר פרא אדם יולד, ואין לו יתרון והתנשאות על הבעלי חיים בפעל בעת צאתו לאויר העולם,

אבל יש לו עליהם יתרון בכח להטיב להסיב במעשיו ולהוציא מה שבכחו אל הפעל ולהכיר מעלת האדון.

63. Fiddes 1991:2.

64. Ibid.

65. Intriguingly, Mircea Eliade, writing in a radically different context, appears to support Albo's thesis that killing animals is crucial for any biblically rooted religion. Indeed, as we saw in chapter 3, Eliade argues in *A History of Religious Ideas* that killing animals is crucial to religion as such. As discussed earlier (see pages 74–81), beyond human verticality Eliade lists two other characteristics that he argues distinguished human beings from our primate ancestors, thus giving birth to religion. The first is the use of tools, fire especially—this we could connect with the question of technology (see previous discussion of technology in note 53). The second is the fact that humans eat other animals and do so by choice. "Man," Eliade argues, "is the final product of a decision to kill in order to live" (Eliade 1981:4). This decision to kill, Eliade goes on to argue, ultimately leads to the production of gender differentiation and the structure of sacrifice, a structure that we saw Derrida place at the center of Abrahamic traditions.

66. Babylonian Talmud tractate Bava Metzia 85a. A variation of the story appears in Bereshit Rabbah 33:3. Also see discussion in the introduction of this book.

67. Rubenstein 1999:3.

68. For an excellent animal-sensitive reading that does just this—that is, tries to read this passage more thoroughly in the larger context of the sugya—see the interpretation of Julia Watts Belser (forthcoming), which builds on the scholarship of Daniel Boyarin. While the reading I propose takes a smaller swath of the tractate into consideration than does Watts Belser, her principle conclusion that "moral certainty" is thwarted by an "aggadic dialectic" is also at the heart of what I wish to show.

69. For a helpful discussion of the rabbinic self-understanding of the "Dual Torah"— that is both "written" and "oral," see Ouaknin 1995:5–40.

70. Bleich 2001a:356–357.

71. Gross 2013.

72. In bringing critical theory—the analytic of the humane subject—in dialogue with the Talmud, I follow Daniel Boyarin's suggestion that "contemporary theory opens

up possibilities for reunderstanding midrash" (Boyarin 1990:x). Like Boyarin, I can also say that this project, is "roughly—very roughly—speaking" Derridean (ibid.).

73. Cohen 1989:184.

74. The question of whether an *am ha-aretz* ("one of the people" rather than the rabbinic intelligentsia) has the same right to eat meat as a scholar is in fact considered in Pesachim 49b, where Judah ha-Nasi rules that an *am ha-aretz* should not eat meat. The passage containing this ruling is quite interesting as an example of several binary oppositions working together: human/animal (the *am ha-aretz* is likened to animals), permitted meat/nonpermitted meat, and torah scholar/*am ha-aretz*. Moreover, the story of Judah ha-Nasi and the calf, the story of this ruling, and the idea that one should eat meat only if there is craving are all brought into dialogue in Bereishit Rabba 33:3.

75. Steinsaltz 1990:133.

 דההוא עגלא דהוו קא ממטו ליה לשחיטה, אזל תליא לרישיה בכנפיה דרבי, וקא בכי. אמר ליה: זיל, לכך נוצרת. אמרי:
הואיל ולא קא מרחם, ליתו עליה יסורין.

76. Ibid., 134.

יומא חד הוה קא כנשא אמתיה דרבי ביתא, הוה שדיא בני כרכושתא וקא כנשא להו, אמר לה: שבקינהו. כתיב ורחמיו על
כל מעשיו. אמרו: הואיל ומרחם, נרחם עליה.

77. Significantly, כנפ, which is, following Steinsaltz, translated as "garment" can also mean wing—as in, perhaps, "taking someone under your wing." The image operating here, perhaps, is that of a mother hen or other bird protecting her young—a powerful image in many cultures, including Israelite (we can think of Jesus in Matthew 23:37 expressing his longing to gather his disciples under his wing like a hen). This is a story, then, about an animal taken from its mother that seeks protection "under the wing" of Judah ha-Nasi. This reading is made more likely by the central use of the root רחם in the passage, which, as noted later in the text, can mean womb.

78. Eliade 1981:5.

79. Cassirer 1972 [1944]:100.

80. Lieberman 1994:158–159.

81. Tanhuma, Numbers 10:6.

82. This is found in tractate (treatise) Parah 3 (seder Tohorot) in the Mishnah and is not obvious on a quick reading.

83. I speculate that the image here is of "infant" rats (or some other rodent) dislodged from their nest. Anyone who as ever stumbled upon a nest of baby rats (or, for that matter, a variety of other rodents) will surely remember the extreme helplessness of the creatures, who for a time cannot see or move with any speed. The emotional response most people would have to such כרכושתא בני is quite different to that which the adult animals would elicit and I believe this is significant for our story. As I

will argue in the main text, several features of the story emphasize the vulnerability of animals and, if we were to look at the text surrounding our story, bodily vulnerability more broadly. Beyond the explicit reference to the animals in question being "children of" and the passage's emphasis on vulnerability, the fact that the animals are described as "scattered" and that the servant is capable of "sweeping them up" (try that with adult rats!) suggest to me that the proper image is not simply of small animals, but some kind of rodent in the first weeks when they are especially helpless and mobility impaired.

84. Schofer 2005:259. Also on the theme of vulnerability in this passage and surround ones see Watts Belser forthcoming.

85. See earlier discussion of carnophallogocentrism in chapter 5 pages 141–144.

86. Watts Belser forthcoming:8.

87. Ibid., 33.

88. Dresner emphasizes not only that reverence for life helps us understand the meaning of kashrut, but that kashrut is the main vehicle for teaching reverence for life. "There is hardly a more powerful or more effective means of teaching the lesson of reverence for life than the proper observance of the mitzvah of kashrut." The text continues, "A. Leroy Beaulieu [a nineteenth-century historian] believes that the practice of kashrut has contributed to the merciful nature of the Jewish people. 'Consider the one circumstance,' he wrote almost a century ago, 'that no Jewish mother ever killed a chicken with her own hand, and you will understand why homicide is so rare among the Jews'" (Dresner 2000:28–30).

89. Ibid., 16.

90. See discussion of ethics in chapter 1 of this book, page 19.

91. Dresner 2000:25.

92. Ibid., 16.

93. Ibid., 13 (emphasis added).

94. Ibid., 28–30.

95. Other examples Dresner uses include the selection of *shochatim,* the removal of blood as symbolic restraint from consuming life essence (explicitly following the analysis of Milgrom), rabbinic prohibitions on hunting, Deuteronomy's various laws protecting animals (22:6, 10, 25:4), the participation of animals in Sabbath rest (Exodus 20:8–10), God's refusal to destroy Nineveh in the book of Jonah not only because of the human residents but because there were "many beasts as well" (4:11), the practice of forgoing the usual blessing over a new piece of clothing if it is made with leather, the custom of not wearing leather on Yom Kippur, and the prevention of the callousness implied in cooking a kid in its mother's milk (Dresner 2000).

96. Ibid., 20.

97. Dresner's sense of a living tradition is visible in particular as he relates how a tale about the Baal Shem Tov was transmitted from a gentile who worked near the mas-

ter to an old *shochet* "of about eighty" to the writer S. Y. Agnon and finally to Dresner himself:

> "Did you ever hear of anyone who actually saw the Baal Shem," inquired Agnon. "Not a Jew," was the reply, "but a gentile. I will tell you about it. I worked on a large farm next to a farm owned by a gentile. One day I was whetting the stone on which I sharpened my slaughtering knife, when the gentile farmers' ancient grandfather, close to a hundred years of age, who was observing me, began to shake violently. I noticed that this happened several times when I was whetting the stone. I did not know whether he was just shaking from old age or shaking his head in disapproval of something I was doing. The next time this happened, I asked him if I was doing something he did not approve of, and this is what he said: 'When Yisroleke [Israel Baal Shem Tov] would whet his stone, he did so with his tears!'"
>
> (ibid., 25)

98. Bland 2010:190.

99. Ibid., 187; see discussion of Derrida, this volume, pages 124–125.

100. Bland 2010:190–197.

101. Bland 2009:166.

102. See earlier discussion of Derrida, pages 131–137.

103. The Hebrew word *dvar* (דבר) has a wide semantic range that can include both word or utterance and deed or act.

104. Emmanuel Levinas has argued that the "face" of the other is the foundation of ethics (see note 44 to the introduction) and that the first thing that this face does is say to us "don't kill me." Levinas's own view of animals is not highly developed, and he tended to deny that they could have a face. Nonetheless, I think his theorization of the face, by which he means a nonempirical structure that is not equivalent with a literal face, can help us appreciate the ethical demands animals place upon us. The face of the other does indeed say "don't kill me," and in this regard human faces do not differ from the faces of cattle. See my discussion of Levinas's views of animal ethics (Gross 2009).

105. Pachirat 2011:3.

106. Ibid., 4.

107. Bauman 1989:95.

108. Derrida 2008a:4, for the French, see 1999:254.

109. The idea of the "public secret" is examined by Michael Taussig in a way that may be helpful here: "Such is the labor of the negative, as when it is pointed out that something may be obvious, but needs stating in order to be obvious. For example, the public secret. Knowing is essential to its power, equal to the denial. Not being able to say anything is likewise testimony to its power" (Taussig 1999:6).

110. Rank 2004a.

111. Foer 2006.

112. Gross 2005.

113. Regarding videos and songs, see the irreverent Orthodox blogger Heshy Fried (2011), who draws special attention to a video by Bentzi Marcus and Dovid Dachs entitled *Yedid Nefesh* ("Yedid Nefesh" is the name of a Jewish liturgical poem). One can also find a number of such homages by searching for "Rubashkin" on YouTube.

114. For a fuller study of the limitations of economic and social explanations for modern meat eating, see Fiddes 1991:chapters 3, 6, 12.

115. For further discussion of the relationship between ethics and kashrut in Orthodoxy, see Myers 2012:2013.

116. McNeil 2004b.

117. McNeil 2004a.

118. Ibid.

119. This article generated a large and positive response in Internet discussions, largely within the Orthodox, if not always Haredi, community, as is evident in the fifty-plus comments on the original article. It has also been reprinted on a number of other Orthodox Web sites; for example, see Menken 2004; Shafran 2007; *Kosher Today,* staff 2008.

120. Though Shafran's views of PETA were corrected by respondents more than once (for example, Goldsmith 2004), he repeats this understanding of PETA's principles in a 2005 article (Shafran 2005b), which itself has been reprinted (for example, see Shafran 2005a).

121. Shafran 2004.

122. For a foundational discussion of links between violence against women and animals, see Adams and Donovan 1995; Adams 1993, 1994, 2003, 2010 [1990]; for a discussion of racialization, see Omi and Winant 1986; Hosang, LaBennett, and Pulido 2012.

123. *Ish* is "man" in Hebrew.

124. Derrida 2008a:17, for the French, see Derrida 1999:268.

125. Lincoln 1992:chapter 8. Lincoln concludes, "the claim is advanced that they [taxonomies] make possible knowledge of the underlying patterns of the natural order. But insofar as taxonomies are also instruments for the organization of society, the patterns are extended to—better yet, imposed upon—social groupings, as the social module (whether explicit or not) is associated to the modules of the natural world, being treated as if it were but one more instance of a general cosmic law. More than legitimate, arbitrary social hierarchies are thus represented as if given by nature, and agitation against their inequities—which tends to come from those who have been subordinated and marginalized by these systems—is made to seem but the raving of lunatics" (ibid., 140–141).

126. This deployment of "the animal" to evade ethical responsibility is structurally parallel to an evasion of race-based injustice by insistence on "individuals' rights" (or "state's rights") insofar as both work to tolerate violence under the shroud of defending a type of (carnophallogocentric) subject. For the racist implications of "state's rights" language, see Omi and Winant 1986:133; and, for more recent discussion, Hosang, LaBennett, and Pulido 2012:introduction.

127. For connections between race and gender, see, for example, Hosang, LaBennett, and Pulido 2012:chapters 1–2; Feagin 2013:41, 73, 81, 105–106, 156–157, 173, 179–181, 185.

128. Often abuse of animals will occur in full light and provide insights into what is happening when no one is looking. Charles Siebert, informally acknowledged as the *New York Times Magazine* "animal writer," has documented many of the most substantial examples of this kind of pragmatic use in "The Animal-Cruelty Syndrome." In this article Siebert explains that the link between animal abuse and

> interpersonal violence is becoming so well established that many U.S. communities now cross-train social-service and animal-control agencies in how to recognize signs of animal abuse as possible indicators of other abusive behaviors. In Illinois and several other states, new laws mandate that veterinarians notify the police if their suspicions are aroused by the condition of the animals they treat. The state of California recently added Humane Society and animal-control officers to the list of professionals bound by law to report suspected child abuse.   (Siebert 2010)

There is a wide body of literature that discusses these connections; for further discussion, see Anderson 2006; Arluke 2007; Ascione 1998, 2005; Ascione and Arkow 1999; Heide 2003; Luke 2007; Roberts 2008. For an opposing position, see Lea 2007.

129. Rashi's Commentary on Genesis 1:28; Bava Metzia 114a (my translations from Bar Ilan's Judaic Library Plus Responsa Version 12 CD rom).

130. Agamben 2004:16, 80, 16.

131. Agamben 2004:16.

132. Ibid., 22.

133. Bauman 1989:113.

134. Coetzee 2004:79.

135. Agamben 2004:16.

136. Ibid., 92. The "suspension of the suspension" is the suspension of the Western tradition of imagining the human as suspended between, on the one hand, humanity, spirituality, and divinity and, on the other hand, animality, physicality, and body.

137. Calarco 2008:4.

138. Derrida 2008a:126, for the French, see Derrida 2006:173.
139. Haraway 2008:74.
140. Derrida 2008a:28, for the French, see Derrida 2006:50.

EPILOGUE

1. Singer 1983:40.
2. Ibid.
3. Ibid., 5.
4. For discussion of Singer's vegetarianism, see Hadda 2003:64, 139–148, 180, 277n40. Harold Bloom, in fact, blasted the English publication of the book in a *New York Times* review, claiming, "The voice is indistinguishable from Singer's own" (1983). Bloom underestimates the literary nature of *The Penitent's* Joseph, but I concur that much of the social critique leveled by the character Joseph is Singer's own.
5. Singer 1983:41.
6. Ibid.
7. In traditional Jewish prayer, Jews appeal to God daily to restore the ancient temple so that the sacrificial system may continue again. It is a passage that contemporary Jews—and Jews going back at least as far as Maimonides in the thirteenth century—found troubling. Although the prayer is found in all Orthodox prayer books, Conservative prayer books have tended to reinterpret it through deliberate mistranslation, and Reform prayerbooks have tended to simply excise it.
8. For an erudite discussion of "vegetarian ideology" in the Talmud, see Shemesh 2006.
9. Singer 1983:41.
10. Derrida 2002:86.
11. Agamben 2004:16.
12. Bittman 2011.
13. Humane Society of the United States 2013.
14. Pachirat 2011:3 (emphasis added).
15. This conclusion complements a long-standing observation that Orthodox Judaism has proved remarkably compatible with consumerist culture: "the expansion of a consumerist culture, far from being even loosely incompatible with Orthodox Judaism, actually made it easier to maintain traditional Jewish practice" (Diamond 2003).
16. Derrida 2008a:28; for the French, see Derrida 1999:279.
17. Fiddes 1991:65.
18. See Fiddes 1991. For the inadequacy of taste as an explanation, see chapter 3; for economics, see chapter 11; for health, see chapter 12.

19. Ibid., 1.

20. Ibid., 65.

21. Derrida 1995:281.

22. Fiddes 1991:65.

23. As of the publication of this book, the OU also certifies kosher meat imported from South America that has been slaughtered by the widely condemned method referred to as "shackle and hoist." The OU itself will not certify U.S. plants that use this practice out of concerns with its cruelty, but they tolerate it from abroad because to do otherwise would prove too disruptive to the U.S. meat supply. This is the unofficial but *self-conscious* understanding of OU officials. A regular supply of kosher meat is more important than even their own principles regarding what constitutes cruelty, which is precisely what Fiddes argues. Moses Pava appropriately asks, "how much of our emotional reactions and intuitive ethical response are based on our uneasiness regarding our own consumption of meat and our own responsibility as consumers, always demanding the lowest possible prices, in supporting the entire production process? The Orthodox Union has taken the position consistently that *its most important goal is to ensure low-cost*, high-quality meat for the kosher consumer. This seems to be a relatively straightforward mission . . . but perhaps its taken-for-granted status covers up an ambivalence and uncertainty among (at least) some kosher consumers" (Pava 2011:131 [emphasis added]).

24. Doniger 2011:24.

25. Ibid., 23.

26. Food and Agriculture Organization of the United Nations 2006:xxi.

27. Pew 2008:27, Food and Agriculture Organization of the United Nations 2006:xxi, 112, 267.

28. Foer 2009:32.

29. See the discussion on pages 141–142 of this volume.

30. Schulz 1992:73.

31. For discussion see chapter 4 of this volume.

32. Lévi-Strauss 1963:89.

33. For discussion see Smith 1993:299.

34. Ingold 1996:119, 2012b:33.

Bibliography

Acampora, Ray. 2006. *Corporal Compassion*. Pittsburgh: University of Pittsburgh Press.

Adams, Carol J. 1993. *Ecofeminism and the Sacred*. New York: Continuum.

——. 1994. *Neither Man Nor Beast: Feminism and the Defense of Animals*. New York: Continuum.

——. 2003. *The Pornography of Meat*. New York: Continuum.

——. 2010 [1990]. *The Sexual Politics of Meat: A Feminist-Vegetarian Critical Theory*. 20th anniversary ed. New York: Continuum.

Adams, Carol, and Josephine Donovan. 1995. *Animals and Women: Feminist Theoretical Explorations*: Duke University Press.

Agamben, Giorgio. 2004. *The Open: Man and Animal*. Trans. Kevin Attell. Stanford: Stanford University Press.

Albo, Joseph. 1946. *Sefer ha-'ikkarim; Book of Principles*. Vol 3. Trans. Isaac Husik. Philadelphia: Jewish Publication Society of America.

Alexander, Jeffrey C. 1988. *Durkheimian Sociology: Cultural Studies*. Cambridge: Cambridge University Press.

Allen, Greg. 2004. "PETA Footage Puts Kosher Slaughterhouse on Defensive." NPR.

American Jewish Legacy. 2004. *From the Mountains to the Prairie: 350 Years of Kosher and Jewish Life in America (1654–2004), Outline of Nineteen Exhibit Panels*. American Jewish Legacy 2004 (cited September 7, 2004). Available from www.ajlegacy.org/exhibitpaneloutline.asp.

Anderson, David C. 2006. *Assessing the Human-Animal Bond: A Compendium of Actual Measures*. West Lafayette, IN: Purdue University Press.

Argueta, Luis. 2010. *AbUSed: The Postville Raid.*

Arluke, Arnold. 2007. *Brute Force: Policing Animal Cruelty*. West Lafayette, IN: Purdue University Press.

Ascione, Frank. 1998. *Cruelty to Animals and Interpersonal Violence: Readings in Research and Application*. West Lafayette, IN: Purdue University Press.

——. 2005. *Children and Animals: Exploring the Roots of Kindness*. West Lafayette, IN: Purdue University Press.

Ascione, Frank R., and Phil Arkow. 1999. *Child Abuse, Domestic Violence, and Animal Abuse: Linking the Circles of Compassion for Prevention and Intervention*. West Lafayette, IN: Purdue University Press.

Associated Press. 2009. "Slaughterhouse Manager Convicted in Fraud Case." *New York Times*, November 12.

Bartlett, Joel (People for the Ethical Treatment of Animals). 2009. Statistics on Viewings of 2004 AgriProcessors Video Footage (e-mail subject line). Norfolk, VA, November 30.

Bauman, Zygmunt. 1989. *Modernity and the Holocaust*. Ithaca, NY: Cornell University Press.

Bekoff, Marc. 2007. *The Emotional Lives of Animals: A Leading Scientist Explores Animal Joy, Sorrow, and Empathy—and Why They Matter*. Novato, CA: New World Library.

Bellah, Robert Neelly. 2011. *Religion in Human Evolution: From the Paleolithic to the Axial Age*. Cambridge: Belknap.

Benjamin, Andrew. 2011. *Of Jews and Animals, Frontiers of Theory*. Edinburgh: Edinburgh University Press.

Benjamin, Walter. 2004a [1931]. "Franz Kafka: *Beim Bau der Chinesischen Mauer*." In *Walter Benjamin: Selected Writings*, vol. 2, part 1, *1927–30*. Ed. Michael W. Jennings and Gary Eiland. Cambridge: Belknap.

——. 2004b [1934]. "Franz Kafka: On the Tenth Anniversary of His Death." In *Walter Benjamin: Selected Writings*, vol. 2, part 2, *1931–34*. Ed. Walter Benjamin, Michael W. Jennings, Gary Smith, and Howard Eiland. Cambridge: Belknap.

——. 2004c [1938]. "Letter to Gershom Schalem on Franz Kafka." In *Walter Benjamin: Selected Writings*, vol. 3, *1935–38*. Ed. Michael Bullock and Michael W. Jennings. Cambridge: Belknap.

——. 2004d [1916]. "On Language as Such and on the Language of Man." In *Walter Benjamin: Selected Writings*, vol. 1, *1913–1926*. Ed. Marcus Bullock and Michael W. Jennings. Cambridge: Bellknap.

Berger, Peter L. 1990. *The Sacred Canopy: Elements of a Sociological Theory of Religion*. New York: Anchor.

Biale, David. 2011. *Not in the Heavens: The Tradition of Jewish Secular Thought*. Princeton: Princeton University Press.

Bittman, Mark. 2011. "Who Protects the Animals." *New York Times*, April 26.

Black, Edwin. 2010. "Is a Life Sentence for Iowa Butcher Disproportionate Justice?" *Cutting Edge News*, April 19.

Bland, Kalman. 2009. "Cain, Able, and Brutism." In *Scriptural Exegesis, the Shapes of Culture and the Religious Imagination: Essays in Honour of Michael Fishbane*, 165–185. Ed. Deborah Green and Laura Lieber. Oxford: University of Oxford.

———. 2010. "Construction of Animals in Medieval Jewish Philosophy." In *New Directions in Jewish Philosophy*, x. Ed. Aaron W. Hughes and Elliot R. Wolfson. Bloomington: Indiana University Press.

Blech, Benjamin. 2004. "High Steaks." *Kosher Spirit* (Winter): 1.

Bleich, David J. 2001a. "Judaism and Animal Experimentation." In *Judaism and Environmental Ethics*, 333–370. Ed. Martin D. Yaffe. Lanham, MD: Lexington.

———. 2001b. "Vegetarianism and Judaism." In *Judaism and Environmental Ethics*. Ed. Martin D. Yaffe. Lanham, MD: Lexington.

Bloom, Harold. 1983. "Issac Bashevis Singer's Jeremaid." *New York Times*, 3.

Bloom, Stephen G. 2000. *Postville*. New York: Harcourt.

———. 2005. E-mail Regarding Slaughter Observations, January 5.

Boesch, Christophe. 2003. "Is Culture a Golden Barrier Between Human and Chimpanzee?" *Evolutionary Anthropology*, no. 12, pp. 82–91.

Borowitz, Eugene B. 1991. *Renewing the Covenant: A Theology for the Postmodern Jew*. Philadelphia: Jewish Publication Society.

Bourdieu, Pierre. 1990. *Logic of Practice*. Trans. Richard Nice. Stanford: Stanford University Press.

Boyarin, Daniel. 1990. *Intertextuality and the Reading of Midrash*. Bloomington: Indiana University Press.

Brown, Culum. 2004. "Not Just a Pretty Face." *New Scientist,* no. 2451, pp. 1–13.

Brueggemann, Walter. 1982. *Genesis*. Atlanta: John Knox.

Brumberg-Kraus, Jonathan. 2004. "Meals as Midrash: A Survey of Ancient Meals in Jewish Studies Scholarship." In *Food and Judaism*. Ed. Leonard Greenspoon, Ronald Simkins, and Gerald Shapiro. Omaha: Creighton University Press.

Bshary, R., W. Wickler, and H. Fricke. 2002. "Fish Cognition: A Primate Eye's View." *Animal Cognition* 5, no. 1, pp. 1–13.

Buber, Martin. 1975 [1947]. *Tales of the Hasidim: Early Masters*. Trans. Olga Marx. New York: Schocken.

———. 1996 [1970]. *I and You*. Trans. Walter Kaufmann. New York: Touchstone.

Buchanan, Brett. 2012. "Being with Animals." In *Animal Others and the Human Imagination,* 265–288. Ed. Aaron Gross and Anne Vallely. New York: Columbia University Press.

Burkert, Walter. 1983. *Homo Necans: The Anthropology of Ancient Greek Sacrificial Ritual and Myth*. Berkeley: University of California Press.

———. 1996. *Creation of the Sacred: Tracks of Biology in Early Religions*. Cambridge: Harvard University Press.

Burns, Douglas. 2008. "After Postville Raid, Mystery Advertiser in Guatemala Sought Meatpackers." *Iowa Independent,* June 27.

Calarco, Matthew. 2008. *Zoographies: The Question of the Animal from Heidegger to Derrida*. New York: Columbia University Press.

Caputo, John. 1997. *The Prayers and Tears of Jacques Derrida: Religion Without Religion*. Bloomington: Indiana University Press.

Carlson, Thomas A. 2008. *The Indiscrete Image: Infinitude and Creation of the Human*. Chicago: University of Chicago Press.

Cassirer, Ernst. 1972 [1944]. *An Essay on Man: An Introduction to a Philosophy of Human Culture*. New Haven: Yale University Press.

Cassuto, U. 1998 [1961]. *A Commentary on the Book of Genesis. Part One, From Adam to Noah: A Commentary on Genesis I—VI*. Trans. Israel Abrahams. Jerusalem: Magnes.

Chidester, David. 2005. *Authentic Fakes: Religion and American Popular Culture*. Berkeley: University of California Press.

Coetzee, J. M. 1999. *The Lives of Animals*. Princeton: Princeton University Press.

———. 2004. *Elizabeth Costello*. New York: Penguin.

Cohen, Jeremy. 1989. *Be Fertile and Increase, Fill the Earth and Master It: The Ancient and Medieval Career of a Biblical Text*. Ithaca, NY: Cornell University Press.

Cooperman, Alan. 2004. "USDA Investigating Kosher Meat Plant: Advocacy Group's Grisly Video Sparked Outcry." *Washington Post*, December 31.

Crane, Jonathan. 2007. "Why Rights? Why Me." *Journal of Religious Ethics*, no. 4, pp. 559–589.

Dan, Joseph. 1996 [1986]. *Jewish Mysticism and Jewish Ethics*. Northvale, NJ: Jason Aronson.

Delitzsch, Franz. 1978 [1888]. *A New Commentary on Genesis*. Trans. Sophia Taylor. Vol. 1. 2 vols. Minneapolis: Klock and Klock.

Derrida, Jacques. 1978a. "Violence and Metaphysics." In *Writing and Difference*. Chicago: University of Chicago Press.

———. 1978b. *Writing and Difference, Writing and Metaphysics*. Chicago: University of Chicago Press.

———. 1986. "Geschlecht II: Heidegger's Hand." In *Deconstruction and Philosophy*. Ed. J. Sallis. Chicago: University of Chicago Press.

———. 1987. *De l'esprit: Heidegger et la question*. Paris: Galilée.

———. 1988. "La structure, le signe et le jeu dans le discours des sciences humanines." In *L'écriture et la différence*. Ed. Jacques Derrida. Paris: Seuil.

——. 1989. *Of Spirit: Heidegger and the Question*. Trans. Geoffrey Bennington and Rachel Bowlby. Chicago: University of Chicago Press.

——. 1992a. "How to Avoid Speaking: Denials." In *Derrida and Negative Theology*. Ed. Harold G. Coward, Toby Foshay, and Jacques Derrida. Albany, NY: State University of New York Press.

——. 1992b. *Points de suspension*. Paris: Galilée.

——. 1995. "'Eating Well,' or the Calculation of the Subject." In *Points . . . Interviews, 1974–1994*. Ed. Elisabeth Weber. Stanford, CA: Stanford University Press.

——. 1999. "L'animal que donc je suis." In *L'animal autobiographique: Autour de Jacques Derrida*. Ed. M. L. Mallet. Paris: Galilée.

——. 2002a. "The Animal That Therefore I Am (More to Follow)." *Critical Inquiry* 28, no. 2: 369-419.

——. 2002b. "Faith and Knowledge: The Two Sources of 'Religion' at the Limits of Reason Alone." In *Acts of Religion*, vi. Ed. Gil Anidjar. New York: Routledge.

——. 2004a. "Violence Against Animals." In *For What Tomorrow . . . a Dialogue*, 62–76. Ed. Elisabeth Roudinesco. Stanford: Stanford University Press.

——. 2004b. "Vivre 'ensemble'—living 'together.'" In *Public Lecture*. University of California Santa Barbara.

——. 2006. *L'animal que donc je suis*. Paris: Galilée.

——. 2008a. *The Animal That Therefore I Am*. Ed. Marie-Louise Mallet. Trans. David Wills. New York: Fordham University Press.

——. 2008b. *Séminaire: La bête et le souverain Volume 1 (2001–2002)*. Paris: Galilée.

——. 2009. *The Beast and the Sovereign*, vol. 1. Ed. Michel Lisse, Marie-Louise Mallet, and Ginette Michaud. Trans. Geoffrey Bennington. Chicago: University of Chicago Press.

de Waal, Frans. 2009. *The Age of Empathy: Nature's Lessons for a Kinder Society*. New York: Harmony.

Diamond, Etan. 2003. "The Kosher Lifestyle: Religious Consumerism and Suburban Orthodox Jews." *Journal of Urban History* 28, no. 4: 488-506.

Dillmann, A. 1897. *Genesis Critically and Exegetically Expounded*. Vol. 1. Trans. Wm. B. Stevenson. 2 vols. Edinburgh: Clark.

Doniger, Wendy. 1982. *Women, Androgynes, and Other Mythical Beasts*. Chicago: University of Chicago Press.

——. 1995. "The Mythology of Masquerading Animals, or, Bestiality." In *Humans and Other Animals*. Ed. Arien Mack. Columbus: Ohio University Press.

——. 1999. "Reflections." In *The Lives of Animals*. Ed. J. M.Coetzee. Princeton: Princeton University Press.

——. 2005. "Zoomorphism in Ancient India: Humans More Bestial Than Beasts." In *Thinking with Animals: New Perspectives on Anthropomorphism*. Ed. Lorraine Daston and Greg Mittman. New York: Columbia University Press.

———. 2006. "A Symbol in Search of an Object: The Mythology of Horses in India." In *A Communion of Subjects*. Ed. Paul Waldau and Kimberley Patton. New York: Columbia University Press.

———. 2011. *The Implied Spider*. New York: Columbia University Press.

———. 2012. "Epilogue." In *Animals and the Human Imagination*, 349–353. Ed. Aaron Gross and Anne Vallely. New York: Columbia University Press.

Dorff, Elliot. 1977. "The Interaction of Jewish Law and Morality." *Judaism* 26:455–466.

Dorff, Elliot, and Jonathan Crane. 2013. *The Oxford Handbook of Jewish Ethics and Morality*. New York: Oxford University Press.

Dorff, Elliot, and Joel Roth. 2002. Shackling and Hoisting. Ed. Committee on Jewish Law and Standards. New York Rabbinical Assembly.

Douglas, Mary. 1966. *Purity and Danger*. New York: Routledge.

———. 1999. *Leviticus as Literature*. Oxford: Oxford University Press.

Dresner, Samuel. 2000. *Keeping Kosher: A Diet for the Soul*. Rabbinical Assembly, United Synagogue of Conservative Judaism Commission on Jewish Education.

Driver, S. R. 1954 [1904]. *The Book of Genesis with Introduction and Notes*. 12th ed. London: Methuen.

Dujack, Stephen R. 2003. "Animals Suffer a Perpetual 'Holocaust.'" *Los Angeles Times*, April 21.

Durkheim, Émile. 1995. *The Elementary Forms of Religious Life*. Trans. Karen E. Fields. New York: Free Press.

Durkheim, Émile, and Marcel Mauss. 1963. *Primitive Classification*. Chicago: University of Chicago Press.

Eby, Charlotte. 2004. "Ag Secretary Judge: Postville Slaughter Video Is 'Disturbing' " *GlobeGazette.com*, December 7.

Elchonon, Y. 2004. "Group Campaigns Against Kosher Meat." *Yated Ne'eman*, December 3.

Eliade, Mircea. 1981 [1978]. *A History of Religious Ideas,* vol. 1: *From the Stone Age to the Eleusinian Mysteries*. Trans. Willard R. Trask. 3 vols. Chicago: University of Chicago Press.

———. 1984 [1969]. *The Quest: History and Meaning in Religion*. Chicago: University of Chicago.

———. 1998. *Myth and Reality*. Prospect Heights, IL: Waveland Press. Original edition, 1963.

Farm Forward. 2010. *Keeping Kosher* 2010 (cited October 15, 2010). Available from www.farmforward.com/features/kosher_investigation.

———. 2013. *Homepage* 2013 (cited March 20, 2013). Available from www.farmforward.com/.

Feely-Harnik, Gillian. 1981. *The Lord's Table: Eucharist and Passover in Early Christianity, Symbol and Culture*. Philadelphia: University of Pennsylvania Press.

Feagin, Joe. 2013. *The White Racial Frame: Centuries of Racial Framing and Counter-Framing*. New York: Routledge.

Feldman, Emmanuel. 1994. *Why Eat Kosher*. Artscroll/Mesorah Publications 1994 (cited September 7, 2004). Available from www.star-k.com/cons-keep-basics-why. htm.

Feyerabend, Paul. 1993 [1975]. *Against Method: Outline of an Anarchistic Theory of Knowledge*. 3d ed. London: Verso.

Fiddes, Nick. 1991. *Meat: A Natural Symbol*. New York: Routledge.

Fishbane, Michael A. 1989. *Biblical Interpretation in Ancient Israel*. Oxford: Oxford University Press.

Fishkoff, Sue. 2008. "Jewish Food Movement Comes of Age." *JTA*.

——. 2009. "Reform Leader Urges Followers to Adopt Jewish Dietary Practice." *Jewish Telegraph Agency*, November 9.

——. 2010a. *Kosher Nation*. New York: Schocken.

——. 2010b. "Red, White, and Kosher." *New York Times*, July 3.

Foer, Jonathan Safran. 2006. "If This Is Kosher . . . " Norfolk, VA: PETA.

——. 2009. *Eating Animals*. New York: Little, Brown.

Food and Agriculture Organization of the United Nations. 2006. Livestock's Long Shadow: Environmental Issues and Options. Rome.

Food Marketing Institute and National Council of Chain Restaurants. 2003. January 2003 Report FMI-NCCR Animal Welfare Program.

Fox, Michael Allen. 1999. *Deep Vegetarianism, America in Transition*. Philadelphia: Temple University Press.

Frank, Adam. 2005. Kashrut in the Industrial Age. *Jerusalem Post*, Feb 3.

Frazer, James George, and Theodor Gaster. 1959. *The New Golden Bough: A New Abridgment of the Classic Work*. New York: Criterion.

Freedman, Samuel. 2010. "A Muckraking Blogger Focuses on Jews." *New York Times*, January 8, A17.

Freeman, Seymour E. 1970. *The Book of Kashruth: A Treasury of Kosher Facts and Frauds*. New York: Bloch.

Freud, Sigmund. 1950. *Totem and Taboo: Some Points of Agreement Between the Mental Lives of Savages and Neurotics*. Trans. James Strachey. New York: Norton.

——. 1963. "Fixation to Traumas—The Unconscious: Lecture XVIII." In *The Standard Edition of the Complete Psychological Works of Sigmund Freud, vol. 16, (1916–1917): Introductory Lectures on Psycho-Analysis (Part 3)*. Ed. James Strachey and Anna Freud. London: Hogarth.

Fried, Heshy. 2011. "Are We Making Rubashkin Into Some Sort of Hero?" In *FrumSatire.net*. Ed. Heshy Fried.

Friedman, Maurice. 1988. *Martin Buber's Life and Work, vol. 1: The Early Years, 1878–1923*. Detroit: Wayne State University Press.

Gastwirt, Harold P. 1974. *Fraud, Corruption, and Holiness: The Controversy Over the Superviosn of Jewish Dietary Practice in New York City, 1881–1940*. Port Washington, NY: National University Publications.

Genack, Menachem. 2004. "Setting the Record Straight on Kosher Slaughter." *Jewish Press*, December 29.

Gibbs, Robert. 2000. *Why Ethics? Signs of Responsibilities*. Princeton: Princeton University Press.

Goldsmith, Ben. 2004. PETA Responds to Rabbi Avi Shafran. In *FailedMessiah.com*. Ed. Shmarya Rosenberg.

Grandin, Temple. 1988. "Commentary: Behavior of Slaughter Plant and Auction Employees Toward the Animals." *Anthrozoos* 1, no. 4, pp. 205–213.

——. 1994. Religious Slaughter and Animal Welfare: A Discussion for Meat Scientists. *Meat Focus International* (March): 115-123. Available from www.grandin.com/ritual/kosher.slaugh.html.

——. 1995. *Thinking in Pictures: And Other Reports from My Life with Autism*. New York: Doubleday.

——. 2004. *Evaluation of 2004 Slaughter Video*. Fort Collins, Colorado.

Gross, Aaron S. 2004. "Continuity and Change in Reform Views of Kashrut 1883–2002: From the Treifah Banquet to Eco-Kahrut." *CCAR Journal* 51, no. 1, pp. 6–29.

——. 2005. "When Kosher Isn't Kosher." *Tikkun* 20, no. 2, pp. 52–56.

——. 2009. "The Question of the Creature: Animals, Theolgy and Levinas' Dog." In *Creaturely Theology*, 121–137. Ed. Celia Deane-Drummond and David Clough. London: SCM.

——. 2010. "The Question of the Animal and Religion: Dietary Practice, Ethics, and Subjectivity." Ph.D. diss., Religious Studies, University of California.

——. 2013. "Jewish Animal Ethics." In *The Oxford Handbook of Jewish Ethics and Morality*, xx. Ed. Elliot Dorff and Jonathan Crane. New York: Oxford University Press.

——. Forthcoming. "Factory Farming (Confined Animal Feeding Operations)." In *Encyclopedia of Food Issues*. Ed. Ken Alba. Thousand Oaks, CA: Sage.

Gross, Aaron S., and Anne Vallely. 2012. *Animals and the Human Imagination*. New York: Columbia University Press.

Gunkel, Hermann. 1997 [1922]. *Genesis*. Trans. Mark E. Biddle. Macon: Mercer University Press.

Hadda, Janet. 2003 [1997]. *Isaac Bashevis Singer: A Life*. Madison: University of Wisconsin Press.

Halivni, David Weiss. 1978. "Can a Religious Law Be Immoral?" In *Perspectives on Jews and Judaism: Essays in Honor of Wolfe Kelman*, 165–170. Ed. Aurthor A. Chiel. New York: Rabbinical Assembly.

Hallmark. 2004. *The Way Home: Stories of Forgiveness*.

Handelman, Susan A. 1982. *The Slayers of Moses*. Albany: State University of New York Press.

Haraway, Donna. 1978a. "Animal Sociology and a Natural Economy of the Body Politic, Part I. A Political Physiology of Dominance." *Signs* 4, no. 1, pp. 21–36.

———. 1978b. "Animal Sociology and a Natural Economy of the Body Politic, Part II. The Past Is the Contested Zone: Human Nature and Theories of Production and Reproduction in Primate Behavior Studies." *Signs* 4, no. 1, pp. 37–60.

———. 1984. "Primatology Is Politics by Other Means." *PSA: Proceedings of the Biennial Meeting of the Philosophy of Science Association* 2:489–524.

———. 1989. *Primate Visions: Gender, Race, and Nature in the World of Modern Science*. New York: Routledge.

———. 1991. *Simians, Cyborgs, and Women: The Reinvention of Nature*. New York: Routledge.

———. 2003. *The Companion Species Manifesto: Dogs, People, and Significant Otherness*. Chicago: Prickly Paradigm.

———. 2008. *When Species Meet, Posthumanities*. Minneapolis: University of Minnesota Press.

Harrison, Robert Pogue. 2003. *The Dominion of the Dead*. Chicago: University of Chicago Press.

Hartman, Geoffrey, and Sanford Budick. 1986. *Midrash and Literature*. New Haven: Yale University Press.

Hayden, Dallas. 2005. AgriProcessors, Inc. Ed. United States Department of Agriculture. Kansas City: United States Department of Agriculture Office of Inspector General.

Heide, Kathleen M. 2003. *Animal Cruelty: Pathway to Violence Against People*. Lanham, MD: AltaMira.

Heidegger, Martin. 1983a. *Die Grudbegriffe Der Metaphysik*. Frankfurt: Vittorio Klostermann.

———. 1983b. *The Fundamental Concepts of Metaphysics: World, Finitude, Solitude*. Trans. McNeill, William and Nicholas Walker. Bloomington: Indiana University Press.

Heilman, Samuel C. 2006. *Sliding to the Right: The Contest for the Future of American Jewish Orthodoxy*. Berkeley: University of California Press.

Hersh, Tzvi, and Menachem Genack. 2004. *Message from Rabbi Dr. Tzvi Hersh Weinreb and Rabbi Menachem Genack*. Orthdox Union, December 9 (cited April 2, 2014). Available from http://oukosher.org/blog/news/message-from-rabbi -dr-tzvi-hersh-weinreb-and-rabbi-menachem-genack/.

Heschel, Abraham Joshua. 1994 [1955]. *God in Search of Man: A Philosophy of Judaism*. New York: Farrar, Straus and Giroux.

Hosang, Daniel Martinez, Oneka LaBennett, and Laura Pulido. 2012. *Racial Formation in the Twenty-First Century*. Berkeley: University of California Press.

Hrdy, Sarah Blaffer. 2009. *Mothers and Others: The Evolutionary Origins of Mutual Understanding*. Cambridge: Belknap.

Humane Society of the United States. 2013. "An HSUS Report: Welfare Issues with Gestation Crates for Pregnant Sows."

Ingold, Tim. 1987. *Hunters, Pastoralists and Ranchers: Reindeer Economies and Their Transformations*. Cambridge: Cambridge University Press.

——. 1988. *What Is an Animal?* London: Unwin Hyman.

——. 1996a. "Hunting and Gathering as Ways of Perceiving the Environment." In *Redefining Nature: Ecology, Culture, and Domestication*. Ed. Roy Ellen and Katsuyoshi Fukui. Washington, DC: Berg.

——. 1996b. "The Optimal Forager and Economic Man." In *Nature and Society: Anthropological Perspectives*. Ed. Philippe Descola and Gísli Pálsson. New York: Routledge.

——. 2001a. "Animals and Modern Cultures: A Sociology of Human-Animal Relations in Modernity." *Society and Animals* no. 9, p. 2.

——. 2001b. "From Complentarity to Obviation: On Dissolving the Boundaries Between Social and Biological Antrhopology, Archeaology, and Pyschology." In *Cycles of Contingency: Developmental Systems and Evolution*, 255–279. Ed. Susan Oyama, Paul E. Griffiths, and Russel D. Gray. Cambridge: MIT Press.

——. 2002 [1994]. Humanity and Animality. In *Companion Encyclopedia of Anthropology*. Ed. Tim Ingold. New York: Routledge.

——. 2008a [2000]. "From Trust to Domination: An Alternative History of Human-Animals Relations." In *The Perception of the Environment: Essays in Livelihood, Dwelling and Skill*, 61–76. Ed. Tim Ingold. London: Routledge.

——. 2008b [2000]. "Hunting and Gathering as Ways of Perceiving the Environment." In *The Perception of the Environment: Essays in Livelihood, Dwelling and Skill*, 40–60. Ed. Tim Ingold. London: Routledge.

——. 2008c [2000]. "Making Things, Growing Plants, Raising Animals and Bringing Up Children." In *Perception of the Environment: Essays on Livelihood, Dwelling and Skill*, 77–88. Ed. Tim Ingold. New York: Routledge.

——. 2010a. "The Man in the Machine and the Self-Builder." *Interdisciplinary Science Reviews* 35, nos. 3-4, pp. 353–364.

——. 2010b. "No More Ancient; No More Human: The Future Past of Archaeology and Anthropology." In *Archaeology and Anthropology*. Ed. Duncan Garrow and Thomas Yarrow. Oakville, CT: Oxbow.

——. 2012a. Personal e-mail to Aaron Gross. August 21.

——. 2012b. "Hunting and Gathering as Ways of Perceiving the Environment." In *Animals and the Human Imagination*, 31–54. Ed. Aaron Gross and Anne Vallely. New York: Columbia University Press.

——. 2013. "Walking with Dragons." In *Animals as Religious Subjects: Transdisciplinary Perspectives*, 35–58. Ed. Celia Deane-Drummond, Rebecca Artinian-Kaiser, and David Clough. New York: T&T Clark.

Iowa Attorney General's Office. 2008. *Sept. 9, 2008: Statement of the Iowa Attorney General's Office.* Iowa Department of Justice 2008. Available from www.state.ia.us /government/ag/latest_news/releases/sept_2008/Child_Labor .html.

Iowa Public Television. 2001. "Postville: When Cultures Collide."

Jacob, Benno. 1974. *The First Book of the Torah, Genesis.* New York: Ktav.

Jacobs, Joseph. 1941. *The Jewish Culture: and What It Means to the American Manufacturer in the Marketing of His Products.* New York: Joseph Jacobs.

Jane, Norman. 2008. "Immigration Raid: Plant Official Is GOP Contributor." *DesMoinesRegister.com*, May 13.

Jerusalem Post. 2004. "The Kosher Way." *Jerusalem Post*, December 9.

Joselit, Jenna Weissman. 1995. "Jewish in Dishes: Kashrut in the New World." In *The Americanization of the Jews.* Ed. Robert M. Sletzer and Norman J. Cohen. New York: New York University Press.

Kalof, Linda, Steven Bryant, and Amy Fitzgerald. 2010. *Animal Studies Bibliography.* Animal Studies Program and the Ecological and Cultural Change Studies Group in the Department of Sociology at Michigan State University 2010 (cited October 15, 2010). Available from www.animalstudies.msu.edu/asbib.html.

Koenig, Leah. 2010. "Grow and Behold: A New Line of Kosher Chicken Launches a Conversation Around Jewish Food Ethics." *Jewish Daily Forward*, June 28.

Kosher Today, staff. 2003. "Market for Kosher Foods Continues to Grow Among Mainstream Consumers." *Kosher Today*, October 1.

——. 2008. *Leading Orthodox Jewish Organizations Vow to Preserve Schechita in the U.S. Yeshiva World News,* December 5 (accessed June 28, 2010). Available from www.theyeshivaworld.com/article.php?p=26826.

Koslow, J. Anthony. 2007. *The Silent Deep: The Discovery, Ecology, and Conservation of the Deep Sea.* Chicago: University of Chicago Press.

Kraemer, David Charles. 2007. *Jewish Eating and Identity Through the Ages.* New York: Routledge.

Kubrick, Stanley. 1968. *2001, a Space Odyssey.* Warner Brothers.

Lawlor, Leonard. 2007. *This Is Not Sufficient: An Essay on Animality and Human Nature in Derrida.* New York: Columbia University Press.

Lea, Suzanne R. Goodney. 2007. *Delinquency and Animal Cruelty: Myths and Realities About Social Pathology.* El Paso, TX: LFB Scholarly Publishing.

Leach, Edmund Ronald. 1989. *Claude Lévi-Strauss.* Chicago: University of Chicago Press.

Legal Info. 2009. "Manager of Kosher Slaughterhouse Found Guilty on 86 Charges of Fraud." December 1. Available from www.legalinfo.com/legal-news/manager-of -kosher-slaughterhouse-found-guilty-on-86-charges-of-fraud.html.

Lévi-Strauss, Claude. 1962. "La pensée sauvage." Paris: Plon. Available from www .archive.org/details/lapenseesauvage00levi.

———. 1963. *Totemism*. Toronto: Saunders/Beacon.

———. 1973. *The Savage Mind*. Chicago: University of Chicago Press.

———. 1983 [1969]. *The Raw and the Cooked: Mythologiques*. Chicago: University of Chicago Press.

———. 1990a [1981]. *The Naked Man: Mythologiques*. Chicago: University of Chicago Press.

———. 1990b [1978]. *The Origin of Table Manners: Mythologiques*. Chicago: University of Chicago Press.

———. 2000 [1963]. *Structural Anthropology*. Basic Books.

———. 2001 [1973]. *Tristes Tropiques*. New York: Penguin.

Levinas, Emmanuel. 1990a. "The Name of a Dog, or Natural Rights." In *Difficult Freedom: Essays on Judaism*. Baltimore: Johns Hopkins University Press.

———. 1990b [1977]. *Nine Talmudic Readings*. Trans. Annette Aronowicz. Bloomington: Indiana University Press.

———. 1995 [1969]. *Totality and Infinity: An Essay on Exteriority*. Trans. Alphonso Lingis. Pittsburgh: Duquesne University Press.

———. 2004 [1981]. *Otherwise Than Being, or, Beyond Essence*. Trans. Alphonso Lingis. Pittsburgh: Duquesne University Press.

Lewin, Nathan. 2004. "The Assault on Shechita." *Jewish Press*, December 15.

Lewin and Lewin (Nathan Lewin). 2003. Letter from Lawyer Nathan Lewin to PETA Prior to 2004 Investigation. Washington, DC, August 26.

Lieberman, Saul. 1994. "Hellenism in Jewish Palestine." In *Greek in Jewish Palestine/ Hellenism in Jewish Palestine*. Ed. Saul Lieberman. New York: Jewish Theological Seminary of America.

Lincoln, Bruce. 1992. *Discourse and the Construction of Society: Comparative Studies of Myth, Ritual, and Classification*. New York: Oxford University Press.

Linzey, Andrew. 1987. *Christianity and the Rights of Animals*. New York: Crossroad.

Lipschutz, Yacov. 1988. *Kashruth: A Comprehensive Background and Reference Guide to the Principles of Kashruth*. Brooklyn: Mesorah.

Luke, Brian. 2007. *Brutal: Manhood and the Exploitation of Animals*. Urbana: University of Illinois Press.

Lynton, Michael, Gary Ginsberg, and Jay Sanderson. 2008. "Top 25 Pulpit Rabbis in America." *Newsweek Web Exclusive*, April 11.

McNeil, Donald. 2004a. "Kosher Authority Seeks Change in Steer Killings." *New York Times*, December 3.

———. 2004b. "Videos Cited in Calling Kosher Slaughterhouse Inhumane." *New York Times*, December 1.

Mehaffey, Trish. 2012. "Former Agriprocessors Manager Appeals Extradition." *Waterloo Daily Courier*, April 19.

Meir, Asher. 2004. *Meaning in Mitzvot* (cited September 8, 2004). Available from www.ou.org/torah/tt/5763/bechukotai63/specialfeatures_mitzvot.htm.

Menken, Yaakov. 2004. "Why Did PETA Target Jews?" *Cross-Currents*. Available at http://www.cross-currents.com/archives/2004/12/25/why-did-peta-target-jews/.

Milgrom, Jacob. "The Biblical Diet Laws as an Ethical System." *Interpretation* 17 (1963): 288–301.

———. 1991. *Leviticus 1–16*. New York: Doubleday Dell.

———. 2000. *Leviticus 17–22*. New York: Doubleday Dell.

Mintel Consumer Intelligence. 2009a. *Kosher Foods—US—January 2009—Market Research Report* 2009b (cited June 21, 2009). Available from http://oxygen.mintel .com/sinatra/reports/display/id=393508/display/id=121162/display/id=393508.

———. 2009b. 3 in 5 Kosher Food Buyers Purchase for Food Quality, Not Religion (press release, cited June 21, 2009). Available from www.mintel.com/press-centre/press -releases/321/3-in-5-kosher-food-buyers-purchase-for-food-quality-not-religion.

Myers, Jody. 2012. "Purity, Charity, Community: The Power of Kashrut in an Orthodox Jewish Neighborhood." In *Reconstructing Jewish Identity in Pre- and Post-Holocaust Literature and Culture*, 97–110. Ed. Lucyna Aleksandrowicz-Pędich and Małgorzata Pakier. Frankfurt: Peter Lang.

Newman, Louis E. 1998. *Past Imperatives*. Albany: State University of New York Press.

Newsweek. 2012. "Wolpe Tops Newsweek List of 50 Influential U.S. Rabbis." *Jewish Telegraphic Agency*, April 2.

Nietzsche, Friedrich. 1989. *On the Genealogy of Morals*. Trans. Walter Arnold Kaufmann. New York: Vintage.

———. 2005. *Friedrich Nietzsche: Gesammelte Werke*. Bindlach: Gondrom.

Norwood, F. Bailey, and Jayson Lusk. 2011. *Compassion, by the Pound: The Economics of Farm Animal Welfare*. New York: Oxford University Press.

Nuttall, M. 2009. "Living in a World of Movement: Human Resilience to Environmental Instability in Greenland." In *Anthropology of Climate Change: From Encounters to Actions*, 292–310. Ed. S. A. Crate and M. Nuttal. Walnut Creek, CA: Left Coast.

OK Kosher Certification. 2004. Y2K. OK Kosher Certification Undated (cited September 7, 2004). Available from www.okkosher.com/Content.asp?ID=22.

———. 2010. About OK—OK in Brief. OK Kosher Certification Undated (cited January 29, 2010). Available from www.ok.org/Content.asp?ID=2.

———. 2012. Corporate Profile. OK Kosher Certification Undated (cited January 1, 2012). Available from www.ok.org/Content.asp?ID=157.

Omi, Michael, and Howard Winant. 1986. *Racial Formation in the United States: From the 1960s to the 1980s, Critical Social Thought*. New York: Routledge and Kegan Paul.

Orbach, Michael. 2008. "A Kosher Quandary: Panel Discusses Ethics and Kashrut." *The Jewish Star* (December 17). Available at www.thejewishstar.com/stories/A

-kosher-quandary-panel-discusses-ethics-and-kashrut,414?page=1&content
_source=.

Orthodox Union, Kashrut Division. 2004a. *The Kosher Primer*. Kashrut Division of
the Orthodox Union Undated-a (cited September 7, 2004). Available from http://
oukosher.org/index.php/articles/single/the_kosher_primer/P1/.

———. 2004b. *Thinking Kosher, An Introduction*. Kashrut Division of the Orthodox
Union Undated-b (cited September 7, 2004). Available from http://oukosher.org
/index.php/articles/single/1310/P0/.

Pachirat, Timothy. 2011. *Every Twelve Seconds: Industrialized Slaughter and the Politics of Sight*. New Haven: Yale University Press.

Patton, Kimberley. 2006. "'Caught with Ourselves in the Net of Life and Time': Tra-
ditional Views of Animals in Religion." In *A Communion of Subjects: Animals in
Religion, Science, and Ethics*. Ed. Paul Waldau and Kimberley Patton. New York:
Columbia University Press.

Pauly, Daniel, Reg Watson, and Jackie Adler. 2005. "Global Trends in World Fisheries:
Impacts on Marine Ecosystems and Food Security." *Philosophical Transactions of
the Royal Society* 360, no. 1453, pp. 5–12.

Pava, Moses L. 2011. *Jewish Ethics in a Post-Madoff World: A Case for Optimism*. New
York: Palgrave Macmillan.

Payne, Mark. 2010. *The Animal Part: Human and Other Animals in the Poetic Imagination*. Chicago: University of Chicago Press.

PETA. 2009. *Investigation Reveals Slaughter Horrors at AgriProcessors*. PETA Undated (cited January 12, 2009). Available from www.goveg.com/feat/AgriProces-
sors/index.asp.

———. 2010a. *AgriProcessors Denies Health Care to Employee*. PETA Undated (cited June 21, 2010). Available from www.petatv.com/tvpopup/Prefs.
asp?video=agri_campy.

———. 2010b. *General FAQs*. PETA Undated (cited June 28, 2010). Available from
www.peta.org/ABOUT/faq.asp.

PETA (Steven Jay Gross). 2003. Letter from PETA to AgriProcessors, Inc. Norfolk,
VA, June 18.

PETA (Lori Kettler). 2004. Letter from PETA to Dr. Elsa A. Murano, Under Secretary
for Food Safety, United States Department of Agriculture. RE: Violations of the
Humane Methods of Livestock Slaughter Act at Agriprocessors, Inc., Postville,
Iowa. Norfolk, VA, November 29.

PetfoodIndustry.com. 2013. *APPA Releases 2010 Pet Industry Spending Figures, 2011
Pet Owners Survey*. PetfoodIndustry.com, 2011 (cited March 18, 2013). Available
from www.petfoodindustry.com/6896.html.

Pew Commission on Industrial Animal Production. 2008. Putting Meat on the Table:
Industrial Farm Animal Production in America. Pew Charitable Trusts, Johns
Hopkins Bloomberg School of Public Health.

Popper, Nathaniel. 2006a. "Conservative Rabbis Pledge Groundbreaking System for Monitoring Working Conditions at Kosher Plants." *Forward*, December 22.

———. 2006b. "In Iowa Meat Plant, Kosher 'Jungle' Breeds Fear, Injury, Short Pay." *Forward*, May 26.

———. 2009. "As New Owners Take Over Meat Plant, Battered Postville Waits and Worries." *Forward*, September 18.

Postville Resource Center. 2012. *La Historia de Nuestras Vidas* 2009. Available from https://sites.google.com/site/postvilleiowavista/may-12–2009/la-historia-de -nuestras-vidas.

Preston, Julia. 2008a. "Large Iowa Meatpacker in Illegal Immigrant Raid Files for Bankruptcy." *New York Times*, November 6.

———. 2008b. "Rabbis Debate Kosher Ethics at Meat Plant." *New York Times*, August 23.

———. 2010. "27-Year Sentence for Plant Manager." *New York Times*, June 22.

Ouaknin, Marc-Alain. 1995. *The Burnt Book: Reading the Talmud*. Princeton: Princeton University Press.

Quine, Willard V. 1969. "Natural Kinds." In *Ontological Relativity and Other Essays*, viii. New York: Columbia University Press.

Rad, Gerhard von. 1974. *Genesis: A Commentary*. Trans. John H. Marks. Philadelphia: Westminster.

Rank, Raphael. 2004a. E-mail from Rabbinical Assembly president Rabbi Rank to all Conservative rabbis, December 8.

———. 2004b. E-mail from Rabbi Rank to Aaron Gross, December 20.

Regenstein, Joe. 2010. "Religious and Non-Religious Slaughter or Slaughtering Religious Dialogue?" Diarel, Girona, Spain.

Roberts, Mark S. 2008. *The Mark of Beast: Animality and Human Oppression*. West Lafayette, IN: Purdue University Press.

Ronell, Avital. 2002. *Stupidity*. Urbana, IL: University of Illinois Press.

Rosen, David. 2004. E-mail from Rabbi David Rosen to Aaron Gross regarding statement on AgriProcessors, November 30.

Rosenberg, Shalom. 1987. "Ethics: Musar." In *Contemporary Jewish Religious Thought*, 195–202. Ed. Arthur A. Cohen and Paul Mendes-Flohr. New York: Free Press.

Rosenberg, Shmarya. 2004a. Agudath Israel Did Not See PETA Video—Voted Without Seeing Evidence. *Failedmessiah.com*.

———. 2004b. Iowa's Ag Secretery Accepted $10K From Rubashkin While USDA Investigation Open. *FailedMessiah.com*.

———. 2004c. KAJ's Position On Postville. *FailedMessiah.com*.

———. 2004d. The OU's Rabbi Belsky on the Postville Scandal. *FailedMessiah.com*.

———. 2004e. Rabbi Shear-Yashuv Cohen, Chief Rabbi of Haifa. *FailedMessiah.com*.

———. 2005. BREAKING! Rubaskin Passes AWAP Audit—OU Claims Audit Done Under New Procedures "Vindicates" AgriProcessors, Implies Horror Seen on PETA Video Humane. *FailedMessiah.com*.

———. 2008a. Most Wanted: The Big, Bad Butchers and Bullies of Agriprocessors. *Jewcy.com*, July 24.

———. 2008b. Rubashkin Family Members Large Republican Campaign Contributors. *FailedMessiah.com*.

———. 2009. The Alternative Universe of Agriprocessors Former Counsel, Nathan Lewin. *FailedMessiah.com*.

———. 2013. About Me: My Name is Shmarya Rosenberg and I Publish FailedMessiah. com. *FailedMessiah.com* undated (cited August 25, 2013). Available from http:// failedmessiah.typepad.com/failed_messiahcom/about-me.html

Rosenberg, Zachary. 2004f. *Dietary Laws in Parshas Shemini*. Kof-K Kosher Supervision undated (cited September 7, 2004). Available from www.kof-k.org/dietary .htm.

Rosenblum, Jordan. 2010. *Food and Identity in Early Rabbinic Judaism*. New York: Cambridge University Press.

———. Forthcoming. "Bacon, Banquets, and Bras: Rabbinic Food Regulations and Boundary Formation" *Journal of Indo-Judiac Studies*.

Rothenberg, Jennie. 2004. "Torah Amid Corn." *Hadassah* 85, no. 8.

Rubashkin, Sholom Mordechai. 2010. Rubashkin's Response to the PETA Video [transcript of 2004 lecture by Sholom Rubashkin].Shmais.com (cited February 9, 2010). Available from www.shmais.com/jnewsdetail.cfm?ID=148.

Rubenstein, Jeffrey L. 1999. *Talmudic Stories: Narrative Art, Composition, and Culture*. Baltimore: Johns Hopkins University Press.

Ruttenberg, Danya. 2001. *Yentl's Revenge: The Next Wave of Jewish Feminism*. Seattle: Seal.

Ryder, Richard D. 2000. *Animal Revolution: Changing Attitudes Toward Speciesism*. Oxford and New York: Berg.

Sanders, Gabriel. 2004. "Animal-Rights Activists Take Aim at Glatt Kosher Meat Plant." *Forward*, December 3.

Sarna, Jonathan D. 2004. *American Judaism : A History*. New Haven: Yale University Press.

Sarna, Nahum M. 1989. *Genesis: The Traditional Hebrew Text with the New JPS Translation*. Philadelphia: Jewish Publication Society.

Savage, Nigel. 2010. "10 Years Ago in Postville, Iowa/Shabbat Hazon." *Hazon*.

Schofer, John. 2005. "Theology and Cosmology in Rabbinic Ethics: The Pedagogical Significance of Rainmaking Narratives." *Jewish Studies Quarterly* 12, no. 3, pp. 227–259.

Schofer, Jonathan Wyn. 2005. *The Making of a Sage: A Study in Rabbinic Ethics*. Madison: University of Wisconsin Press.

Schulz, Bruno. 1992. *The Street of Crocodiles and Other Stories*. Trans. Celina Wieniewska. New York: Penguin.

Schwartz, Barry L. 2004. "Abusing Animals." *Chicago Tribune*, December 6.

Sears, David. 2003. *The Vision of Eden: Animal Welfare in Jewish Law and Mysticism.* New York: Orot.

Sellbach, Undine. 2012. "Wittgenstein, Coetzee, and the Extent of the Sympathetic Imagination." In *Animals and the Human Imagination*, 307–330. Ed. Aaron Gross and Anne Vallely. New York: Columbia University Press.

Serpell, James. 1996. *In the Company of Animals: A Study of Human-Animal Relationships.* Cambridge: Cambridge University Press.

Shafran, Avi. 2005a. "Did PETA Identify Problems with Kosher Slaughter Plant? No." *New Standard*, January 12.

——. 2005b. "Who Will Determine Humane Animal Slaughter, Rabbis or PETA?" *Wisconsin Jewish Chronicle*, January 7.

——. 2007. "Much Ado About Shmittah." *Cross-Currents.*

——. 2010. "The 'PETA Principle,' the Moral Equating of Animals and Humans, Is an Affront to the Very Essence of Jewish Belief." Aish.com 2004 (cited June 28, 2010). Available from www.aish.com/jw/s/48894162.html.

Shapiro, Samantha M. 2008. "Kosher Wars." *New York Times Magazine*, October 12.

Shemesh, Yael. 2006. "Vegetarian Ideology in Talmudic Literature and Traditional Biblical Exegesis." *Review of Rabbinic Judaism* no. 9, pp. 141–166.

Siebert, Charles. 2010. "The Animal-Cruelty Syndrome." *New York Times*, June 11.

Simon, Stephanie. 2004. "Cattle Video Stirs Kosher Meat Debate: Graphic Images from an Iowa Slaughterhouse Are Posted Online by an Animal Rights Group. Rabbis Disagree About the Techniques' Merits." *Los Angeles Times*, December 28.

Singer, Isaac Bashevis. 1983. *The Penitent.* New York: Farrar, Straus, Giroux.

Singer, Peter. 1991 [1975]. *Animal Liberation.* Rev. ed. New York: Avon.

Singer, Peter, and Jim Mason. 2006. *The Way We Eat: Why Our Food Choices Matter.* New York: Rodale.

Singer, Saul. 2004. "Interesting Times: Cutting-edge Kashrut." *Jerusalem Post*, December 16.

Skinner, John. 1930. *A Critical and Exegetical Commentary on Genesis.* 2d ed. Edinburgh: Clark.

Smith, Jonathan Z. 1988a. "The Bare Facts of Ritual." In *Imagining Religion: From Babylon to Jonestown*, 53–65. Chicago: University of Chicago Press.

——. 1988b. *Imagining Religion: From Babylon to Jonestown.* Chicago: University of Chicago Press.

——. 1993. *Map Is Not Territory: Studies in the History of Religions.* Chicago: University of Chicago Press.

Staal, Frits. 1990. *Rules Without Meaning: Ritual, Mantras, and the Human Sciences*, vol. 4. New York: Lang.

Star-K Kosher Certification. 2004. *Kosher 101*. Star-K Kosher Certification undated (cited September 7, 2004). Available from www.star-k.com/cons-keep-basics-101 .htm.

——. 2010. *Star-K Online—Who is Star-k?—In the Beginning*. Star-K Kosher Certification undated (cited June 29, 2010). Available from www.star-k.org/ind -whatisstark-begin.htm.

Steinfeld, Henning, Pierre Gerber, Tom Wassenaar, Vincent Castel, Mauricio Rosales, and Cees de Haan. 2006. "Livestock's Long Shadow. Food and Agriculture Organization of the United Nations." Available at www.fao.org/docrep/010/a0701e /a0701e00.HTM.

Steinsaltz, Adin. 1990. *The Talmud: the Steinsaltz Edition (Bava Metzia) with Commentary by Adin Steinsaltz*. Trans. Israel Institute for Talmudic Publications and Milta Books. Vol. 2. New York: Random House.

Taussig, Michael T. 1999. *Defacement: Public Secrecy and the Labor of the Negative*. Stanford: Stanford University Press.

Taves, Ann. 2009. *Religious Experience Reconsidered: A Building Block Approach to the Study of Religion and Other Special Things*. Princeton: Princeton University Press.

Thomas, Keith. 1983. *Man and the Natural World: A History of the Modern Sensibility*. New York: Pantheon.

Tillich, Paul. 1959. *Theology of Culture*. New York: Oxford University Press.

Tony, Leys. 2008. "Packers Taking Advantage of Workers Nettle Obama." *Des Moines Register*, August 26, 4B.

Union for Reform Judaism. 2011. *Green Table, Just Table*. Available from http://urj .org/life/food/.

Union of American Hebrew Congregations. 1995 [1885]. "The Pittsburgh Platform." In *Critical Documents of Jewish History: A Sourcebook*, pp. 58–60. Eds. Ronald H. Isaacs and Kerry M. Olitzky. Northvale, NJ: Jason Aronson.

United Jewish Community in Cooperation with the Mandell L. Berman Institute– North American Jewish Data Bank. 2003. *National Jewish Population Survey 2000–01: Strength, Challenge and Diversity in the American Jewish Population*. United Jewish Communities and the Jewish Federation System.

USDA Technical Service Center. 2004. *Humane Interactive Knowledge Exchange (HIKE) Scenario 03–04*. United States Department of Agriculture Food Safety and Inspection Service 2004 (cited December 29, 2004). Available from www.fsis.usda .gov/ofo/tsc/hike_03–04.htm.

Vonnegut, Kurt. 1990. *Hocus Pocus*. New York: Putnam's.

Waddington, Lynda. 2008a. "Culver Compares Agriprocessors to Sinclair's Jungle, Outlines State Response." *Iowa Independent*, August 24.

——. 2008b. "Professor, PETA: When No One Is Looking, Agriprocessors Does 'Bad Things.'" *Iowa Independent*, Sept 5.

——. 2008c. "Slaughter Expert Calls AgriProcessors "Sloppy" " *Iowa Independent*, Sept 11.

Wagner, Matt. 2004a. "Not Kosher: Rabbinate Backs PETA." *Jerrusalem Post*, December 2.

——. 2004b. "Rabbis Unite Against Wider Anti-'shehita' Campaign." *Jerusalem Post*, December 12.

——. 2006. "Rabbinate OKs Meat Despite Cruelty to Animals." *Jerusalem Post*, March 14.

Waldau, Paul, and Kimberley Patton, eds. 2006. *A Communion of Subjects: Animals in Religion, Science, and Ethics*. New York: Columbia University Press.

Watts Belser, Julia. *Forthcoming*. "Suffering Rabbis and Other Animals: Women, Wickedness, and the Construction of Rabbinic (In)Humanity in Bavli Baba Metsia 83b–85a."

Wenham, Gordon J. 1987. *Genesis 1–15*. 2 vols. Waco, TX: Word Books.

Westermann, Claus. 1994 [1984]. *Genesis 1–11: A Continental Commentary*. Trans. J. J. Scullion. Minneapolis: Fortress.

Wolfson, Ben. 1998. "Kosher Slaughter." *Mishpahah*, 364 (August 30): 16–17. Available at http://failedmessiah.typepad.com/failed_messiahcom/2004/12/the_expert_ruba.html.

Wolfson, David, and M. Sullivan. 2005. "Foxes in the Henhouse." In *Animal Rights: Current Debates and New Directions*. Ed. Cass R. Sunstein and Martha Nussbaum. Oxford: Oxford University Press.

Wolfson, Elliot R. 2006. *Venturing Beyond: Law and Morality in Kabbalistic Mysticism*. Oxford: Oxford University Press.

Worm, Boris, Edward B. Barbier, Nicola Beaumont, J. Emmett Duffy, Carl Folke, Benjamin S. Halpern, Jeremy B.C. Jackson, Heike K. Lotze, Fiorenza Micheli, Stephen R. Palumbi, Enric Sala, Kimberley A. Selkoe, John J. Stachowicz, and Reg Watson. 2006. "Impacts of Biodiversity Loss on Ocean Ecosystem Services." *Science* 314, no. 5800, pp. 787–790.

Yoav, Eitan. 2013. *Information and Communication Technologies (ICT) Contribution to Broiler Breeding* 2008 (cited March 22, 2013). Available from http://departments.agri.huji.ac.il/economics/gelb-broiler.pdf.

Zirkind, Elie. 2009. A Lawyer, a Legend—an Interview with Nathan Lewin. *Where, What, When*, November.

Index

Abrahamic tradition, 140–41, 143, 193

Acampora, Ralph, 118

Activism, 139, 165–66; *see also* People for the Ethical Treatment of Animals

Agamben, Giorgio, 12, 91–94, 99, 187–89, 228n9, 229n11

Agency or agent, 113–14, 115–20, 176, 227n3

"Ag-gag" laws, 196

AgriProcessors, Inc., 222n66; Conservative movement's response to, 47, 50–52, 178–79, 222n74; definition and nature of, 203; following AgriProcessors scandal, 43–44; Hazon's identity linked to, 54; history and function of, 27; in kosher industry, 27; liberal Judaism and criticism of, 50; Orthodox leaders' criticism of, 47–48, 49–50; PETA letter and response of, 30–31; political support for, 36; Reform Judaism and response to, 51–52; USDA oversight of, 33

AgriProcessors, Inc., footage and scandal, 1, 211n1; AgriProcessors after, 43–44; AgriProcessors procedures and impact of, 46–47; animal abuse and suffering in, 4–5, 6, 25, 26, 31, 33–34, 40–42, 57, 58–59, 176–77, 180–82, 212n15, 218nn12–13; animals in religious studies through, 9–10; animal welfare community's reaction to, 3–4; consciousness or sensibility in, 41–42, 181, 218n14; depth dimension of, 175–83; economic and symbolic in, 148; ethical kosher meat as result of, 52–53; ethics articulated by, 17–18, 56–57, 147–48, 178–83; food ethics from, 56; HMSA violations in, 33, 211n6; humane subject in, 152–53, 178, 185–87; hyperdominionist ethical response to, 179–83, 184, 196–97; Jewish and human identity impacted by, 2–4, 182–83, 211n8; Jewish community's reaction to, 2–4, 25–26,